Limiting Leviathan

Limiting Leviathan

*Hobbes on Law and
International Affairs*

Larry May

OXFORD
UNIVERSITY PRESS

OXFORD
UNIVERSITY PRESS

Great Clarendon Street, Oxford, OX2 6DP,
United Kingdom

Oxford University Press is a department of the University of Oxford.
It furthers the University's objective of excellence in research, scholarship,
and education by publishing worldwide. Oxford is a registered trade mark of
Oxford University Press in the UK and in certain other countries

© Larry May 2013

The moral rights of the author have been asserted

First Edition published in 2013

Impression: 1

All rights reserved. No part of this publication may be reproduced, stored in
a retrieval system, or transmitted, in any form or by any means, without the
prior permission in writing of Oxford University Press, or as expressly permitted
by law, by licence or under terms agreed with the appropriate reprographics
rights organization. Enquiries concerning reproduction outside the scope
of the above should be sent to the Rights Department, Oxford University Press,
at the address above

You must not circulate this work in any other form
and you must impose this same condition on any acquirer

Published in the United States of America by Oxford University Press
198 Madison Avenue, New York, NY 10016, United States of America

British Library Cataloguing in Publication Data
Data available

Library of Congress Control Number: 2013937548

ISBN 978–0–19–968279–9 (Hbk.)

ISBN 978–0–19–968280–5 (Pbk.)

Printed and bound in Great Britain by
CPI Group (UK) Ltd, Croydon, CR0 4YY

Links to third party websites are provided by Oxford in good faith and
for information only. Oxford disclaims any responsibility for the materials
contained in any third party website referenced in this work.

Acknowledgments

This book on Hobbes began life 35 years ago when I wrote my doctoral dissertation on Hobbes's political and legal philosophy, which started under the supervision of Hannah Arendt and concluded under Anthony Quinton's direction after Arendt's death. Upon completing the dissertation I revised it and sent it to Oxford University Press, which, after taking a year to review the revised dissertation, turned it down. I then did something I have told my graduate students never to do: I put the manuscript in a drawer. I had not thought again about producing a book-length treatment of Hobbes's legal philosophy until 2011, when Bernard Gert's kind words convinced me that I should return to my book on Hobbes's legal theory. I am grateful to Bernie, who died far too young, for bringing back to life this project on Hobbes.

The first five chapters of this book are mainly interpretive, offering a distinctly different view of Hobbes than is often presented in the literature. The other five chapters occupy various topics in political and legal philosophy and work out a Hobbesian position in those debates. Two of the chapters are based on my unpublished doctoral dissertation. Parts of eight of the chapters have been published over the years.[1] These appeared in a somewhat different form, and derive from the following essays:

"Hobbes's Contract Theory," *Journal of the History of Philosophy*, vol. 18, no. 2, April 1980, pp. 195–207.
"Hobbes on Equity and Justice," *Hobbes's Science of Natural Justice*, ed. Craig Walton and Paul Johnson, Dordrecht: Martinus Nijhoff Publishing Co., 1987, pp. 241–252.
"Hobbes on the Attitudes of Pacifism," *Thomas Hobbes: De La Metaphysique A La Politique*, ed. Martin Bertman and Michel Malherbe, Paris: Libraire Philosophique J. Vrin, 1989, pp. 129–140.
"Hobbes on Fidelity to Law," *Hobbes Studies*, vol. V, 1992, pp. 77–89.

These pieces have been revised extensively for the current book.

---

[1] The three essays on contract theory, equity, and fidelity were reprinted in *Hobbes on Law*, ed. Claire Finkelstein, Surrey: Ashgate Press, 2005.

I am grateful for the help my research assistants have given me, and also to those graduate students who have taken my courses on Hobbes over the years. I would like to single out Andrew Forcehimes, who worked tirelessly to help me put the first draft of the manuscript together out of a very large number of disparate parts that I had accumulated over the years, and for providing superb comments. I would also like to thank Paul Morrow, Elizabeth Edenberg, and Emily McGill for providing me with excellent feedback on a late draft. Over the years, my graduate students at Vanderbilt University, Washington University, and Purdue University have convinced me that my radical reinterpretation of Hobbes can be made plausible. These students have also helped me to take account of many objections to my views as well as alternative readings of Hobbes's texts.

Contents

Introduction	1
I. Limitations on Sovereign Law-Making	2
II. Summary of Arguments of the Book	15
1. Law, Morality, and Prudence	20
I. Sovereignty and Assumpsit	21
II. Self-Interest and Natural Right	25
III. Moral Epistemology and the Laws of Nature	28
IV. Conscience, Promise, and Contract	32
V. Law and Morality	38
VI. Prudence and Morality	42
VII. Conclusions	46
2. Social Contract	48
I. The Legal Background	49
II. The Original Contract	52
III. The Constitutional Contract	56
IV. Conclusions	65
3. Equity and Justice	67
I. The Earlier View	68
II. The Later View	76
III. Conclusions	81
4. Concept of Law	85
I. Hobbes's *Dialogue*	86
II. Knowledge of the Law	89
III. The Origins and Sources of Law	93
IV. The Nature of Law	99
V. Aquinas and Hobbes on the Typology of Law	108
VI. Common Law	113
VII. Natural Law and Equity	117
5. Fidelity to Law	122
I. Obligation to Obey the Law	122

II.	Limits on Legal Authority	125
III.	The Soldier and the Condemned Man	127
IV.	Mere Obedience versus Fidelity to Law	132
V.	Conclusions	135

6.	Sovereignty and Artificial Reason	139
I.	Natural Reason and Sovereignty in *Leviathan*	140
II.	Edward Coke on Artificial Reason	142
III.	Artificial Reason and Sovereignty in the *Dialogue*	146
IV.	Matthew Hale's Defense of Artificial Reason	149
V.	Divided Sovereignty and the Rule of Law	151

7.	Authorization, Joint Action, and Representation	156
I.	Grotius's Consent Principle	157
II.	Hobbes on Artificial Persons and Authority	160
III.	The Multitudes	163
IV.	A Hobbesian Account of Mass Action	167
V.	Objections	170

8.	Crimes and the International Order	173
I.	Hobbes and International Relations Theory	174
II.	Trust and the First Performer	178
III.	International Civil Society	180
IV.	International Law in Kant's *Perpetual Peace*	184
V.	A Hobbesian Defense of International Criminal Law	187
VI.	Objections	190

9.	Rules of War	195
I.	The Laws of Nature	196
II.	Hobbes on Self-Preservation and Cruelty	199
III.	Rationality in War	204
IV.	A Hobbesian View of Cruelty	207
V.	Minimalist Rules of War	211
VI.	The Laws of War	214
VII.	Objections	219

10.	The Attitude of Pacifism	224
I.	Attitudes and Moral Psychology	225

II. Trust, First Performance, and Peace	227
III. The Reasonableness of Developing Pacifist Attitudes	230
IV. The Choice between Peace and War	233
V. The Problem of the First Peace-Seeker	235

Concluding Thoughts   240

Bibliography   249
Index   255

Most men grant, that a government ought not to be divided; but they would have it moderated and bounded by some limits. Truly it is very reasonable it should be so… for my part, I wish that not only kings, but all other persons, endued with supreme authority, would so temper themselves…within the limits of natural and divine law.

Thomas Hobbes, *De Cive*, EW II 96 note

Introduction

Thomas Hobbes wrote extensively about law and was strongly influenced by developments and debates among lawyers of his day. And Hobbes is considered by many commentators to be one of the first legal positivists. Yet there is no book in English that focuses on Hobbes's legal philosophy. Indeed, Hobbes's own book-length treatment of law, his *Dialogue Between a Philosopher and a Student of the Common Laws of England*, has also not received much commentary over the centuries. I will seek to fill a gap in the literature by addressing Hobbes's legal philosophy directly and by often comparing *Leviathan* to the *Dialogue* as I seek to provide an interpretation of Hobbes's views about the connections among law, politics, and morality.[1]

The thesis of the book is that Hobbes is much more amenable to moral, and even legal, limits on law-making—indeed closer to Lon Fuller than to today's legal positivists—than he is often portrayed.[2] I also argue that Hobbes's views can provide a solid grounding for the rules of war and international relations generally, contrary to the near universal belief that Hobbes is the *bête noire* of international law. To support these views, I argue that Hobbes places greater weight on equity than on justice, and that understanding the role of equity is the key to his legal philosophy. Equity also is the moral concept that provides restrictions on what a sovereign can legitimately do, and if violated is the kind of limitation on sovereignty that could open the door for possible international institutions.

This book does not present a view of the whole of Hobbes's corpus. But in focusing on Hobbes's legal philosophy most of the major topics in his scholarship are at least touched on. I am not an historian. I do not read texts in the history of philosophy with an eye primarily toward the political or rhetorical

---

[1] The portrait of Hobbes on the cover of my book is from the end of Hobbes's life. This seems to me to be appropriate, since I will argue throughout the book that we should understand *Leviathan* in light of Hobbes's last work, his *Dialogue*, which would have been composed shortly before the cover portrait was painted.

[2] See Lon Fuller, *The Morality of Law*, New Haven, CT: Yale University Press, 1964.

debates at their time.³ So, while I will sometimes discuss some of the legal debates at Hobbes's time, as well as some of his fellow seventeenth-century philosophers, I come to these debates as a political and legal philosopher interested to see what kind of Hobbesian view could be successfully defended today.

I will be primarily guided by trying to resolve conceptual puzzles that I find in Hobbes's texts in a way that makes him more plausible to contemporary readers. And here one of the most significant puzzles is how Hobbes could come nearly to the end of Part II of *Leviathan*, in Chapter 30, and claim that the sovereign had rather stringent duties, while at the beginning of Part II, in Chapter 17, he had claimed that the sovereign received only rights but no duties from the social contract. I will try to make sense of such puzzles in *Leviathan* by looking to one of Hobbes's last works, his *Dialogue between a Philosopher and a Student of the Common Laws of England*. In the next section I will explore the various ways that sovereignty is seemingly limited in key passages from Hobbes's works. I will then summarize the remaining chapters of this book.

I. Limitations on Sovereign Law-Making

In Chapter 16 of *Leviathan*, Hobbes says that the sovereign is authorized to act in behalf of the subjects or citizens and that such authorizing is "without stint."⁴ Commentators have interpreted this as meaning that there are no limitations on sovereignty. I regard this statement as having considerably less scope than many commentators believe. But in any event, from the fact that the subjects or citizens have given up the authority to criticize the sovereign for what the sovereign does, since it is really their own doing, it does not follow that the sovereign is without limitations. Instead it is merely that limits are not imposed on the sovereign by the subjects or citizens. In this section I will explain where other limits might come from.

---

³ See the treatment of Hobbes's changing views of liberty in terms of the raging rhetorical debates in the middle of the seventeenth century, in Quentin Skinner, *Hobbes and Republican Liberty*, Cambridge: Cambridge University Press, 2008. Also see Quentin Skinner, *Reason and Rhetoric in the Philosophy of Hobbes*, Cambridge: Cambridge University Press, 1996.

⁴ EW III 151, Tuck 114. Throughout I will refer to *Leviathan* first by the pagination of the English Works (EW) edition, *The English Works of Thomas Hobbes*, ed. Sir William Molesworth, 11 vols. (London: John Bohn, 1839), and then by the pagination of the edition of *Leviathan* ed. Richard Tuck (Tuck) in 1996 for Cambridge University Press, which is one of the most readily available versions.

One obvious way that a sovereign could be limited is by laws instead of by humans who are subjects or citizens. Hobbes does dispute the idea that laws rather than men should govern in various places in *Leviathan*, including Chapter 46. But in Hobbes's *Dialogue*, as I will show later, he endorses the idea that it is the King in Parliament that is sovereign. The idea that it is the King in Parliament, not merely the King, that rules seems to open the door to thinking that laws, or at least the specifically law-making Parliament, could limit what the King does. So, if the sovereign is associated with the King, then there appear to be texts that show that Hobbes understood and even may have embraced in his later life the idea of limitations on sovereignty. But I will argue that even in *Leviathan* and *De Cive*, there are passages to make us think that Hobbes embraced limitations on sovereign law-making.

Hobbes is relatively clear in saying that there are no substantive limits on sovereignty and that there should not be any, since the sovereign needs to be as strong as possible in order to secure the peace. But Hobbes also says that there are things the sovereign should not do, such as punishing the innocent or acting cruelly, also in part because these things would weaken the sovereign and make it harder for the sovereign to protect the people. So limiting the sovereign makes it harder to protect the people—the chief duty of the sovereign—but not limiting the sovereign also makes it harder for the sovereign to secure the safety of the people. One obvious way to interpret Hobbes that saves him from this inconsistency is to distinguish types of limitation of sovereignty. And it seems to me that what might be called substantive limits on sovereignty, where subjects or citizens could restrict what the sovereign does, need to be distinguished from other types of limitation that would not weaken the sovereign, at least not concerning the sovereign's ability to secure the peace.

It should be noted that Hobbes is extremely clear in Chapter 30 of *Leviathan*, and many other places, that the sovereign has duties, and that the chief duty is *salus populi*, the safety of the people.

> The Office of the sovereign, be it a monarch or the assembly, consisteth in the end, for which he was trusted with the sovereign power, namely the procuration of *the safety of the people;* to which he is obliged by the law of nature; and to render an account thereof to God, the author of that law, and to none but him.

> But by safety here, is not meant a bare preservation, but also all other contentments of life…and in the making and executing of good laws.[5]

While this point is utterly unambiguous, especially due to the use of the term "obliged," it is not well appreciated that the mere having of obligations or duties is in a sense an admission that the sovereign is limited, even if the sovereign is not answerable to the people. Duties, after all, are just the sort of things that create limits on what can be done generally.

Hobbes also is just as clear that there are many things that are both beyond the sovereign's power and also beyond the sovereign's *legitimate* exercise of power. Next, I shall briefly explore five types of limitation on sovereign law-making power, and in each case discuss to what extent these limitations have teeth in the sense that they would be recognized as serious limitations on sovereignty today. The more developed argument on these topics will be the subject of the chapters that compose the rest of this book.

a. Moral Limitations

Hobbes is often quite straightforward in saying that morality limits legality, contrary to the way he is normally portrayed. The main evidence for saying this comes from the fact that all of the laws of nature, which are the main basis of morality for Hobbes, are said still to be binding after the institution of sovereignty. In addition, Hobbes says that some of these laws of nature, especially equity, clearly bind the sovereign. Hobbes discusses this often, as when he says that the sovereign cannot be said to be unjust but can be said to be iniquitous.

> It is true that they that have sovereign power may commit iniquity; but not injustice or injury in the proper signification.[6]

I take it that it is uncontroversial that iniquity for Hobbes is the violation of equity. And I also take it that commentators have generally not taken Hobbes at his word here when they have claimed that the sovereign can do no wrong in Hobbes's view. What Hobbes says is that the sovereign cannot do injury—that is, cannot violate justice—but that the sovereign can nonetheless commit iniquity.

[5] EW III 322–323, Tuck 231.
[6] EW III 163, Tuck 124.

There is controversy nonetheless about what kind of bindingness there is here, since Hobbes says that all of the laws of nature bind only *in foro interno*, in conscience, not *in foro externo*, in terms of putting them into effect. I will argue that when something binds in conscience it is truly binding. In any event, despite whether laws of nature are binding *in foro externo*, they can still function as limits to sovereignty. Indeed, the laws of nature form the basis for the sovereign's duties that Hobbes clearly sets out in Chapter 30 of *Leviathan*, when he says that the sovereign is obliged by the law of nature, and especially that the sovereign is required to make good laws.[7] The list of the duties of the sovereign includes the duty not to make superfluous laws but only those that are "*needful* for the *good of the people*, and withal *perspicuous*." And Hobbes is clear that the requirement that sovereigns only make good laws is to be distinguished from the making of just laws, "for no law can be unjust."[8] These limitations on sovereignty are not captured by considerations of justice, as this is narrowly defined by Hobbes, but extend to the moral domain of making good laws.

In *De Cive*, Hobbes endorses the idea that government is bounded by some limits, and then singles out those of the natural and divine law. Natural law is equivalent to what Hobbes means by morality, as he makes clear at the end of Chapter 15 of *Leviathan*. There is a bit of confusion in that Hobbes says that the laws of nature restrict civil law, and yet he also says that the laws of nature contain and are of the same extent as the civil law.

> The law of nature, and the civil law, contain each other, and are of equal extent. For the laws of nature, which consist in equity, justice, gratitude, and other moral virtues on these depending, in the condition of mere nature, as I have said before...are not properly laws, but qualities that dispose men to peace and obedience. When the commonwealth is once settled, then are they actually laws, and not before...The law of nature is therefore part of the civil law in all commonwealths of the world. Reciprocally also, the civil law is part of the dictates of nature...Civil and natural law are not different kinds, but different parts of law; whereas one being written is called civil, the other unwritten, natural.[9]

The problem of how to interpret these passages will have to be addressed in more detail later. At the moment, suffice it to say that in Hobbes's later

---

[7] EW III 322–323, Tuck 231.
[8] EW III 335, Tuck 239.
[9] EW III 253–254, Tuck 185.

work, where equity comes to such prominence, it is said to be the main law of nature that binds the sovereign, and hence also thus limits the sovereign's law-making.

In this section of my introductory chapter, equity is being regarded as primarily a moral limitation on sovereign law-making. As such, to say that Hobbes accepted limitations on sovereignty may not seem to be controversial, unless one sees Hobbes as the kind of legal positivist who keeps to a strict separation of law and morality. And this would turn on whether the kind of limitation that morality places on law-making concerns the law's validity, not merely the law's strength.

The discussion of the duties of the sovereign is linked to what is required of the sovereign in terms of equity, which is a law of nature.

> The safety of the people, requireth further, from him, or them that have the sovereign power, that justice be equally administered to all degrees of people; that is that as well the rich and mighty, as poor and obscure persons…for in this consisteth equity, to which as being a precept of the law of nature, a sovereign is as much subject, as any of the meanest of his people.[10]

So there are clear moral limits on the sovereign.

And yet at the end of Chapter 30 of *Leviathan*, Hobbes seemingly muddies the waters when he says:

> the law of nations and the law of nature, is the same thing…And the same law, that dictateth to men that have no civil government, what they ought to do…dictateth the same to commonwealths, that is to the consciences of sovereign princes and sovereign assemblies; there being no court of natural justice, but in the conscience only.[11]

It will be especially interesting to see how Hobbes talks of the Court of Equity in his *Dialogue*, especially since he recognizes that this is very much like a court of natural justice. So, the question of how much teeth such moral limitations have is left uncertain and will require further investigation in later chapters. But the other kinds of limitation of sovereign law-making will relate to the moral limitations and can provide the beginning of an

---

[10] EW III 332, Tuck 237.
[11] EW III 342–343, Tuck 244.

answer about to what extent Hobbes thought that the moral limitation on sovereign law-making was in some sense binding.

b. Prudential Limitations

There are also uncontroversial prudential limits on sovereignty that Hobbes endorses. He argues that sovereigns would be foolish if they were to create superfluous laws or *ex post facto* laws, for example. Hobbes spends much time in Chapter 30 of *Leviathan* and elsewhere discussing the kinds of things that sovereigns should not do if they do not want to risk rebellion or serious dissent in the society where they govern. Indeed, after discussing the prudential limits on sovereign law-making, Hobbes says:

> Take away in any kind of state, the obedience, and consequently the concord of the people, and they shall not only not flourish, but in short time be dissolved.[12]

Hobbes often counsels the sovereign not to act in ways that create dissent in the people because this will weaken, and ultimately undermine, sovereignty.

But as with moral limitations it is unclear to what extent these are binding limits on the sovereign. Prudence is not issued as a matter of commands as law is; rather, prudence is counsel and one can take it or leave it.

> Command is where a man saith, *do this*, or *do not this*, without expecting any other reason than the will of him that says it…Counsel is, where a man saith, do, or do not this, and deduceth his reasons from the benefit that ariveth by it to him he saith it…a man may be obliged to do what he is commanded…but he cannot be obliged to do what he is counseled, because the hurt of not following it is his own[13]

So, in this sense prudence does not seem to be a limitation on sovereignty that has any institutional teeth. Indeed, prudence and morality are such closely allied notions for Hobbes, as most commentators have recognized, that if the moral limits on sovereign law-making are weak it is highly probable that that will also be true of prudential limits on sovereignty. Yet such a view fails to note how concerned Hobbes is that sovereign law-makers

---

[12] EW III 326, Tuck 234.
[13] EW III 241, Tuck 176–177.

not act in ways that jeopardize their sovereignty. Indeed, Hobbes is often put into the same camp as Machiavelli for the prescient advice that they provided to princes and other sovereigns who wanted to continue to hold on to power.

Throughout *Leviathan*, as well as Hobbes's other works, sovereigns are strongly advised not to abuse their power. For instance, in Chapter 18 of *Leviathan*, Hobbes argues that sovereigns must be guided by the strictures of "prevention of discord at home, and hostility from abroad."[14] And in Chapter 24 he advises that sovereigns not be negligent when it comes to monetary affairs in the commonwealth, and specifically that sovereigns avoid "a long and costly war."[15]

Prudential limitations on sovereign law-making are only as strongly limiting as are other forms of prudence in Hobbes's system. But as we will see in subsequent chapters, prudence should be regarded as strongly limiting. Indeed, many commentators have seen Hobbes as effectively substituting prudence for morality in his normative theory. Hobbes talks of these prudential limits as what any sovereign should respect if that sovereign wishes to remain in office. And there is an obligation, which seems to be one of prudence, to do that which will keep the sovereignty from being dissolved.

> if the essential rights of sovereignty…be taken away, the commonwealth is thereby dissolved…it is the office of the sovereign to maintain those rights, and consequently against his duty, first, to transfer to another, to lay from himself any of them[16]

Of course, this limitation on sovereignty, which is clearly a duty, only has strength, as a matter of counsel, insofar as the sovereign wants to benefit from his sovereignty, where this requires that sovereignty not be dissolved.

c. Legal and Structural Limitations

The most controversial, and in many ways the most significant, of the limitations I will address in this book are legal limitations, which take the form of either being straightforward procedural limits on the sovereign, or structural limits on the nature of sovereignty. Structural limits on sovereignty

---

[14] EW III 164, Tuck 124.
[15] EW III 173, Tuck 236.
[16] EW III 323, Tuck 231.

appear, as with the other limitations, not to have any teeth for Hobbes. But insofar as the structural limits are also in some sense legal limits, things get more interesting. This issue is interesting in the context of how Hobbes understands equity, especially in his *Dialogue* written at the end of his life.

There are significant discussions of structural limitations on sovereign law-making in *Leviathan* as well as in the *Dialogue*, as when Hobbes states:

> No law made after a fact done, can make it a crime: because if the fact be against the law of nature, the law was before the fact; and a positive law cannot be taken notice of, before it be made; and therefore cannot be obligatory.[17]

In addition, Hobbes argues:

> when that man, or assembly, that have the sovereign power, commandeth a man to do that which is contrary to a former law, the doing of it is totally excused…when the sovereign commandeth anything to be done against his own former law, the command, as to that particular fact, is an abrogation of the law.[18]

These are what David Dyzenhaus has rightly called structural limits on sovereignty. These are formal or procedural limits of the sort that we will see to be of the same sort as rule of law limitations discussed in contemporary times by theorists such as Lon Fuller. It is a good question, to which we will return, whether such limitations that Hobbes discusses commit him to the kind of rule of law constraints as are so often discussed today.

Hobbes also discusses somewhat more substantive legal limits on sovereignty, most significantly when he discusses the limits on the right of punishment by sovereigns.

> All punishments of innocent subjects, be they great or little, are against the law of nature; for punishment is only for transgression of the law, and therefore there can be no punishment of the innocent.[19]

In this discussion from Chapter 28 of *Leviathan*, Hobbes seems to endorse something like substantive due process, especially as he seeks to link the

---

[17] EW III 281, Tuck 203–204.
[18] EW III 289, Tuck 208–209.
[19] EW III 304, Tuck 219.

prohibition on punishing the innocent with the laws of nature and hence moral considerations. Indeed, Hobbes explicitly links this prohibition with equity when he says: "the law that commandeth equity…which in punishing the innocent is not observed."[20]

In the *Dialogue*, Hobbes talks of equity as a legal basis, grounded in fairness, to challenge otherwise valid law-making. Equity is a legal as well as a natural law category for Hobbes: for he acknowledges that the courts of equity are where one goes to deal with iniquitous or demonstrably unfair judicial acts. Recently, there has been some discussion about whether Hobbes even recognized that a subject or citizen could go to court to seek redress from an action by the sovereign that violated the limits on sovereign law-making. Since the courts of equity are controlled by the sovereign, this likelihood would seemingly not provide limitations of sovereignty with the kind of teeth that many commentators have said to be lacking in Hobbes's system. This is because the sovereign is in control of the court of equity, not someone who can be summoned before it. Yet, Hobbes often says that nonetheless the sovereign is bound by equity.

For Hobbes, structural and due process limitations on sovereign law-making are efficacious, as is true of most procedural or formal matters, not because of explicit sanctions but because of what the people recognize and act upon. Retroactive laws, for instance, can be promulgated. In some contexts it may be possible to challenge these laws in court. But other ways for these laws to be constrained are for them not to be enforced by members of the government who have the task to enforce the law, or not recognized, and hence not obeyed, by members of the populace, especially by government ministers. Indeed, Hobbes says:

> A body of councillors, are never without some authority, either of judicature, or of immediate administration.[21]

To what extent government ministers will uphold such limitations on sovereignty as are involved in the prohibition on ex post fact laws is not easy to figure out in Hobbes's texts, but there does seem to be a kind of structural limitation on sovereignty, as I will argue in more detail later.

---

[20] EW III 304, Tuck 219.
[21] EW III 231, Tuck 170.

One of the things that makes Hobbes so interesting to me is the continuing relevance of his thought to today's problems. It remains a matter of theoretical concern how to characterize the way that structural limitations on law-making are binding. Hobbes's discussions about the limits on sovereign law-making have not previously been well recognized and are insufficiently studied. These discussions are especially interesting because Hobbes did not recognize that the people retain a right to disobey the sovereign, except in certain special cases such as when the sovereign tries to kill one of his or her subjects. But there are duties of the sovereign nonetheless, and they seem to correspond to those discussed today that fall under the label of due process, contrary to the way Hobbes is normally understood.

d. International Limitations

I wish next to consider some of the things that Hobbes discusses that could provide limitations on sovereignty in terms of international relations. Hobbes is often interpreted as saying that the sovereign can pretty much do as he or she pleases *vis-à-vis* other sovereigns. Indeed, it is clear that if a sovereign would consider himself or herself to be limited by other sovereigns, it is these other sovereigns who are really sovereign. This discussion occurs in Chapter 29 of *Leviathan*, when Hobbes discusses the nature of sovereignty and says that when sovereign power is divided it destroys itself.[22]

Another initial place to turn is where Hobbes strongly endorses the idea that a sovereign cannot punish the innocent. In that discussion in Chapter 28, he also makes it clear that if the person to be punished is not one of the sovereign's subjects the one to be punished should be treated differently.

> But the infliction of what evil soever, on an innocent man, that is not a subject, if it be for the benefit of the commonwealth, and without violation of any former covenant, is no breach of the law of nature.[23]

Notice, though, that the excerption here concerns where a sovereign has made a covenant with another sovereign. The law of nature concerning contracts and covenants apparently binds sovereigns when interacting with other sovereigns, or at least seems to govern the international arena. If this is

---

[22] EW III 313, Tuck 225.
[23] EW III 313, Tuck 225.

a reasonable interpretation of the above passage, then it is very hard indeed to continue to think that Hobbes is the great defender of seeing the international arena as one of pure anarchy, as he has often been interpreted, especially by realists in international relations theory.

In Chapter 22 of *Leviathan*, Hobbes allows that there can be a "league between commonwealths" that is "not only lawful, but also profitable." And here he talks about such a league being formed by mutual covenants.[24] Yet because there is no international power to keep them all in awe, Hobbes rejects the idea that there can be a true world sovereign. Nonetheless, his discussion of how States can be bound to keep covenants among themselves certainly appears to set the stage for external limitations on sovereignty. As with our earlier discussion of other limitations on sovereignty, those that occur in the international arena may not have the teeth for which one would hope. Yet, that is also certainly the state of things today in international relations, where States nonetheless restrict themselves by their mutual covenants.

Non-consensual forms of international law, such as international criminal law, are also not ruled out by Hobbes, since it turns out that sovereigns in effect abdicate their sovereignty when they seek to oppress or kill sections of their own populace.

> The obligation of subjects to the sovereign, is understood to last as long, and no longer, than the power lasteth, by which he is able to protect them. For the right men have by nature to protect themselves, when none else can protect them, can by no covenant be relinquished. The sovereignty is the soul of the commonwealth; which once departed from the body, the members no more receive their motion from it.[25]

As I will argue in great detail later, a Hobbesian could support international criminal law as a means to allow for such gaps in sovereignty that open when sovereigns have abdicated their sovereignty by attacking or failing to protect their subjects.

I will also argue that the kind of rules of war that are characterized in the Geneva Conventions can also be accommodated from a Hobbesian perspective, especially concerning limitations on cruelty that Hobbes clearly

---

[24] EW III 222–223, Tuck 163.
[25] EW III 208, Tuck 153.

supports. Indeed in *De Cive*, as well as in *Leviathan*, Hobbes says that cruelty can never be justified.

> But there are certain natural laws, whose exercise ceaseth not even in the time of war. For I cannot understand what drunkenness or cruelty, that is, revenge that respects not the future good, can advance toward peace, or the preservation of any man.[26]

Here is a limitation that has been at the center of contemporary attempts by the International Committee of the Red Cross to restrict certain kinds of tactics during war and other international relations.

At the end of the book I argue, in addition, that Hobbes, or at least a Hobbesian, would support the restriction of war-like attitudes that are sometimes displayed by people and sovereigns, so that peace can be achieved and sustained. I suggest that this can be characterized as support for pacifist attitudes and the restriction of pro-war attitudes by subjects and sovereigns alike. This thesis is probably the most controversial of all my theses concerning how to interpret Hobbes's views of limitations on sovereignty in international affairs. But even in this case I believe that Hobbes recognized how important it was especially for sovereigns to restrict themselves, and to accept limitations, on the exercise of their sovereign law-making power.

e. Self-limitations

Let me now return to the quotation from *De Cive* that serves as the epigram for my book and that is one of the clearest statements Hobbes made about limitations on sovereignty.

> Most men grant, that a government ought not to be divided; but they would have it moderated and bounded by some limits. Truly it is very reasonable it should be so…for my part, I wish that not only kings, but all other persons, endued with supreme authority, would so temper themselves…within the limits of natural and divine law.[27]

In this quotation, Hobbes makes it clear that he is speaking of limitations on governments, and it is also clear that he thinks some such limitations

---

[26] EW II 45 ch. 3, para 26, note. I will refer to *De Cive* by citing the version reprinted in *The English Works of Thomas Hobbes*, ed. Sir William Molesworth, 11 vols. (London: John Bohn, 1839), vol. II, and then by chapter and paragraph number.

[27] EW II 96 ch. 7, para. 4, note.

are reasonable. The limits that are addressed here are those that come from "natural and divine law" and are hence primarily moral limits on what a government can do. Hobbes is equally clear in this *De Cive* quotation that he does not support divided government, where sovereignty is spread among several branches of government.

So, what did Hobbes mean by supporting the idea that government should be "moderated and bounded by some limits"? One clear possibility is that these are limits that sovereigns should impose on themselves, which is presumably why Hobbes talks of Kings and other sovereigns tempering themselves. Self-limitations seem to be quite weak, at least by comparison with normal structural and legal limitations on sovereignty that are often written into constitutions today. But there is good reason to believe that Hobbes is not thinking of such a comparison.

Then there is the question of why Hobbes refers to natural and divine law if the limits under discussion are merely those that are self-imposed. One would think that moral limits would not be merely self-imposed limits. Yet it is clear that Hobbes often talks about morality as simply a matter of what we are obliged to do as a matter of conscience, *in foro interno*, as he says at the end of Chapter 15 of *Leviathan*. Indeed, Hobbes often talks of how conscience should not be placed over considerations of obedience to law on the part of subjects or citizens. Hobbes is clearly skeptical of those who thought that conscience was so strongly binding that in all cases it could and should override obedience and fidelity to law.

Yet when conscience is linked with the natural and divine law, there is an opening for an interpretation of what Hobbes means by self-imposed limitations on sovereignty that sees these limits as not merely internal limits. After all, Hobbes believed that the natural and divine law is "immutable and eternal"[28] as well as applicable to all people in all circumstances. Indeed, the distinction between internal and external does not capture what Hobbes means by distinguishing *in foro interno* from *in foro externo*. Hobbes says that the former bind "to a desire they should take place" but not always "to the putting them in act."[29] But there is little doubt that Hobbes thinks that the laws of nature bind all people, including the sovereign, since concerning

---

[28] EW III 145, Tuck 110.
[29] EW III 145, Tuck 110.

"the law of nature, a sovereign is as much subject, as any of the meanest of his people."[30]

Hobbesian self-imposed limitations, grounded in natural or divine law, may be binding in ways that one might not expect. As I will argue later, the way in which the third law of nature is binding on conscience is similar, Hobbes says, to the way that one is bound not to contradict oneself. Hobbes even talks of a specific fear here: the fear of absurdity that would result when someone engaged in self-contradiction. Should the self-imposed limits that Hobbes discusses in *De Cive* and elsewhere be similarly seen as just as binding as are limits based on the fear of self-contradiction? Hobbes certainly suggests this much in his discussion of certain laws of nature in Chapter 14 of *Leviathan*.

> And the same are the Bonds, by which men are bound, and obliged: bonds, that have their strength, not from their own nature, for nothing is more easily broken than a man's word, but from fear of some evil consequence upon the rupture.[31]

In any event, the limitations on sovereign law-making that Hobbes discusses can still be somewhat binding even as they are self-imposed, as I shall argue in the chapters that follow.

II. Summary of Arguments of the Book

Let me now briefly set out the topics and theses I develop in the ten chapters that make up this small book on Hobbes. In Chapter 1 I set out a sketch of most of the issues I take up in greater detail in the rest of the book, and I emphasize especially how morality is related to prudence as well as to law. Throughout this chapter I compare Hobbes's views to those philosophers and lawyers who were his contemporaries. Here I make use of various legal concepts that were discussed during Hobbes's time, including the idea of assumpsit (that a bare promise, without consideration, can have legally binding effect) and of a third-party beneficiary contract (where a person who is not a party to a contract can nonetheless have rights from the contract),

---

[30] EW III 332, Tuck 237.
[31] EW III 119, Tuck 93.

as well as the emerging doctrine of sovereignty that was developed by Jean Bodin and Richard Hooker.

In Chapter 2 I discuss Hobbes's two contract theories as found in *Leviathan* and the *Dialogue*. Hobbes is normally interpreted as holding only one type of contract theory: a hypothetical social contract theory. But I argue that Hobbes is best interpreted to be advancing an actual constitutional contract theory as well. The difference between the hypothetical and constitutional contract lets Hobbes avoid some of the most important problems faced by other social contract theorists. Here I set the stage for Hobbes's conversation with Edward Coke and Matthew Hale, the leading lawyers of his day.

In Chapter 3 I argue that equity, not justice, is the central moral concept for Hobbes, at least concerning his legal philosophy. I draw heavily on differences between *Leviathan* and Hobbes's *Dialogue*. In the *Dialogue*, Hobbes is much clearer about what equity entails as far as limitations on the sovereign, and also that equity is to have pride of place in his political and legal system. Equity considerations place rather stringent constraints on what the sovereign law-maker can do, making the whole system both procedurally and substantively fairer. Such a conception allows us to portray Hobbes in a far more palatable way than he is normally drawn.

In Chapter 4, I present an extended discussion of Hobbes's *Dialogue* as I set out the main features of his legal philosophy. This chapter provides one of the very few commentaries on the *Dialogue* since Hobbes wrote this work 350 years ago. One author was so bold as to say that Hobbes's doctrine in the *Dialogue* was certainly clear, but inadequate. In this chapter I dispute that interpretation. I discuss Hobbes's views of the nature and sources of law as well as how the various types of law relate to each other. Aquinas's system of law is contrasted with that of Hobbes, and I also discuss some of the differences between Hobbes and leading legal theorists of his time.

Chapter 5 completes the largely exegetical chapters of the book with a close look at what Hobbes says about obedience and fidelity to law. In this chapter I argue that Hobbes is not a strict legal positivist. Indeed, the view of Hobbes's legal philosophy, at least concerning obedience to law, is closer to Lon Fuller than is normally believed. I spend much time examining what Hobbes says about those who choose to disobey legal authority when condemned to death or when sent off to battle.

Chapter 6 discusses sovereignty, and examines in detail Hobbes's debates with the two leading legal theorists of his day, Coke and Hale—both Lord

Chief Justices of the King's Bench. I argue that Hobbes came to change his mind somewhat about the desirability of divided sovereignty by the time, near the end of his life, that he wrote the *Dialogue*. But I also argue that Hobbes should have developed more than a very thin conception of the rule of law. Hobbes should have been more open to the ideas that the jurists of his day were developing, especially the idea that the judiciary should have independent status.

In Chapter 7 I address one of the most enduring legacies of Hobbes, his account of authority and representation, and draw out its significance for today's debates about how best to understand the limits of the authority of representative agents such as sovereign rulers. I attempt to provide a characterization of mass or group agency and responsibility. I am interested in extending Hobbes's discussion of how a multitude becomes unified to set the stage for answering questions about how sovereign States should interact with groups. I attempt to construct a Hobbesian view of mass action such as the mass uprisings we have seen in the so-called Arab Spring, where thousands of people were able to organize themselves apparently without a leader. I also consider the case of the storming of the Bastille, where people gathering in the street were able to destroy a fortress that armies could not topple previously.

In the last three chapters I explore themes in international legal theory. In Chapter 8 I develop a Hobbesian defense of international criminal law. The centerpiece of this defense is the idea, taken rather directly from *Leviathan*, that if a sovereign cannot or will not protect its people then sovereignty is undermined and the people can seek "outside" forces for their protection and redress of their wrongs—even an international institution. Here I confront directly the long line of theorists, including Hans Morgenthau and Hedley Bull, who argue that Hobbes would reject any international institution because the world of international affairs is one of anarchy.

In Chapter 9 I continue the line of argument begun in the previous chapter by explaining how a consistent Hobbesian could support the rules of war—some of the key rules governing international order today. I argue that Hobbes was keenly aware that cruelty needed to be outlawed even in the state of war, and I indicate that Hobbes can provide the grounding for contemporary international agreements on the rules of war, especially the St Petersburg Declaration, the Lieber Code, and the Geneva Conventions.

In Chapter 10 I end the book with an attempt to explain to what extent a consistent Hobbesian, and even Hobbes himself, could be seen as supporting pacifist attitudes. This is in some ways the chapter that runs most directly against people's general sense of Hobbes's views. But it is also, perhaps surprisingly, the chapter of the last set that is most closely connected to what Hobbes says about the first and most fundamental law of nature: to seek peace. In ending on this note I complete a reappraisal of Hobbes and Hobbesian legal and political philosophy that might cause a change in the debates about how to understand arguably the greatest systematic philosopher to have written in the English language.

We are currently experiencing yet another resurgence of interest in Hobbes—which was also true 35 years ago just after I finished my doctoral dissertation at the time of the three-hundredth anniversary of Hobbes's death. That students and readers continue to find Hobbes and Hobbesian ideas fascinating is, of course, a testament to Hobbes, but also to the very distinguished group of philosophers who have written on Hobbes over the years. My own modest contribution to that literature is to explicate Hobbes's generally neglected legal philosophy, and to work out what a Hobbesian approach to international law would look like.

Over the years I have tried out these ideas on fellow philosophers and political theorists. In nearly every case, people have said that they admired my imagination but that surely the standard interpretation of Hobbes has survived for so long because it best accounts for the texts. But once we have sat and looked at the texts, these scholars have often come to see, what most of my graduate students have also seen, that Hobbes's views are both more complex and more palatable than they had thought previously. This is a shame if one wants to use Hobbes as a foil. Perhaps we can use the old term "Hobbist" so that this foil is still available. But I will argue that this is not Hobbes, and not even a plausible Hobbesian theory.

I hope that at the very least readers will be surprised at how useful Hobbes is for understanding and justifying international law, even international criminal law—the area of research in which I have worked most closely over the past decade. Indeed, my work on the moral foundations of international criminal law is completely indebted to a Hobbesian way of viewing the world, although, as will become clear in this book, what I take to be such a Hobbesian perspective will probably be very different from what most of my readers think. Even if I do not convince people to change their views of Hobbes, I hope readers will enjoy thinking with me about the ideas of the first great philosopher to write in English.[32]

---

[32] I thank Emily McGill for help especially with the middle part of this chapter.

I
Law, Morality, and Prudence

In this chapter I will set out a general sketch of Hobbes's moral, political, and legal philosophy, emphasizing how the legal side influenced the other two. I will have occasion to develop this sketch in more detail in subsequent chapters. But here I want to present the overall view of morality, politics, and law that I take Hobbes to have held in order to show how different I see him from the way he is normally portrayed. The differences will become acute in later chapters, especially where I argue that it is equity, not justice, that is the central legal and political concept for Hobbes, and much later yet, where I argue that Hobbes can be seen as a theorist who would support the rules of war as well as international institutions. In this introductory chapter I will also discuss some of Hobbes's immediate predecessors.

Changes in legal theory in the late sixteenth and early seventeenth century, especially concerning contract and obligation, had a profound impact on Hobbes's political and moral philosophy as well. The seventeenth century was a period of radical change, and by its end, Hobbes's espousal of a legally oriented, prudential, social contract theory was recognized to be the most radical normative philosophy of the time. In this chapter I will attempt to assess, and at least partially reject, the portrait of Hobbes sketched by his contemporaries—namely, as the chief exponent of an amoral philosophy which challenged all that was good in the classical natural law tradition, epitomized by Aquinas.

While Hobbes did break with classical traditions in ethics, his break was consistent with certain developments in political and legal theory at his time. Indeed, it is my contention that rather than rejecting the natural law tradition, Hobbes is best appreciated as having found a non-theological basis for the doctrine of moral obligation. In Hobbes's view, the dictates of conscience, encapsulating the voice of God, were not the sole or even the most important source of morality. Instead, prudentially-based consent and conformity to the properly authorized dictates of the sovereign lawmaker were the chief ingredients in Hobbes's theory of obligation. Thus Hobbes's critics were not fully justified in regarding him as the chief enemy of the classical tradition. It is true that Hobbes came to moral and political disputes from a starting point very different from that of classical authors, but the conclusions that he reached were often not so greatly at odds with these authors as his contemporaries claimed. Finally, I will also consider the extent to which Hobbes's views are unique, and whether or not those views lead us to a plausible basis for law, politics, and ethics.

I. Sovereignty and Assumpsit

In the late sixteenth and early seventeenth century, two concepts, sovereignty and assumpsit, were developed which seem to have greatly affected Hobbes's understanding of the contractual obligation a citizen owed to a ruler. In this section I will briefly survey the development of these two concepts. First, I will look at the writings of Jean Bodin and Richard Hooker on sovereignty—a concept which epitomized the modern turn in political and moral thought. From Bodin, Hobbes probably borrowed the new concept of sovereignty; and from Hooker he probably borrowed the notion that the social contract was an agreement between individuals, not between a people and a ruler. I will then look at various legal writings on the emerging doctrine of assumpsit which significantly changed contract law in England at Hobbes's time, and may have been a model for Hobbes's own understanding of the social contract.

At the end of the sixteenth century the social contract was linked with a new notion of rulership, which the French theorist Jean Bodin called sovereignty. Bodin argued that a ruler derived unlimited power from a transfer of power from the people; that is, he argued that the people, by a contract, gave up any claim to retain rulership in their own hands by contracting with and subjecting themselves to a ruler. He defined sovereignty as "the most high, absolute, and perpetuall power over the citisens and subjects in a commonwealle...that is to say, the greatest power to command."[1] There had been many theories of absolute rulership before Bodin; and there had been many

---

[1] Jean Bodin, *The Six Bookes of a Commonweale*, K. D. McRae (ed.), Cambridge, MA: Harvard University Press, 1962, p. 84

theories of obligation based on contract. But Bodin was one of the first to combine these two notions to form the modern notion of sovereignty.

The main feature of Bodin's contract-based sovereignty was that it was not limited by other persons or political bodies, although it remained limited by various natural law factors. Here is how Bodin put it: "the chiefe power given unto a prince *with charge and condition* is not properly soveraigntie, nor power absolute."[2] Power must be given absolutely, that is, given as unlimited, in order to be properly sovereign power. Hobbes's own notion of sovereignty seems to have drawn heavily on that of Bodin. But Bodin and Hobbes were not in complete agreement. Bodin, like his predecessors, continued to cling to the natural law foundation of rulership. He saw the relationship between sovereign monarch and subjects as an extension of the relation between a father and his family. Bodin also retained the idea that the subjects, as a "people," relinquished power to the sovereign, rather than relinquishing power as individual citizen-subjects. The people had a position analogous to the family, and as a result the individual members had no status apart from their group in respect to the grant of sovereignty. For Bodin, the people were a type of "corporation." But he gave little indication how this corporation, as a body, related to its individual members. This was typical of the writers prior to Hobbes: the people were not seen as a collection of individuals each giving assent to the ruler.

On the other side of the English Channel, Richard Hooker's notion of a covenant-based rulership varied from that of Bodin, as did his view of sovereignty. Hooker introduced the idea that covenants, especially the covenant between God and man, needed to be conceived in individualistic terms. In both religious and political contexts there must be a compact between individual subject and sovereign ruler, and the terms of this compact must be well understood in order for the subject to be obligated to obey the dictates of the ruler. Here is the way he put it:

> the articles of compact between them must shew: not only the articles of the first beginning, which for the most part are clean worn out of knowledge, or else known unto very few, but whatsoever hath been after in free and voluntary manner condescended unto, whether by express consent, whereof positive laws

---

[2] *The Six Bookes of a Commonwealle*, p. 89.

are witnesses, or else by silent allowances famously notified through custom reaching beyond the memory of man.[3]

For Hooker, moral obligation is created by the explicit or implicit consent of individuals. Unless the individual person, not merely that person's group, consents to the law-maker, the individual is not properly obligated. On this point, Hobbes and Hooker were in complete agreement.

But Hooker also held that the "best established dominion [is] where the law doth most rule the king." Hooker wanted not only to establish the contractual basis of the obligations of citizens, but also the contractual limitations on the power of the ruler. Of all the advocates of religious toleration during this period, Hooker presented the most legally oriented attack on the absolute power of the King. His general maxim was that "power may be limited ere it be granted." Hobbes followed Bodin in thinking that sovereignty was not properly so called when it was divided. To divide the powers of rulers is merely to open the door for another person to supplant this ruler. I will argue that Hobbes clearly disfavored divided sovereignty (at least in *Leviathan*), but as the title of my book, *Limiting Leviathan*, indicates, Hobbes did agree that sovereignty could and should be limited.

One other historical development may have had an influence on Hobbes's attempt to ground obligation in a social contract. Contract law before Hobbes's time was seen mainly as a branch of property law. It was not sufficient to show that there had been an agreement between two parties, and a subsequent breach of that agreement, in order to establish that one of the parties had a basis of legal action. In addition, there had to be some "consideration" at stake. Only when there was something done to or given by one party to another, and one had thereby established the *quid* of the *quid pro quo*, could a claim be made for the *quo*. It was not the promise *per se* that created the obligation, but the debt.[4]

By the end of the sixteenth century, contract law was changing in England. The doctrine of assumpsit arose that allowed one to sue merely for

---

[3] Richard Hooker, *The Laws of Ecclesiastical Polity*, ed. R. A. Houk, New York: Columbia University Press, 1931, p. 176.
[4] The English legal historians Sir Frederick Pollock and Frederick William Maitland provide the best treatment of the history of contract law just prior to Hobbes's time. See their monumental study *The History of English Law Before the Time of Edward I*, 2nd ed., vol. 2, Cambridge: Cambridge University Press, 1909.

the violation of a promise, regardless of whether there had been a "consideration" or not. It was thought to be sufficient that one person had raised the expectations of another through the spoken act of promise-making—that is, through beginning an "undertaking" that expressed the voluntary relinquishing of what one would otherwise have been free to do. Once the doctrine of assumpsit established a foundation for legal actions based on promises alone, the stage was set for the creation of obligations, especially in politics, which could not be removed merely by withdrawing from the agreed-on undertaking. By the end of the sixteenth century, assumpsit actions had established the theory that irreversible legal rights and duties resulted from agreements and contracts.[5]

Of equal importance, developments in the doctrine of assumpsit led to the establishment of the legitimacy of "third-party beneficiary contracts." By the middle of the seventeenth century it had become well accepted in English common law that the beneficiary of a promise, even when that person was not one of the contracting parties, had a legitimate right to the benefit. Lever *v.* Heys (1599), for instance, concerns a marriage agreement struck between two fathers. One father promised to pay a certain sum of money as dowry to the second father's son if the second father agreed to give his consent to the marriage and assure that it would take place. Properly, then, the contract was made between the fathers, with the son being only a third party to the contract and incurring no obligations thereby himself. The legal question was this: once the marriage had taken place, did the son have a legal right to the dowry, and could he sue on his own behalf to secure it. The judges of the King's Bench ruled that the son did have standing to sue.[6] We will explore this case, and similar ones, in much more detail later.

---

[5] The American jurist Oliver Wendell Holmes argues quite cogently for the historical thesis that assumpsit developed out of a need for contractual obligation that was not based on debt. See his book *The Common Law*, ed. Mark DeWolfe Howe, Boston: Little Brown, 1963, especially pp. 198–226.

[6] Two other cases are important to consider as well. In Provender *v.* Wood (Hetley 31,124 ER 318, 1631) the court ruled that "the party to whom the benefit of a promise accrews, may bring his action." And in Starkey *v.* Mill (Style 296, 82 ER 723, 1651), the principle articulated in Provender was applied to a commercial situation, and again the third party was said to have the right to sue. "Roll Chief Iustice held, that it is good as it is, for there is a plain contract because the goods were given for the benefit of the plaintiff, though the contract be not made between him and the defendant, and he may have an action upon the case for here is a promise in law made to the plaintiff, though there be not a promise in fact." For an analysis of these and related cases, see G. W. F. Dold, *Stipulations for a Third Party*, London: Stevens and Sons, 1948.

As we will see, Hobbes made his sovereign a third-party beneficiary to the contract that each person makes with each other person in the state of nature. This doctrine, though fraught with problems, constitutes one of the unique contributions Hobbes made to social contract theory. While it is not possible to prove that Hobbes was influenced by the legal developments in assumpsit at his time, his doctrine of contract is so similar to that of the common law defenders of assumpsit that the influence seems probable. In any event, Hobbes explicitly acknowledged his reliance on a large number of other common law doctrines. And as we will see later, his moral concepts of right, justice, and equity are all framed within a legalistic structure.

II. Self-Interest and Natural Right

Psychology is as important to Hobbes as is law and, interestingly, the two combine in an important way. Surely the most famous passages from *Leviathan* deal with the highly imaginative thought experiment, the state of nature, which Hobbes developed to test his views of human nature and the psychological motivation to obey the law. It is quite clear that Hobbes did not envision the state of nature as an historical condition. He said:

> It may peradventure be thought, there was never such a time, nor condition of war as this; and I believe it was never generally so, over all the world…yet in all times, kings, and persons of sovereign authority, because of their independency are in continual jealousies, and in the state and posture of gladiators…[7]

But it is equally clear that Hobbes used this thought experiment to set out his views on the relation between psychology and ethics—especially the centrality of self-interest to the concept of natural right.

Hobbes begins his discussion of the mythical state of nature by drawing our attention to three conditions of equality that exist in nature: equality of strength, equality of prudence or ability, and equality of hope. Equality of strength does not imply that each person possesses the same amount of physical strength as the next person, but only that "the weakest has strength enough to kill the strongest."[8] People are of equal strength in the sense that

---

[7] EW III 114–15, Tuck 89–90.
[8] EW III 110, Tuck 87.

each is endowed with enough physical strength to put the other in fear. Even the strongest must sleep, and then even the weakest can sneak up and thrust a dagger into such a person's back. Hobbes regards this vulnerability as a basis for the motivation of fear in human psychology.

The second equality, of prudence or the ability to pursue one's own interests, is a greater "equality among men, than that of strength."[9] Equality of prudence results from the equal opportunity to learn from experience. "For prudence is but experience; which equal time, equally bestows on all men, in those settings they equally apply themselves unto." Thus, like equality of strength, Hobbes does not claim that all people are equal in the amount of their prudence, but only that they are all equally capable of achieving a certain level of ability if they apply themselves. So not only are people relatively equal in strength, but they are also relatively equal in the ability rationally to pursue their own interests. That people would pursue their own interests, over all else, in the state of nature seems to be based largely on the fear that equality of strength creates.[10]

From this second equality a third develops: the equality of hope, which is simply a synthesis of the first two. When two people desire the same thing, neither one backs away; instead, the two become enemies in striving for it. They become enemies because they both perceive themselves as equal in strength and ability, and they thus come to have an equal hope of prevailing in any conflict. Such competition is rendered even more plausible by Hobbes's contention that it is also natural for individual persons to seek gain, safety, and reputation, and that it is not uncommon for people to resort to violence to achieve these basic ends.[11] All of these natural psychological conditions lead to such a fear among persons as to transform the state of nature into a state of war, "and such a war as is of every man against every other man."[12]

This state of war is totally devoid of all the aspects of society and civilization that we have come to accept as synonymous with human life itself. By

---

[9] EW III 110, Tuck 87.
[10] Here I take no stand on the debate that has raged recently about the extent to which Hobbes was an egoist. The two most recent books on this issue are in S. A. Lloyd's *Morality in the Philosophy of Thomas Hobbes: Cases in the Law of Nature*, New York: Cambridge University Press, 2009; and Bernard Gert's *Hobbes: Prince of Peace*, Cambridge: Polity Press, 2010. I will discuss this issue in some detail later in the text.
[11] See EW III, 112, Tuck 88; and also see EW II 6n.
[12] EW III 113, Tuck 88.

so stating his case, Hobbes explicitly challenges the Aristotelian identification of human life with social life.[13] In this state of war, says Hobbes, the continual fear of our neighbors would make our lives reducible to a simple formula: "solitary, poor, nasty, brutish and short."[14] It would be solitary because we have no reason to trust anyone else; poor because we have no possible benefit of commerce in such a war; nasty because we are continually threatened and fearful of one another; brutish because we only have time to act on our passions like our fellow animals; and short because the war of every man against every man results in many untimely and violent deaths.

This incredibly pessimistic account of the nature of human life, Hobbes says, is borne out in part by the actions of all of us, when, without any provocation we arm ourselves and lock our doors.

> Does [a person] not there as much accuse mankind by his actions as I do with my words? But neither of us accuse man's nature in it. The desires and the other passions of man, are in themselves no sin. No more are the actions, that proceed from those passions, till they know a law that forbids them: which till laws be made they cannot know: nor can any law be made, till they have agreed upon the person to make it.[15]

The key to getting out of this miserable condition is the agreement, the contract, to allow for a common power which can make and enforce laws on us, thereby ending the natural war.

Hobbes singles out one particular consequence of the lack of law enforcement in the state of nature:

> Where there is no common power, there is no law: where no law, no justice...Justice, and injustice, are none of the faculties of body, nor mind...They are qualities, that relate to men in society, not in solitude.[16]

This particular consequence is taken up at greater length subsequently in *Leviathan* in a general discussion of the relation between justice and law.

---

[13] EW II 2–3, ch. I, para. 2.
[14] EW III 113, Tuck 89.
[15] EW III 114, Tuck 89.
[16] EW III 115, Tuck 90.

As a final note on this discussion of our natural self-interested dispositions, it is worth mentioning that Hobbes also identifies three passions which would incline individual persons to seek peace and therefore to seek some way out of the misery of the state of nature. These passions are: (1) "fear of death;" (2) "desire of such things as are necessary to commodious living;" and (3) "hope by their industry to obtain them."

These passions have the same basis as the threefold equality among persons: strength, prudence, and hope. But now people have a strong reason "which suggesteth convenient articles of peace, upon which men may be drawn to agreement. These articles are they which otherwise are called the Laws of Nature…"[17], and Hobbes later equates the laws of nature with "the true moral philosophy."[18] Hobbes's account of the general epistemic status of moral propositions, such as are embodied in the laws of nature, is the important part of his theory to which I now turn.

III. Moral Epistemology and the Laws of Nature

For Hobbes, understanding is generally characterized as "conception caused by speech."[19] One person is said to understand another's words when one person has various thoughts caused by the hearing of the other's speech, *and* when these thoughts are those which the words of that speech were ordained to signify.[20] But sometimes the equivocation of names makes it

> *difficult* to recover those conceptions for which the name was ordained; and that not only in the language of other men…but also in our discourse, which being derived from the custom and common use of speech, representeth unto us not our own conceptions.[21]

The best example Hobbes offers of equivocation and inconsistency in the meaning assigned to names occurs in ethical discourse. In Chapter 6 of *Leviathan*, Hobbes tells us that the names "good" and "evil" refer to objects

---

[17] EW III 116, Tuck 90.
[18] EW III 146, Tuck 110.
[19] See Philip Pettit, *Made with Words*, Princeton: Princeton University Press, 2008.
[20] EW III 28, Tuck 31.
[21] EW IV 23. ch.V, para. 8. I will refer to Hobbes's *Human Nature or the Fundamental Elements of Policy* by citing the version reprinted in The English Works of Thomas Hobbes, ed. Sir William Molesworth, 11 vols. (London: John Bohn, 1839), vol. IV, and by chapter and paragraph.

of appetite and aversion respectively for the individuals who employ these terms, "there being nothing simply and absolutely" good or evil.[22] And in Chapter 4 he says that all people are "not like affected" and hence they call the same thing by different names.[23] Specifically, with respect to the so-called virtues and vices, we find that

> one man calleth *wisdom* what another calleth *fear;* and one *cruelty,* what another *justice;* one *prodigality* what another *magnanimity;* and one *gravity* what another *stupidity,* &c. And therefore such names can never be true grounds of any ratiocination.[24]

Thus it would appear that a science of ethics leading to correct reasoning and understanding is blocked by the possible equivocation and relativity of ethical names, for terms like "good" are "relative to person, place and time."[25]

But Hobbes also speaks of a kind of deductive knowledge in science, which is not linked to such an uncertain basis because it is *a priori,* not *a posteriori.* We can know various things to be true by right reasoning which proceeds from what we ourselves have made or generated; that is, it is possible to know that a figure will have a certain proportion because through geometry we have constructed that figure and its dimensions. Similarly, politics and ethics "can be demonstrated *a priori;* because we ourselves make the principles—that is, the cause of justice (namely laws and covenants)..."[26] But such knowledge can only be achieved in civil society, because without a power to overawe us all and guarantee that these covenants will be kept, laws and covenants are not practical in the state of nature.[27]

Without such a power to guarantee a common basis for our various feelings of appetite and aversion, ethical propositions must only be contingently true. In Chapter 7 of *Leviathan* Hobbes explains that all *a posteriori* reasoning

---

[22] EW III 41, Tuck 39.
[23] EW III 28, Tuck 31.
[24] EW III 29, Tuck 31.
[25] De Homine Ch. 11; I will refer to *De Homine* by chapter and then by citing the version in Bernard Gert, ed. *Man and Citizen,* 1991, p. 47.
[26] De Homine, Ch. 10; Bernard Gert, ed. *Man and Citizen,* 1991, p. 42.
[27] A number of commentators have written on the importance of the deductive method for Hobbes's philosophy. One of the most accessible of such commentaries was provided by J. W. N. Watkins, *Hobbes's System of Ideas,* London: Hutchinson & Co., 1965, chs. 2 and 3.

of this type is conditional because it is not possible to know absolutely through discourse "that this or that, is, has been, or will be."[28] In ethical discourse, the relativity of understanding is compounded by the fact that we must begin from the opinions we hold of what is conducive to our own pleasure, and we remain uncertain that we will continue to hold the same opinions later or that others will be of the same opinion about the causes of our own pleasures. Thus, for Hobbes, knowledge of what we ought to do remains uncertain and only contingently true.

The notion of obligation in Hobbes's moral epistemology is stabilized by the idea that there are laws of nature or moral precepts found by reason alone.[29] This position reflects, but only to a certain extent, the late-medieval view that human reason could attain knowledge of the moral law. Aquinas had held this position also, but he contended that it was possible for only some humans to whom God had bestowed special powers. Hobbes is much more a forerunner of the Enlightenment moral philosophers than he is a follower in the Thomistic tradition on this issue. This is mainly due to the fact that Hobbes does not think that human reason needs to be aided in order to be able to come to a full knowledge of the moral law embodied in the laws in nature.[30] For Hobbes, natural right and law of nature are derived from reasonable, prudential maxims known to all.[31] Here again we see that Hobbes is attempting to ground morality in strictly non-theological terms, though not necessarily in terms at odds with traditional natural law concerns.

---

[28] EW III 52, Tuck 47.

[29] EW III 116, Tuck 90.

[30] There has been a lively debate about how reason is related to the laws of nature in Hobbes's system. See John Deigh, "Reason and Ethics in Hobbes's Leviathan," *Journal of the History of Philosophy*, vol. 34, 1996; Mark Murphy, "Desire and Ethics in Hobbes's Leviathan: A Response to Professor Deigh," *Journal of the History of Philosophy*, vol. 38, 2000, pp. 259–268; and Kinch Hoekstra, "Hobbes on Law, Nature, and Reason," *Journal of the History of Philosophy*, vol. 41, no. 1, 2003, pp. 111–120.

[31] There is a significant group of interpreters of Hobbes who do not share my views on whether God is needed to aid us in knowing the laws of nature. A. E. Taylor, Howard Warrender, F. C. Hood, and more recently A. P. Martinich, have each advanced the thesis that God plays a central role in Hobbes's moral philosophy. Warrender presents the strongest argument against the interpretation I urge throughout my chapter. In *The Political Philosophy of Thomas Hobbes*, Oxford University Press, 1957, p. 100, Warrender says: "In the present work, Hobbes's statements regarding the place of God will be taken as a necessary part of his theory, and it will be contended that this allows the most probable construction to be put upon his text. Thus it will be held that with regard to natural law, the ground of obligation is always present as this derives from the commands of God in his natural kingdom, and does not depend in any way upon the covenant and consent of the individual or upon the command of the civil sovereign."

In *Leviathan*, Hobbes contrasts a law of nature with a right of nature. The latter is defined as

> the liberty each man hath to use his own power, as he will himself, for the preservation of his own nature; that is to say, of his own life; and consequently, of doing anything, which in his own judgment, and reason, he shall conceive to be the aptest means thereunto.[32]

And in the next paragraph he defines a law of nature to be

> a precept or general rule, found out by reason, by which a man is forbidden to do what is destructive of his life, or taketh away the means of preserving the same; and to omit that, by which he thinketh it may be best preserved.[33]

A right of nature and a law of nature, in one and the same matter, are inconsistent for Hobbes. A right "consisteth in liberty to do or to forbear: whereas LAW, determineth and bindeth to one of them."[34]

The conflict between right and law of nature is due to the particular conditions of lawlessness and insecurity in the state of war of each against each. In the state of nature "every man has a right to every thing; even to another's body. And therefore as long as this natural right of every man to every thing endureth, there can be no security to any man."[35] People generally come to see that in order to achieve security they must not exercise their rights to all things, and from this understanding arises the laws of nature. From a desire for security, the first general rule of reason is derived:

> that every man ought to endeavor peace as far as he has hope of obtaining it; and when he cannot obtain it, that he may seek, and use, all helps and advantages of war.[36]

Hobbes clearly uses the term "ought" here. Furthermore, the rule of reason spoken of is the basis for the laws of nature which are said to be the very same as morality for Hobbes. It is thus quite plausible, I believe, to suggest

---

[32] EW III 116, Tuck 91.
[33] EW III 116–117, Tuck 91.
[34] EW III 116–117, Tuck 91.
[35] EW III 117, Tuck 91.
[36] EW III 117, Tuck 91.

that Hobbes has here set out a moral "ought"—that is, a precept stipulating a moral obligation, albeit one that is based largely on considerations of prudence.[37]

IV. Conscience, Promise, and Contract

Even though a skeptic about many things concerning morality, Hobbes does allow that there are certain laws or precepts which stipulate how human beings ought to act, and which thereby indicate our moral obligations. Because of the lack of external or authoritative moral pronouncement by others in the state of nature, morality under those conditions would be a matter between oneself and one's conscience. Yet Hobbes holds that laws which bind only *in foro interno* (in our consciences) are not laws properly so called. So in what sense are we bound or obligated by the precepts of reason and morality? It is to this central question in Hobbes's ethics that I now turn.

At the very end of Chapter 15 of *Leviathan* Hobbes clearly states what he believes to be the essence of the laws of nature. The laws of nature "are but conclusions or theorems concerning what conduceth to the conservation and defense of themselves." The laws of nature are thus merely "dictates of reason" and not laws properly so called. For "law, properly, is the word of him, that by right hath command over others."[38] The laws of nature bind the will and not the actions of a person because they tell only what is likely to produce the best results for individuals who follow them. Since each person, as a prudentially rational person, desires what is best, then each person desires what the laws of nature dictate. And while, in general, it would go against our own desires if we failed to conform to the laws of nature, such failure to conform may not go against our desires in certain circumstances. For example, if we had been condemned to death by the State, our desire to live in a peaceful State would be overridden by our desire at the moment to remain alive.[39] If violating the laws of nature does not always go against our prudentially rational desires, then it cannot be that we are obligated always

---

[37] See Stephen Darwall, *The British Moralists and the Internal 'Ought': 1640–1740*, Cambridge: Cambridge University Press, 1995.
[38] EW III 147, Tuck 111.
[39] See my discussion of this issue in Chapter 5, Section III.

to follow those laws. Hobbes's view of moral obligation is that we can be bound only by our own will. We are obligated to act only in those ways which are required, so as not to contradict what we will to do. The paradigm case of moral obligation occurs when a person voluntarily agrees or promises to perform an action, thereby indicating both that he or she has a will so to act, and that not to act in this way would be to contradict the will.

In Chapter 15 of *Leviathan*, Hobbes contends that the "laws of nature oblige *in foro interno;* that is to say, they bind to a desire they should take place: but *in foro externo*, that is, to the putting them in act not always."[40] The main reason offered for this claim is that no one can be bound to act contrary to that which grounds all of the laws of nature: namely, self-preservation. Thus, when one of the laws of nature obligates a person to do that which would risk his or her life, the person's actions are not bound by that law of nature. The laws of nature bind only in the conscience, or as Hobbes also puts it "they require nothing but endeavour, he that endeavoureth their performance, fulfilleth them."[41]

At one crucial point in *Leviathan*, Hobbes constructs an analogy between being obliged to give the correct answer to a mathematical or logical problem, and being bound to follow the law of nature concerning the keeping of one's promises.

> So that *injury*, or *injustice*, in the controversies of the world, is somewhat like to that, which in the disputations of scholars is called *absurdity*. For as it is there called an absurdity, to contradict what one maintained at the beginning: so in the world, it is called injustice, and injury, voluntarily to undo that, which from the beginning he had voluntarily done.[42]

In both cases, one is bound in the sense that one risks self-contradiction—that is, the rejection of what one has a will to do—if one does not assent to the correct answer or action. This doctrine creates a bridge between metaphysics and ethics, between contradiction in the mind and in the will. And it also creates a bridge between Hobbes's moral philosophy which places

---

[40] EW III 146, Tuck 110.
[41] EW III 145–146, Tuck 110. J.W.N. Watkins argues quite cogently that the concept of endeavour is central to Hobbes's whole project of connecting natural philosophy with moral and political theory. See *Hobbes's System of Ideas*, especially ch. 7.
[42] EW III 119, Tuck 93.

high priority on the natural law obligation to keep promises and his political philosophy based on the social contract.

In logic and mathematics we assent to names and definitions, and are thus bound to accept valid conclusions which follow from these. In morality we assent to restrictions on our future conduct when we utter words that make promises, and we are thus bound to will to do the things we have committed ourselves to do. And in politics, we assent to be ruled by a sovereign through the social contract, and we are thus bound to endeavour to obey the laws propounded by that sovereign. In all three cases (logic, ethics, and politics) we bind our wills by what we have previously assented to, although the type of binding may be different, for moral and political terms, as we saw earlier, have a tendentious character not typically associated with mathematical terms. In Chapter 16 of *Leviathan* Hobbes accounts partially for the similarity by saying that "no man is obliged by a covenant, whereof he is not author; nor consequently by a covenant made against, or beside the authority he gave."[43]

In Part II of his *Elements of Law* (*De Corpore Politico*) Hobbes explains that it is consistent with the dictates of conscience to obey the civil law, and even be forced to obey it.

> For the conscience being nothing else but a man's settled judgment and opinion, when he hath once transferred his right of judging to another, that which shall be commanded, is no less his judgment, than the judgment of that other. So that in obedience to laws, a man doth still according to his own conscience, but not his private conscience.[44]

When we assent to be ruled by another, we authorize another person to issue commands to us, and we thereby give this person's commands the authority of our own consciences.[45] As a result, it comes to be contrary to our own consciences to disobey the civil law. There is one exception here: namely, when our public conscience commands us to do something which is at odds with our private conscience. As we will see later, there are

---

[43] EW III 149, Tuck 112–113.
[44] EW IV 186–187. I will refer to Hobbes's *Elements of Law (De Corpore Politico)* by citing the version reprinted in *The English Works of Thomas Hobbes*, ed. Sir William Molesworth, 11 vols. (London: John Bohn, 1839), vol. IV.
[45] See the discussion of authorizing in the next chapter.

relatively few cases that fit into this exceptional class, since in civil society most of one's private conscience has been voluntarily subjugated to the public conscience. Only those things which threaten self-preservation count as exceptions, since it is never rational voluntarily to give up one's right to self-preservation.

The obligation to obey the civil law is generated out of the moral obligation to obey that which we have agreed to do in our consciences. But this moral obligation is a defective type of obligation, since there may be self-interested reasons to disobey particular laws at particular times. The *might* of the sovereign is necessary to make conscience's dictates truly binding. In Chapter 26 of *Leviathan*[46] Hobbes says:

> When a commonwealth is once settled, then are they [the laws of nature] actually laws, and not before; as being then the commands of the commonwealth; and therefore also civil laws: for it is the sovereign power that obliges men to obey them. For in the differences of private men, to declare, what is equity, what is justice, and what is moral virtue, and to make them binding, there is need for the ordinances of sovereign power, and punishments to be ordained for such as shall break them; which ordinances are therefore part of the civil law.

The sovereign power obliges us to obey the civil and also the natural law, Hobbes says, but of course this must be done by a sovereign who has indeed been duly authorized by us to speak in our names. Even so, the power of the sovereign does correct the deficiencies of mere private conscience by adding a layer of motivation to the binding quality of the laws of nature.

But why would anyone first agree to let another rule over one's own conscience? The rule which underlies the laws of nature, Hobbes tells us, has two corollaries:

> The first branch of which rule, containeth the first, and fundamental law of nature; which is *to seek peace and follow it*. The second, the sum of the right of nature; which is *by all means we can to defend ourselves*.[47]

These corollaries point to the opposition of law and right in the state of nature. When reason shows that following the limitations of law will lead to

[46] EW III 253, Tuck 185.
[47] EW III 117, Tuck 92.

insecurity and that it will threaten our self-preservation, then pure natural right resurfaces as the guiding rule of our actions.

Since, in the state of nature, we are always insecure, we should only act to defend ourselves by exercising our right to all things. But this strategy, of course, will lead to insecurity and the perpetuation of the horrible conditions of the "war of every man against every man." Such a situation is the lesser of two evils, but not the option that is preferable to us. We want to have the security of knowing that all of us will obey *the laws* of nature. Thus we come to seek a way out of the miserable condition called *the state* of nature by agreeing to transfer or relinquish our natural right to all, by a contract with our fellows.

The second law of nature states the rationale for the move out of the state of nature, where private conscience is the only moral authority. It holds that:

> a man be willing when others are so too, as far forth as for peace, and defense of himself he shall think it necessary, to lay down his right to all things; and be contented with so much liberty against all other men, as he would allow other men against himself.[48]

Once prudential reason has shown that we are better off seeking peace than continuing in the state of war, people begin to look for the conditions necessary to bring themselves out of the state of nature. The first thing that reason ascertains is that each person must give up the absolute right to all things. But to do so unilaterally would not be prudent, for there would be no assurance that one's neighbor would act likewise.[49]

Without such an assurance, no one should initiate the move out of the state of nature, because of the vulnerability to attack that would result for each person from such a first step. Hobbes sets up the dilemma in this way:

> For as long as every man holdeth his right, of doing any thing he liketh, so long are all men in the condition of war. But if other men will not lay down their right, as well as he; then there is no reason for any one to divest himself of his;

---

[48] EW III 118, Tuck 92.

[49] Many contemporary philosophers trace the origin of decision theory, especially concerning the prisoner's dilemma, directly back to Hobbes. One of the chief defenders of this view is David P. Gauthier. See his important book, *The Logic of Leviathan*, Oxford: Oxford University Press, 1969. Part II is of the most relevance to our concerns, and provides quite an interesting attempt to refute the views of Warrender.

for that were to expose himself to prey, which no man is bound to do, rather than to dispose himself to peace.[50]

Before people will lay down their absolute rights, they seek some sign to show that their fellow neighbors, who also lay down their rights, will not reassert their absolute rights at the first opportunity of their own personal advantage.

Seeking for a sign is the beginning of mutual promising. But such promising still results only in the defective form of obligation addressed above.[51]

> And the same are the bonds by which men are bound and obliged; bonds which have their strength not from their own nature, for nothing is more easily broken than a man's word, but from fear of some evil consequence upon the rupture.[52]

While laying down a right through mutual promising is formally irreversible, on pain of self-contradiction, it is more importantly not reversed for prudential reasons: namely, for fear of punishment at the hands of the sovereign. The motivator of our promise-keeping is the sovereign who is the third-party beneficiary of our acts of mutual promising to restrict our natural rights. We are formally bound or obligated by these promises because we have committed ourselves by our word and deed. But we actually follow through on these obligations because we fear what would happen if we did not.

For Hobbes, a person generally acts in order to achieve "some good to himself." In respect to laying down one's rights, this good can be of two sorts: "it is either in consideration of some right reciprocally transferred to himself; or for some other good he hopeth for thereby."[53] People in the state of nature would not renounce their right to all things for altruistic reasons.

---

[50] EW III 118, Tuck 92.

[51] Perhaps the most telling point in Warrender's favor is Hobbes's own claim that the laws of nature might not be a defective form of moral obligation in the state of nature. For this to be true, there would have to be some authority in the state of nature who issues moral commands. Warrender forcefully argues that God is the only entity that could fill this function (*Political Philosophy of Thomas Hobbes*, p. 98). The chief passage from Leviathan that Warrender relies on is this: "But yet if we consider the same theorems, as delivered in the word of God, that by right commandeth all things; then are [the laws of nature] properly called laws." (EW III 147, Tuck 111) As Warrender himself admits, this passage is conditional and is thus subject to a number of interpretations. Since Hobbes has just said that the laws of nature are not properly called laws, the consequent clause must be something which Hobbes believes to be false. And Hobbes thereby commits himself to believing that the antecedent clause is false also. It is for this reason that I hold that the laws of nature for Hobbes are a defective form of moral obligation.

[52] EW III 119, Tuck 93.

[53] EW III 119–120, Tuck 93.

They would do so only in expectation of some good to be received. Here Hobbes's psychology is key, for he contends that

> the motive and end for which this renouncing, and transferring of right is introduced, is *nothing else* but the security of a man's person, in his life and in the means of so preserving life, as not to be weary of it.[54]

This psychological point has another implication which is later developed into a basis for moral rights in Hobbes's political philosophy. If people act only for their own advantage, then certain rights cannot be given up. For instance, "a man cannot lay down the right of resisting them, that assault him by force, to take away his life; because he cannot be understood to aim thereby, at any good to himself."[55] As we will see later, even in civil society, morality remains firmly rooted in prudence.

V. Law and Morality

From the account presented so far it should be clear that morality is a legally oriented concept for Hobbes. The natural laws, which encompass the precepts of morality, achieve effective force only when they are enforced by the sovereign through incorporation into the civil law. It is for this reason that Hobbes's detractors claimed that he had simply equated law and morality.[56] But this is not the case. There remained a significant, if limited, area of morality (or natural law) which did not overlap with civil law. In what follows I will argue that Hobbes' concept of law, while admittedly central to his views, did not overwhelm all aspects of his morality.

First, let us examine the definition and limitation of law for Hobbes. In the clearest formulation of his legal philosophy, the little-noticed work *A Dialogue Between a Philosopher and a Student of the Common Laws of England*, Hobbes sets out four criteria of a valid law:

(1) the command of him or them that have the sovereign power;
(2) given to those that be his or their subjects;

---

[54] EW III 120, my italics, Tuck 93.
[55] EW III 120, my italics, Tuck 93.
[56] John Eachard is one of the strongest defenders of the view that Hobbes conflated morality and legality. See the quotation from him which occurs near the end of the present chapter.

(3) declaring publicly and plainly;
(4) what every of them may do, and what they must forbear to do.[57]

The first two criteria are fairly straightforward. Like Jean Bodin, Hobbes believes that sovereignty is key to proper law-making. And he also believes that laws are commands that bind only those who are properly subject to these commands. Interestingly, Hobbes thinks that this is also true of what he calls the moral law. "It is true that the moral law is always a command or a prohibition, or at least implieth it..."[58] So, one might think that all of the moral law is contained within the civil law, since the moral law which is outside of the civil law would not meet the requirement imposed by these first two conditions.

But for any law to be binding, two further conditions must be met. The law must be accessible to the people who are to be bound by it. This third criterion requires that the laws be publicly proclaimed so that it is possible for all subjects to know how they are bound. This ties into the fourth criterion: namely, that the law specify, in advance, what the people are to do and what they are not to do. These two requirements taken together form the foundation of various moral and structural limitations on the law of the sort discussed in my introductory chapter. This is first seen when it is realized that these two criteria impose the following procedural limitations on the sovereign: laws will not be valid if they cannot be found and then understood by the people; laws will not be valid if they do not clearly specify what actions lie under the domain of those laws; and laws will not be valid if they are claimed to be retroactively binding. These limitations begin to resemble various constitutional principles of more modern legal systems, as I will discuss in the next chapter.

The individual person retains certain powers which may be legitimately used if the transfer to the sovereign of the right to exercise various powers is somehow rendered void. Hobbes addresses this topic when he attempts to specify the duties of the sovereign. In *De Cive* he states this quite clearly: "Now all the duties of the ruler are contained in this one sentence,

---

[57] EW VI 26, Cropsey 71. I will refer to the *Dialogue* first by referring to it in the version reprinted in *The English Works of Thomas Hobbes*, ed. Sir William Molesworth, 11 vols. (London: John Bohn, 1839), vol. IV and then in Joseph Cropsey's edition, Chicago: University of Chicago, 1971.
[58] EW VI 28, Cropsey 72.

the safety of the people is the supreme law."[59] Hobbes here says that by safety he means "not the sole preservation of life in what condition soever, but in order of happiness...to live delightfully."[60] And in *Leviathan* the safety of the people is said to involve "public instruction, both of doctrine and example; and in making and executing good laws, to which individual persons may apply their own cases."[61] In general, if the sovereign does not provide for the safety of the people, then the social contract, which relied on the assurance of safety by the sovereign, is no longer in effect. And it is at this point that the individual people could legitimately use their own power which they had temporarily agreed not to use in certain matters.[62]

Morality thus sometimes comes to limit the law-making functions of the sovereign in quite an unusual way for Hobbes. The limitation does not appear in the realm of justice, for justice is completely based on what the sovereign says it is. As Hobbes says, "before the names just, and unjust can have place, there must be some coercive power."[63] In regard to justice, the sovereign appears to stand outside of morality. It is for this reason that Hobbes's sovereign is often regarded as being above moral criticism. In this respect, then, Hobbes does provide a basis for making the transfer of right to the sovereign something which cannot be easily taken back. For Hobbes, the sovereign as legitimate law-maker cannot be restricted merely because individuals happen to believe that this sovereign acts in a morally unjust way.[64]

But the sovereign may attempt to exercise power in ways that are not legitimate, and it is at this point that morality re-enters as a limitation on law-making. For Hobbes there are moral categories other than justice that apply to the sovereign. Specifically, there is the concept of equity which is closely related to the sovereign's duty to protect the safety of the people by providing "good" laws. Equity is linked to the duty of providing for the safety of the people in Chapter 30 of Leviathan. At the beginning of this

---

[59] EW II 166, ch. XIII, para. 2.
[60] EW II 166, ch. XIII, para. 2.
[61] EW III 322–323, Tuck 231.
[62] At least at this point in our discussion legitimate and rightful can be assumed to be roughly the same for Hobbes.
[63] EW III 131, Tuck 100.
[64] In Chapter 21 of *Leviathan*, Hobbes says that if the sovereign "demand, or take anything by pretense of his power; there lieth in that case, no action of law" EW III 207, Tuck 153.

chapter, Hobbes says that "the Office of the sovereign...consisteth in...the procuration of *the safety of the people*.[65] And then Hobbes says:

> The safety of the people requireth further...that justice be equally administered...For in this consisteth equity.[66]

And in the *Dialogue*, Hobbes says that "the King is not bound to any other law but that of equity."[67] So, there is a clear connection between equity and the duty to provide for the safety of the people. And equity dictates that the laws are made so that they are perceived to be fair by those who are subject to them. But, for Hobbes, even the bindingness of equity is grounded in prudence. The sovereign should not violate the principles of equity, because to do so would risk the kind of open warfare that would jeopardize sovereignty by undermining the sovereign's ability to ensure the safety of the people.[68]

Unlike most other philosophical views of the moral limits on law-making, Hobbes held the view that only when the immoral actions of the law-maker jeopardize that which grounds sovereignty are they limiting constraints on the law. Nonetheless, these are limits. As we will see the moral limits on sovereign law-making are largely drawn in procedural terms by Hobbes: ruling out laws that are superfluous, contradictory, or secret, as well as laws that cause the citizenry to lose faith in the fairness of the law. Indeed, any laws that have the effect of undermining peace are ones that the sovereign is prohibited from promulgating by the principles of equity that Hobbes defends in *Leviathan* Chapter 30 and in significant discussions in the *Dialogue*.[69]

---

[65] EW III 322, Tuck 231.
[66] EW III 332, Tuck 237.
[67] EW VI 26, Cropsey 70.
[68] Some commentators have also focused on equity, but no one sees equity as the cornerstone of the limitations on sovereign power for which I will argue. Eleanor Curran discusses the relation between equity and the retained right of self-preservation, *Reclaiming the Rights of the Hobbesian Subject*, New York: Palgrave Macmillan, 2007, p. 110. Also of note is the essay by Dennis Klimchuk, "Hobbes on Equity," in *Hobbes and the Law*, ed. David Dyzenhaus and Thomas Poole, Cambridge: Cambridge University Press, 2012, who helpfully sorts out the various usages of equity in Hobbes's writings.
[69] Eleanor Curran has discussed these moral limits in terms of the "requirements of the office of the sovereign" and calls them not moral duties proper, and also says they are only "indirectly" protected. *Reclaiming the Rights of the Hobbesian Sovereign*, p. 113 and 168. Claire Finkelstein has also called attention to the sovereign duties but says they "only play an indirect role" in protecting the citizens. See Claire Finkelstein, "A Puzzle about Hobbes on Self-Defense," *Pacific Philosophical Quarterly*, vol. 82, nos. 3–4, pp. 332–361, especially p. 359.

It is, thus, inappropriate to characterize Hobbes as a defender of the kind of legal positivism which admits no moral limit whatsoever on the lawmaker. I will argue in later chapters that Hobbes's theory of law is closer to that of Lon Fuller than to the legal positivists with whom he is normally associated. And when the sovereign acts against the moral limits on lawmaking, sovereignty is jeopardized to such an extent that the door is opened for international institutions that could come to the defense of the citizens whose sovereign does not or cannot protect them. It will be a matter of some difficulty to ascertain the boundary between the moral and the prudential for Hobbes—a topic to which I will turn next and to which I will return in other chapters.

International institutions and laws are generally thought to be ruled out by Hobbes, but in my view this is not true of Hobbes and certainly not true of a Hobbesian legal philosophy. Just as there are moral limits on sovereignty, so there are also international analogs to the formation of civil society that can tell us why and when international civil society could arise for Hobbes. Indeed, Hobbes discusses the formation of federations in similar terms to those of Kant in his *Perpetual Peace*. To understand fully Hobbes's views about the moral and prudential limitations of sovereignty, we must understand the relation between prudence and morality, the final topic of this chapter.

VI. Prudence and Morality

Hobbes's original contribution to the history of ethics concerns the way in which he links the various components of morality by reference to the concept of prudence. In exploring this point I will contrast Hobbes's views with those of John Locke, whose writings seem to be heavily based on Hobbes's conceptual scheme, but which ended in a more traditional conception of morality.

For Hobbes, moral philosophy involved the study of what was good and the means to achieve the good. To understand the good, one needed first to understand what a person would call good in a situation where there was no society. Hobbes has a relatively easy time showing that self-preservation and self-interest will determine what is good for individuals in this pre-societal state, the state of nature. Thus, at least in the state of nature, prudence, which involves rational self-interested calculation, will be the basis of moral deliberations.

The social contract determines most of the domain of morality in civil society, but prudence still remains important at two levels. First, prudence is the vehicle by which persons decide to limit their natural passions and to establish the social contract. Here Hobbes is quite clear:

> if their actions be directed according to their particular judgments, and particular appetites, they can thereby expect no defense, nor protection, neither against a common enemy, nor against the injuries of one another.[70]

Second, it is prudence which determines when the contract has been rendered void. Each person continues to engage in prudential calculation concerning his or her putative obligations after civil society has been established.

Indeed, even as Hobbes says that it is wrong to break the contract, he explains the wrongness by pointing out the likely prudential harm to be done to individuals who break the contract, and who act in opposition to civil law and morality. Hobbes argues against those who, whenever it seems prudent, would break the contract in the following passages:

> The fool hath said…that every man's conservation, and contentment, being committed to his own care, there could be no reason, why every man might not do what he thought conduced thereunto: and therefore also to make, or not make; keep, or not keep covenants, was not against reason, when it conduceth to one's benefit.[71]

Hobbes responds that this "specious reasoning is nevertheless false." He agrees with the fool that what is reasonable is that which is shown to be beneficial or prudential. But he argues that the fool, through selective obedience to law, could not gain what is sought by all people: namely, long-term security.[72]

---

[70] EW III 155, Tuck 118.
[71] EW III 132, Tuck 101.
[72] Hobbes's refutation of the fool has received very interesting commentary. A number of authors have reassessed Hobbes's attempt to answer the fool, as well as why Hobbes even mentions such a powerful objection to his own theory. Of special note are the following essays: Annette Baier, "Secular Faith," *Canadian Journal of Philosophy*, 10/1 (1980); and David Gauthier, "Three Against Justice: The Foole, The Sensible Knave, and the Lydian Shepherd," *Midwest Studies in Philosophy*, VII (1982). More recently, Lloyd has a good discussion of this issue in her book *Morality in the Philosophy of Thomas Hobbes: Cases in the Law of Nature*, New York: Cambridge University Press, 2009.

He therefore that breaketh his covenant and consequently declareth that he may with reason do so, cannot be received into any society, that unite themselves for peace and defense, but by the error of them that receive him, nor when he is received in it, without seeing the danger of their error, which errors a man cannot reasonably reckon upon as the means of his security...[73]

The social contract, then, is itself justified in terms of prudence, and it serves as the basis of morality in civil society for Hobbes. But since it is never prudent to give up self-preservation, it may sometimes be right for the contract to be broken, especially in those situations where a sovereign power attempts to take the life of an individual. These cases are rare indeed and, as Hobbes says above, the advantages of civil society almost always outweigh whatever inconvenience there might be to an individual by keeping to the terms of the contract.

John Locke,[74] writing slightly later than Hobbes, also held the social contract to be the chief determiner of what is morally right in civil society. But although Locke often speaks of what reason dictates in the state of nature, he does not justify either the legitimacy of the contract or the breaking of the contract in terms of prudence. Consider this central passage from Locke's *Second Treatise*.

The *State of Nature* has a Law of Nature to govern it, which obliges every one: And Reason, which is that Law, teaches all Mankind, who will but consult it, that being all equal and independent, no one ought to harm another in his Life, Health, Liberty, or Possessions. For men being all the Workmanship of one Omnipotent, and infinitely wise Maker...they are his Property, whose Workmanship they are, made to last during his, not one another's pleasure.[75]

Locke denies that reason is equivalent to pure self-interested calculation, and he does so for considerations of a theological nature, as the passage above indicates.

---

[73] EW III 134, Tuck 102.
[74] John Locke (1632–1704) wrote two books which are important in the history of ethics. First, in *An Essay Concerning Human Understanding* he devotes parts of several chapters to the subject of ethical knowledge, arguing that such knowledge cannot be innate. Also, in his *Two Treatises of Government* Locke tries to blend conceptions of natural right with the social contract theory Hobbes had developed a few years earlier.
[75] Second Treatise para. 289.

Locke also comes to the view that the state of nature is not a state of war, based on his belief that God has not placed us on this earth merely to look after ourselves, but to look after those who are innocent and incapable of defending themselves.

> For *by the Fundamental Law of Nature, Man being to be preserved*, as much as possible, when all cannot be preserv'd, the safety of the Innocent is to be preferred. And here we have the plain *difference between the State of Nature, and the State of War*, which however some men have confounded, are as far distant, as a State of Peace, Good Will, Mutual Assistance, and Preservation, and a State of Enmity, Malice, Violence, and Mutual Destruction are from one another.[76]

While Locke agrees with Hobbes that self-preservation is important in the state of nature, he does not share Hobbes's bleak assessment of pre-social life, and Locke therefore does not come to see prudence as the basis for moral evaluation. As we saw above, Locke believes that altruism, especially concerning the innocent, is also a proper basis for moral deliberation. When people leave the state of nature for civil society, Locke similarly does not place prudence as the overriding aspect of moral deliberation.

Locke may have toned down his own views, in part, because of the reaction to Hobbes's writings. Hobbes had been roundly criticized especially for failing to retain any of the traditional natural law considerations in his description of the state of nature, and hence in his account of human nature. Locke seems to have been greatly affected by the hostile reaction that Hobbes's writing received, especially from theologians in England. John Eachard, for example, claimed that Hobbes had not made out his case for thinking that 'Humane Nature (or reason) [is] so very vile and raskally, as he writes his own to be, nor his account of it altogether so demonstrative, as Euclid'[77]

In particular, Eachard says that Hobbes was too hasty in drawing the conclusion that prudence would be the most rational strategy to pursue in the state of nature.

---

[76] Second Treatise paras. 297–298.

[77] John Eachard, *Mr. Hobbes's State of Nature Considered*, 1672, ed. Peter Ure, Liverpool: Liverpool University Press, 1958. p.7.

Wherein he saies, that a great and necessary occasion of quarrelling and war is, that several men oftimes have a desire to the same thing; which thing if it happens not to be capable of being divided, or enjoyed in Common, they must needs draw and fight for't: Instead of which, he should have said; if these men be mad, or void of reason, it is possible they may fight for't: For being that every one of them have a equal right to this same, that is in controversie, they may either compound for it as to its value, or decide it by Lot, or some other way that reason may direct (which is the Law of *reason* and *humane Nature*, and not merely positive, because it is in *Law Books*).[78]

This particular objection to Hobbes is voiced by Eachard, supposedly on behalf of Divine Providence, the Church, and most especially the Clergy, who have been "so vilely aspersed and persecuted by our *Adversaries* malicious suggestions."[79]

VII. Conclusions

Hobbes was the first to attempt to ground the concept of moral obligation on rational self-interest. People are generally bound to do what they have stipulated that they have a will to do. The bindingness is based, in the first place, on the desire that all people have to avoid self-contradiction. Furthermore, in civil society, there is an additional motivation to our moral obligations. Our agreement, through the social contract, to be subject to the rule of the sovereign, further stipulates that we have a will to regard all laws as morally binding. Not only do we risk self-contradiction by failing to do what we are obligated to do, but we also risk the punishment of the sovereign. This fear of punishment is so strongly motivating that what was a defective, or merely self-enforced, sense of being bound becomes a properly binding (in terms of liberty constraining) sense of obligation.

Once civil society is in place, people are morally bound to follow all of the traditional dictates of the natural law, according to Hobbes. And this remains true as long as the sovereign is able to guarantee the safety of the people. If the sovereign indicates that such a guarantee is in jeopardy, then the sovereign's subjects are no longer properly obligated, though they

---

[78] *Mr. Hobbes's State of Nature Considered*, p. 6.
[79] *Mr. Hobbes's State of Nature Considered*, p. 1.

remain obligated in conscience. The attempt to ensure that no one believes that the guarantee of safety is jeopardized leads the sovereign also to feel obligated to make good laws and to treat the subjects equitably, as we shall see in Chapter 3. These results of Hobbes's theory are again consistent with traditional natural law doctrine.

What marks Hobbes out as an extreme radical for his contemporary opponents is that he sought to equate reason and prudence, completely upsetting the tradition since Aquinas of seeing reason not as the servant of self-interest but of God's law. Hobbes was also accused by several of his contemporaries as sowing the seeds of rebellion.[80] It seemed to matter little to his contemporaries that Hobbes did affirm the traditional virtues and found a strong basis for legal obligation in his conception of prudence. Hobbes's moral philosophy is unique in virtue of the central place that prudence takes in all his deliberations. But it is important to note that Hobbes's positions on the great controversies of his day are not much at odds with those of his contemporaries.

Hobbes attempted to provide what he considered to be a less controversial and more reasonable basis for supporting the traditional norms and virtues which, following Aquinas, and his supporters in the seventeenth century, were identified as constituting the substance of the laws of nature. As a result, Hobbes can be seen as the first modern moralist: the reasonable basis for natural law which he espoused did not appeal to theological considerations, except in the final section of *Leviathan*. In a time of ferment, when the authority of Church and State were thrown into question, Hobbes felt that only an appeal to non-theological considerations such as prudence could succeed. Hobbes was wrong about what would persuade his contemporaries, but he was right about what would be persuasive in the long run.

---

[80] The best treatment of this challenge to Hobbes, which is also sympathetic to this as a reasonable interpretation, is Susanne Sreedhar's, *Hobbes on Resistance: Defying the Leviathan*, Cambridge: Cambridge University Press, 2010. Sreedhar says: "Hobbes's right of self-defense is fundamentally a right of *resistance*, although in Hobbes's theory resistance is understood quite broadly; resistance to the sovereign will include simple noncompliance, or the mere refusal to obey his commands." p. 10. Sreedhar's interpretation of Hobbes looks to be even more radical than mine, unless one recognizes this caveat about the understanding of resistance. As Sreedhar characterizes it, Hobbes would not really be critizeable for writing a "Rebells catechism" as John Bramhall claimed at Hobbes's time. See John Bramhall, "The Catching of Leviathan, Or the Great Whale,' in *Leviathan: Contemporary Responses to the Political Theory of Thomas Hobbes*, ed. G. A. J. Rogers, Bristol: Thoemmes Press, 1995, p. 145.

2

Social Contract

Political philosophers have traditionally been interested in contract theory as a hypothetical or potential explanation of political obligation and the origin of the State. Constitutional theorists have been interested in contract theory as an actual explanation of the legitimacy of certain decision-making procedures especially within democracies. Political philosophers have addressed themselves predominantly to the "social contract" that might have been struck among persons in the state of nature. Constitutional theorists have addressed themselves to what has sometimes been called "the contract of government" that exists between the citizens of a State and the sovereign ruler of that State.

Political philosophers who call themselves social contract theorists are often criticized because they do not distinguish between the actual origin of a State and its hypothetical origin, especially when it is clear that a particular State did not come into being by means of a social contract. Constitutional theorists who employ contract-theoretical terms are often criticized because they fail to question the justification of the conditions of the contract of government. Some of this criticism could be met by providing a contract theory with two interrelated but separable parts—one part describing the reasonableness of having a State, and one part describing the rights and limitations of any sovereign ruler who relies on the consent or agreement of the people as the basis of his or her political authority. In this chapter I shall argue that this is precisely what Hobbes's contract theory provides.

Hobbes presented a contract theory that contained both a hypothetical initial situation to illustrate his views on human conduct and social interaction, and a constitutional doctrine describing the legitimacy and limitations on sovereignty. To understand Hobbes properly, I shall argue, it is important to keep these two parts of the contract doctrines separate. The first tells us something, much like John Rawls's own discussion of the original position,[1] about the reasonableness of political obligation. The second doctrine explains the nature of the constitutional authority that political rulers are said to have. The first doctrine, as with most social-contract doctrines, is a doctrine of moral justification for the generation of the State. The second doctrine is properly a jurisprudential doctrine concerning the transfer of right necessary for the institution of any sovereign authority. These two parts of Hobbes's contract doctrine—the first hypothetical and moral, the second jurisprudential and constitutional—are intertwined in the central chapters of *Leviathan* (13–18). It is my intent to separate these two contract doctrines before putting them back together again to show their importance for contemporary legal and political philosophy. Before doing this I shall explain, in more detail than in the first chapter, how to understand the notion of third-party beneficiary contracts, which is very close to the notion of contract that Hobbes employed in both parts of his contract doctrine.

I. The Legal Background

The aspect of legal theory I wish to examine concerns the so-called "third-party beneficiary contracts." By the late sixteenth century a new wrinkle was added to the ideas of assumpsit and contract actions. In a number of cases a party who was not a member of the parties involved in a contract, but who was to receive a benefit from that contract, was given the right to bring an action before the court. Here is what the legal historian G. W. F. Dold says about this situation.

> The present state of English law may be summed up in the statement: "No one can stipulate for a third party so as to give the latter an actionable right unless he stipulates as a trustee for such third party." This was not always so, and the early cases do not support the statement. Thus in Dutton *v.* Poole (1677), 2 Lev. 210; 83 E.R. 523, a donee beneficiary was allowed to sue in assumpsit, though she was not a party to the contract and gave no consideration, nor did the promisee

---

[1] Rawls admits that there is a variety of "possible interpretations of the initial situation." His own interpretation, the original position, "is not intended to explain human conduct except insofar as it tries to account for our moral judgments." It is not intended to be anything other than a hypothetical construct. I will argue that Hobbes viewed his "original contract" in a somewhat similar way. See John Rawls, *A Theory of Justice*, Cambridge, MA: Harvard University Press, 1971, pp. 120–121.

expressly act as a trustee for her, and in the Physician's Case (1680), 1 Ventris 318; 86 E.R. 205, A made a promise to his physician that, if he would effect a certain cure, he would pay a sum of money to the physician's daughter, and it was held that she might sue. There was no mention of trust.[2]

According to Dold, then, the third-party beneficiary actions of assumpsit were recognized in the late seventeenth century but not in the twentieth century. To show that this particular aspect of contract law was part of legal theory when Hobbes wrote *Leviathan* in the middle of the seventeenth century, I must draw on cases a little older than those cited above. In an interesting footnote, Dold lists a number of cases from the late sixteenth and early seventeenth century as also pertaining to this point. Careful examination of these cases might show that third-party beneficiary contracts were recognized in Hobbes's time.

The earliest case, Lever v. Heys, is from 1599.[3] It concerns a dowry and marriage agreement between "pere del file" and "pere le fits" (father of a girl and father of a boy). The father of the girl agreed to pay a sum of money to the boy if the father of the boy would "doner son consent al le marriage" (give his consent to the marriage) and assure that it would take place. The question posed concerns whether the son as well as his father could bring an action of assumpsit if the girl's father failed to make the stipulated dowry payment to the son. Since the agreement was between the two fathers, the boy was not strictly a party to the contract. But he did have a clear interest in the matter because the contract made him the beneficiary of the dowry. The theoretical question was whether the contract created a legal right for the son to receive the dowry, such that, if he did not receive it, he could sue to obtain it. The judges of the King's Bench, Pophan and Fenner, ruled that "le fits ava l'action" (the son has a cause of action); one other judge dissented, and one judge abstained. This was also not a case of a trustee but of a true third-party action. Thus it seems that as early as 1599, fifty years before *Leviathan*, the King's Bench recognized the status of third-party beneficiary contracts.

In a case with very similar circumstances in 1631, Provender v. Wood, the court ruled that "the party to whom the benefit of a promise accrews, may

---

[2] *Stipulations for a Third Party*, London: Steven and Sons, 1948, p. 97.
[3] Moore K. B. 550, 72 E. R. 740 (1599). I have retained all spellings as they originally appeared.

bring his action."[4] This statement is so clear that it needs no elucidation. Twenty years later, at about the time when Hobbes's *Leviathan* appeared, the principle articulated in Provender was applied to a commercial situation, and again the third party was said to have the right to sue.

> Roll Chief Justice held, that it is good as it is, for there is a plain contract because the goods were given for the benefit of the plaintiff, though the contract be not made between him and the defendant, and he may well have an action upon the case for here is a promise in law made to the plaintiff, though there be not a promise in fact....[5]

The distinction between "promise in law" and "promise in fact" raises the question that was to plague Hobbes throughout *Leviathan*: Is there an implied contract between the third party (the sovereign) and the true parties to the contract (each man and each man)? Stated in another way, the question is this: Does the third-party, the sovereign, receive both rights and duties by his status as a beneficiary to a contract he has not made? The duties could be established only if there is some second-level contract operative. Here the third party, while not a party to the "contract in fact," is nonetheless seen as a party to a "contract in law" by his implicit agreement to be made a beneficiary.

Contracts have always been seen as creating both rights and duties;[6] so as soon as a third party is said to be a true party to a contract, he not only has the right to bring an action when the promised benefit does not result, but he himself also is liable, at least in theory, to be brought to court and sued by one of the other parties for not fulfilling his duty. As far as I am able to tell, the courts never drew out this inference from their rulings, by saying, for example, that if the son backed out of the marriage after receiving the dowry, he, rather than his father, could be sued by the girl's father. Just as Hobbes struggled with the idea of the extent of the sovereign's duties as beneficiary of the third-party contract, so did the judges at his time.

---

[4] Hetley 31, 124 E.R. 318(1631)
[5] Starkey *v.* Mill, Style 296, 82 E. R. 723 (1651).
[6] Modern legal historians and scholars recognize this. In one commentary on contract law, contract is defined as follows: "A contract is a promise, or set of promises, for breach of which the law gives a remedy, or the performance of which the law in some way recognizes as a duty." Samuel Williston and George Thompson, *Williston on Contracts*, 2nd ed., New York: Barker, Voorhis and Co., 1936, 1:1.

As I indicated in the first chapter, I believe that Hobbes viewed the sovereign as having a third-party beneficiary status in respect to the contract made between each man and each man. I will soon set out this argument in some detail. Hobbes claims that the sovereign, while not a party to the contract, has certain rights as benefits from that contract. While Hobbes clearly says that the sovereign has duties, he does not seem to want to embrace the idea that this duty was one that subjects could force the sovereign to satisfy. Hobbes wanted to distance himself from those contract theorists who saw the sovereign under certain obligations, which when not honored gave cause for the people or for Parliament to seek redress against him.[7] I will make extensive use of this understanding of the social contract in what follows.

II. The Original Contract

The original contract itself is described by Hobbes as a contracting between individuals in the state of nature. Here is the way Hobbes characterizes it:

> The only way to erect such a common power, as may be able to defend them...is, to confer all their power and strength upon one man, or upon one assembly of men, that may reduce all their wills, by plurality of voices, unto one will....This is more than consent, or concord; it is a real unity of them all, in one and the same person, made by covenant of every man with every man, in such manner, as if every man should say to every man, *I authorize and give up my right of governing myself to this man, or to this assembly of men, on this condition, that thou give up thy right to him, and authorize all his actions in like manner.*[8]

I shall examine this description of the contract by first distinguishing between (a) conferring of power, (b) consenting to be governed, and

---

[7] A number of Hobbes scholars have recognized the similarity between Hobbes's sovereign in *Leviathan* and third persons in contracts. Gierke says: "Thus also the individuals have no rights what ever as against the sovereign power, which is absolute by its very nature; nor can they derive any rights from the original covenant, as they did not contract with the ruler, but simply with all other individuals to renounce, jointly and simultaneously, all rights and all liberties in favor of this third person. Otto von Gierke, *The Development of Political Theory*, trans. Bernard Freyd, New York: W. W. Norton, 1939. Goldsmith also makes the specific point I made above, but again without comment. "Apparently the sovereign is something like a third-party beneficiary of their contracts; each obliges himself to the sovereign by a donation, or conveyance of right, as well as obliging himself to his fellow citizens by covenant." M. M. Goldsmith, *Hobbes's Science of Politics*, New York: Columbia University Press, 1966, p. 158. And by 2002, Malcolm is quite confident in saying that the sovereign "is a third-party beneficiary of their mutual covenanting." Noel Malcolm, *Aspects of Hobbes*, Oxford: Oxford University Press, 2002, p. 446.

[8] EW III 157–158, Tuck 120.

(c) transferring of right. Hobbes here tells us that the original contract is more than (a), or (b), or (c). But the question remains of whether contracting is merely a combination of (a), (b), and (c), or whether it entails the addition of a fourth element.

The idea of consenting to be governed was traditionally tied to the idea of an agreement between "people" and ruler. But Hobbes is not here speaking of a consent of this type, because there is no such group existing as a "people" in the state of nature. Perhaps even more important than this is the fact that Hobbes's notion of original contract is more than just a passive acceptance or consent to allow one person the right of ruling over all of the others. The original contract involves an act of transferring and simultaneously creating a party to be the beneficiary of this transfer. With the creation of this new party, the wills of each party to the contract are united in the will of the new party. This uniting of wills is not a loose association or federation that can be broken up as easily as it was joined together. Instead, a bond is created that cannot be broken, says Hobbes, without self-contradiction.

Conferring of power is also not coextensive with what Hobbes means by contracting. Hooker rightly pointed out that what can be conferred can just as easily be taken back. For Hobbes this was exactly what he did not want. A man can confer his power by agreeing not to impede the power of another. But a man cannot technically transfer his power to another. For transfer implies an irreversibility of action: what is transferred cannot be regained. Power and strength, though, must always remain within the individual himself. He can suspend exercise of his power, or use his power for the benefit of another, but he cannot hand over his power (like a sum of money) to another. Thus the collective power of the sovereign does not result from a transfer of power but from an agreement to do all that one can for the benefit of the sovereign. This is called conferring power. The transfer of right is irreversible, but the conferring of power is not.

The original contract in the state of nature is a combination of conferring of power, consenting to be governed, *and* mutual transferring of right. The third component, as we have seen, is the driving force that actually moves men out of the state of nature and into civil society. The key here is that the transferring act is a mutual one, made by each person with each person. If it were not mutual, then there could be people living side by side, half of whom still lived and acted as in a state of war, and half of whom had laid down their right to exercise their own power indiscriminately over others. In such a situation, it is clear that the members of the former half would easily win out over the members of the latter half and compel them to withdraw to the individualistic position of the state of nature. Thus the transfer is effectual only when mutually agreed to, and when the creation of the sovereign as an artificial entity is also included. This latter condition is the fourth element in the original contract. This element is also closely related to the conferring of power, but the two are not quite the same.

An artificial entity, a sovereign, with power to enforce the contract, is created at the same time that the contracting members confer their power on one man or assembly of men.[9] But even though the two acts are simultaneous they must be seen as different acts. This is because pure conferring of power does not necessarily result in the creation of a sovereign power. For without the additional element of transferring of right,[10] the power conferred could be as easily regained as transferred. A sovereign power, though, cannot be established on such an unsure footing. It requires a separate act, which establishes the entity that will receive the power and have the right to enforce the contract. (Even a dissenter who temporarily withholds his power must obey the sovereign because he has agreed to do so by a prior act.) Thus we have four elements in the original contract: (a) conferring a power, (b) consenting to be governed, (c) transferring of right, and (d) creating a sovereign.

Let us now turn to the terms of the contract itself. Hobbes says at the outset that the words spoken are said only "in such a manner, as if every man should say to every man...." What can Hobbes mean by employing this hypothetical language? There are a number of possible explanations. It might be that Hobbes wishes to establish that the words that follow are not necessarily the exact words used in the original contract. Or it might be that he is pointing to the hypothetical status of original contracts generally. A third possibility would be that Hobbes, while describing the words used in his own myth of the original contract, was arguing that other views of the original contract need not employ the letter, but must employ the intent of these words. In any event, the formulation that follows must be seen in a somewhat approximate manner.

---

[9] But remember the discussion in the previous chapter where it was argued that despite Hobbes's words there is no actual giving of power from one person or entity to another, but rather a willingness to aid or at least to restrain oneself so the sovereign can act.

[10] Again, right, like power, cannot literally be transferred, rather this is a matter of willingness or recognition.

The first words of this contract need some elucidation because of Hobbes's use of two terms that seem particularly crucial. Here he says, "I authorize and give up my right of governing myself...." The term "authorize" has a particularly technical meaning for Hobbes, which had just been given in Chapter 16. This discussion was centered around the general notion of authority and was not restricted nor even directed to authorizing in the original contract. Generally, by authority "is always understood a right of doing any act; and done by authority, done by commission or license from him whose right it is."[11] Thus, for our purposes here "I authorize" is equivalent to saying "I transfer my right to act in particular ways to another." The term "governing" is also, as of yet, unanalyzed. Hobbes has not yet given a technical meaning to this term, and so we can assume that he is using the term in a common way. "Governing myself" is thus synonymous with "controlling myself" or any other like formulation.

The transfer of right is a bestowal on one man or assembly of men. The terms of the contract do not state "I authorize and give up my right of governing myself, to this man or assembly of men, on the condition that this man or assembly of men do x." If Hobbes had used this formulation, the contract would have been between each man and one man—that is, between subject and a designated ruler. Instead, Hobbes says that the terms of the contract are agreed upon "on this condition, that thou give up thy right to him, and authorize all his actions in like manner." Thus the contract is between each man and each man, not between each man and the ruler.

What is the status, then, of this "man" or "assembly of men" to whom my right of "governing myself" is transferred? As Hobbes later tells us, this man, or assembly of men, is not strictly a party to the original contract. This entity is the beneficiary of the act of transfer of each man; but it is also more than this, for before the transfer the entity did not exist. There is no gap between the act of contracting and the creation of the sovereign. The sovereign man, or assembly of men, is actually created by the original contract. It is in fact a condition of the contract that this be the case. It is as if a condition of the

---

[11] EW III 148, Tuck 112. Hobbes uses the term "authorize" to mean the act of giving another the right to be the author of your own words, that is, the act of giving another the right to speak in your name. Authorization involves transfer of right but not transfer of power, since the person authorized obviously already has the power to speak and act on his own. What he lacks, until the authority has been bestowed, is the right to speak and act in behalf of others as well.

contract was the establishment of a corporation that would be the beneficiary of the power and rights each person agrees to bestow upon it.

III. The Constitutional Contract

Now we come to examine the second part of the contract which appears to be formal and legal, as opposed to the hypothetical and largely moral. I shall be particularly interested to show how the sovereign actually achieves his right to rule and how he[12] perpetuates the basis for retaining that right throughout his tenure. Sustaining the right to rule becomes the most important consideration in this scheme. We shall also search for the basis of both duty and right for the sovereign's subjects in the constitutional scheme that Hobbes proposes.

Before turning to our main goal in this section, let me address a potential problem for my interpretation which separates the two parts of the contract. At the beginning of Chapter 18 of Leviathan, Hobbes sets out the complete contract where the two parts are discussed in ways that could lead a reader to think that there is no significant distinction between these two parts. As we will see, there are clear differences between the way the contract is described in Chapters 17 and 18. But remember that my point is not that these are utterly distinct, but rather that one of these concerns a contracting in the state of nature and the other is more like a constitutional contracting in that the people already constitute a "multitude" where votes are cast. In part, what I am claiming is that Hobbes's contract doctrine more closely resembles that of Locke, in having two parts, than is normally recognized. Even if one disagrees that the two parts of the contract are separate in the end, there is value in analyzing them separately for a full understanding of Hobbes's project.

We move now to Hobbes's discussion of the characteristics of contract in Chapter 14 of *Leviathan*. Hobbes begins by making certain distinctions between types of contract (or transfer of right).

> There is a difference between transferring of right to the thing; and transferring, or tradition, that is delivery of the thing itself. For the thing may be delivered together with the translation of the right; as in buying and selling with

---

[12] Of course, one could say instead of "he": "she," or "they" and perhaps even "it." I will employ all these pronouns to refer to the sovereign at various points in the text.

ready-money; or exchange of goods, or lands: and it may be delivered some time after.[13]

This first type of contract is the least interesting for Hobbes's political scheme. In a sale of goods there is always a contract between buyer and seller. The seller agrees to transfer her right to a thing to the buyer in exchange for a sum of money.

The simplest form that this contract can take is when the seller hands over the thing to the buyer and the buyer simultaneously hands over the sum of money to the seller. Here the exchange of thing for money implies an exchange of right to that thing for a right to that money. As Hobbes points out, the delivery of the thing and the delivery of the right to the thing are performed in the same act, and at the same time. This simple contract must then be distinguished from contracts where the transference of the right to the thing and the transference of the thing itself are not performed in the same act or at the same time. These more complex contracts resemble the constitutional contract because of the introduction of future time to the considerations.

Before leaving this simple contractual relation it should be noted that Hobbes has abruptly changed his style of discourse. Here he makes no mention of people contracting in the state of nature, which had been the main theme of the preceding pages of *Leviathan*. Instead, he explicitly draws our attention to concrete contractual situations in business and commerce. Once again we see the clear demarcation of subject matters: from fictional to real contracts.

Hobbes next examines two types of complex contract where considerations of future time enter in. First is the type of contract called covenant.

> Again, one of the contractors, may deliver the thing contracted for on his part, and leave the other to perform his part at some determinate time after, and in the mean time be trusted; and then the contract on his part, is called Pact, or Covenant…[14]

Covenants are contracts where one party performs and the other party is trusted to perform later. In the state of nature this type of contract would

---

[13] EW III 120–121, Tuck 94.
[14] EW III 121, Tuck 94.

have been seen as ridiculous. If you gave a man a pig and trusted him to give you a bushel of grain later, you would wait a very long time for the delivery of that grain because, since he already had possession of the pig, there was no incentive for him to perform. But now, in Hobbes's formal discussion of this type of contract, covenant is reinstated as legitimate. This is because Hobbes is now discussing the actual conditions in which men find themselves in civil society. And, in fact, this type of contract is to be the basis for Hobbes's constitutional contract. I shall return to this point below.

It seems that the covenant implies a promise by the party who is not presently performing. Without the promise there would be no basis for the trust that the reciprocal performance will be forthcoming, which Hobbes says must exist in the party who is performing. Hobbes explicitly mentions promise in his next case: where both parties promise to perform.

> Both parts may contract now, to perform hereafter: in which case, he that is to perform in time to come, being trusted, his performance is called keeping of promise, or faith; and the failing of performance, if it be voluntary, *violation of faith*.[15]

This type of contract, like the previous one, has two distinct steps: (1) a mutual transfer of right in the present, and (2) a present promise to transfer the thing in the future. An example of the contract where both parties are trusted would be the case where I contract with you to deliver a bushel of wheat to you at the end of the summer, if you will deliver to me a bushel of corn also at the end of the summer. The contract takes place here in the present. The transfer of my ownership right of a bushel of wheat to you, and the transfer of your ownership right of the bushel of corn to me, also takes place in the present. But the actual transfer of the wheat and the corn (the acts that complete the contract) is promised now to be performed in the future.

This analysis of the second type of complex contract enables us better to understand the first type: the covenant. In a covenant, there is a mutual transfer of right. For the first party there is also a transfer of the thing; and for the second party there is a promise to transfer the thing. The first party performs now in exchange for the promise of the second party to perform also, but not immediately. Thus there are two considerations that lead the

---

[15] EW III 121, Tuck 94.

first party to perform: (1) the transfer of right to the thing by the second party, and (2) the promise of performance itself, made by the second party. The former is the more important because it means that the second party no longer retains his ownership right to the thing promised. If he fails actually to deliver the thing promised, he still has no basis for claiming a right to retain possession of the thing promised. Without this transfer of right there is no contract at all.

If there is only promise, without present transfer of right, the transfer can be considered only as a free gift from the first party to the second. The promise by itself is an insufficient sign of a contract and is not seen as establishing an obligation, because by itself it does not create a right or a corresponding duty. The mere promise is like a television call-in fund-raising pledge. A pledge made by a caller is not legally binding, because there is no commonly recognized sign that the pledge involved a present transfer of right.

A promise is only one type of accompanying sign of a contract. Hobbes distinguishes two possible signs:

> *either express*, or *by inference*. Express, are words spoken with understanding of what they signify: and such words are either of the time *present*, or *past*; as, *I give, I grant, I have* given, I have granted, I will that this be yours: or of the future; as, I will give, I will grant: which words of the future are called Promise.[16]

True to his own nominalism, Hobbes says that the most explicit form of contractual sign is the spoken word. By saying "I grant that this be yours" I have transferred my right to that thing to you, regardless of whether you actually take possession of that thing now or not. The mere words were sufficient to indicate that there had been a transference of right. More important than this, though, was Hobbes's claim that a promise was simply words spoken in the future tense about an intended performance. As with the fund-raising pledge, the promise when performed provided a free gift to the charitable organization. But since there was no corresponding duty on the part of the performer, if she does not perform, the charity has no recourse.

As in Hobbes's previous discussion, a promise and a covenant are distinguished. This ran counter to the tradition of political theorists who had

---

[16] EW III 121, Tuck 94.

virtually equated covenant, contract, agreement, and promise. Hobbes, though, following the legal theorists of his day, saw that these terms were quite different.

> The second type of sign is that of inference. Signs by inference, are sometimes the consequence of words; sometimes the consequence of silence; sometimes the consequence of actions; sometimes the consequence of forbearing an action: and generally a sign by inference, of any contract, is whatsoever sufficiently argues the will of the contractor.[17]

With the introduction of this second type of sign, Hobbes is able to account for contracts based on tacit consent. Not only can my words be a sign of a contract, but my silence can also be a sign of a contract. Thus, in certain situations (like the constitutional one we will soon examine) the fact that I do not speak to the contrary is a sign that I have agreed to the terms of a contract. The important element here is that I have demonstrated what I have a will to do. This demonstration does not need words, although words often do provide a clearer demonstration of one's will.

As a matter of fact, though, words alone are not enough to constitute a true contract if the words are of a future time. The words must be of the present time: that is, they must state that the transfer is by these words carried out in the present. Hobbes spends a good deal of time making this subtle distinction. To help illustrate this point it should be noted that the fund-raising pledge mentioned above was not binding because the words were spoken in the future tense: "I shall give $100 to your charity." If there had been a present-tense wording, "I pledge that $100 will be yours," then it might have been binding in Hobbes's view.

> Words alone, if they be of the time to come, and contain a bare promise, are an insufficient sign of a free-gift, and therefore not obligatory. For if they be of the time to come, as tomorrow I will give, they are a sign I have not given yet, and consequently that my right is not transferred, but remaineth till I transfer it by some other act.[18]

Any transfer requires some present-tense sign for it to be legitimate. If the sign is in words, then the words must at least indicate that one has the

[17] EW III 121–122, Tuck 94.
[18] EW III 122, Tuck 94.

will now to engage in the transfer, even if the actual doing of it must wait until later. Thus, as Hobbes says, there is a great difference in signification between "I will that this be thine tomorrow" and "I will give it thee tomorrow." The former is a present act of the will concerning a future doing. The latter is only a promise of an act of the will in the future, and this can signify no obligation of the will on the part of him who speaks it. Therefore, "the former words, being of the present, transfer a future right; the latter, that be of the future, transfer nothing."[19]

At this point a question arises. How is it that contracts can be said always to entail transfers of right? The answer, in respect to times past and present, is quite obvious. By giving a thing to another (when done without stipulation) we do not have the right to seize it back. Thus, along with the transfer of a thing, is the transfer of the right to that thing: that is, the right of calling it one's own (ownership). But in the case of promises we must deal with future time. Here the answer to the above question is not so easy. In the case of covenant, the first party transfers a thing, and thus also the right of ownership of a thing to a second party. The second party makes a promise as a sign that she will transfer a thing to the first party.

How is it that this future-tense sign implies a transfer of right? Hobbes's answer here is quite interesting:

> he that promiseth only, because he hath already received the benefit for which he promiseth, is to be understood as if he intended the right should pass: for unless he had been content to have his words so understood, the other would not have performed his part first.[20]

The only reason for the first party to perform first is that she has received two guarantees of the eventual performance by the second party. The promise as a mere future-tense verbal sign of intent is not enough. It must be accompanied by an actual present-tense transfer of right (of ownership) to the thing contracted for. Otherwise, there would be no reason for the first party to trust the second party's word. Trust based solely on a mere promise would be an imprudent basis for first performance. But when the promise is accompanied by a transfer of right, "it is equivalent to a covenant; and therefore obligatory."

[19] EW III 121, Tuck 94.
[20] EW III 123, Tuck 95.

In covenants, and in other contracts involving a promise, he that performs first "is said to Merit that which he is to receive by the performance of the other; and he hath it as his *due*."[21] That is, in a covenant a duty is created for the second party to perform because of the performance of the first party. But in a free-gift transfer the situation is different. The receiver of the gift also gets the performance as a merit; but not in the same sense as that of a proper contract like a covenant. In a free-gift transfer "I am enabled to merit only by the benignity of the giver;" whereas in contract "I merit by virtue of my own power, and the contractor's need."[22] In free-gift transfers I have no basis for claiming that the giver should relinquish his right to me; but only that if she should do so, then I should be the recipient rather than someone else. In contracts, I have a basis for claiming that I should be the recipient and that the right should be relinquished. These considerations are of interest in regard to the status of parties to contracts, both in general and in respect to constitutional contracts. We will also begin to see how the constitutional arrangement places limitations on the sovereign—perhaps what might even be described as constitutional limitations on the sovereign.

At the beginning of this chapter I spoke of the status of third-party beneficiaries to contracts in law in Hobbes's time. There the third party received a legal right to that thing promised in the contract. This right itself was not owed to the third party in any way except insofar as it had been stipulated in the contract. Since the third party was not strictly a contracting party to the contract, he did not receive the right as a consequence of a performance on his own part. Rather, he gained it, as it were, because of someone else's performance. That is, he gained it as a free gift. The right was owed to him only because of the performance of another, not because of the exercise of his own power. Once the right had been established, though, the third party was owed the thing promised, and the right to the thing was transferred to the third party because of the performance of the first party.

The distinction Hobbes draws between actual contract and free gift is not only related to his own political concepts; it is also related to the distinctions drawn by the lawyers and jurists between the statuses of the actual parties

---

[21] EW III 123, 95.
[22] EW III 121, Tuck 94.

to a contract and the third party. The actual contracting parties to a contract received both a right and a duty from that contract. In a covenant the first party can expect the second party to perform because the first party, by performing, has discharged his duty and now awaits the fulfillment of his corresponding right. The second party has received the fulfillment of his right to the thing for which he contracted (by the actual transference of that thing), and now is bound by his corresponding duty to fulfill his part of the contract.

So far we have no mention of the third and non-contracting party. This party enters into the considerations only when the promised performance concerns benefitting someone other than the first party to the contract. In other words, the third party is to benefit from the performance of the second party because the first party (who would normally benefit from the second party's performance) has designated the third party as his stand-in. This was the stipulated condition for which the first party performed first, and thus discharged the duty necessary to create that right for the third party. The right must then be transferred due to an act of the first party, not the third party. Once this is established, though, the third party has the right to be the beneficiary of the performance of the second party, as opposed to any other claimants.

It is in this way that Hobbes mixes the notion of covenant and free-gift transfer to form the notion of third-party beneficiary contract. Due to the subtlety of the construction, the third party receives a right due to no action of his own, and with no corresponding duty on his part.[23] These highly complex relations between parties form the basis for Hobbes's discussion of the status of parties to the constitutional contract, to which we now turn.

> A commonwealth is said to be instituted, when a multitude of men do agree, and covenant, every one, with every one, that to whatsoever man, or assembly of men, shall be given by the major part, the right to present the person of them all, that is to say, to be their representative; every one, as well he that voted for it,

---

[23] The sovereign, as a third party, has no corresponding duty from the contract, because the duty has already been assigned (and discharged) by one of the contracting parties. This contracting party would have been entitled to the right the sovereign now claims if he had not relinquished it to the sovereign as a free gift. Thus the bestowal of the right to rule is literally free and clear for the sovereign and entails no corresponding duty on the sovereign's part. Whatever duties or offices the sovereign has do not stem directly from the contract that established his right to rule. The duties of the sovereign will be discussed in Chapter 3.

as he that voted against it,[24] shall authorize all the actions and judgments, of that man, or assembly of men, in the same manner, as if they were his own, to the end, to live peaceably amongst themselves, and be protected against other men. From this institution of a commonwealth are derived all the rights, and faculties of him, or them, on whom the sovereign power is conferred, by the consent of the people assembled.[25]

It is important to note the difference between this formulation of the contract and that of Chapter 17, which was discussed in Section II. The formulation of the contract in Chapter 17 concerned the *generation* of the commonwealth, whereas this formulation in Chapter 18 concerns the *institution* of a commonwealth. The generation is carried out in the state of nature and must be conceived as involving a unanimity. The specific institution requires only a majority. In both the original and the constitutional contracts a multitude is united in one person. The specific difference between the compositions of these multitudes and the persons who receive rights and unite these multitudes is my next concern.

In the original contract a unanimity was demanded because, in the state of nature, any person standing outside the contract was a threat to all the others. The multitude is seen as existing in that depraved state where only their passions or appetites control their actions. Thus none can be trusted to join the rest later in contracting. Instead, all must contract simultaneously or not at all. In the constitutional contract, Hobbes introduces the idea of imposing the will of the majority on the minority. Even though the "original" contract constituting the commonwealth is by every man with every man, the agreement to appoint a particular person or persons to be the entity benefitting from the contract need not receive the explicit support of each person. That is, the contract is unanimously agreed to in principle by the mere fact that all participate in the commonwealth.

But the choice of the third party (to whom the sovereignty is granted) need not also be unanimous,[26] as we see by the terms of the constitutional contract above. To be a representative actor and unifying agent, the sovereignty needs to be authorized by all the people assembled. But the

---

[24] Those who vote against the particular person who is to become sovereign are bound by the decisions of the majority because of the prior unanimous consent to be governed by majority rule.
[25] EW III 159, Tuck 121.
[26] Although there must be unanimity to establish the office of the sovereign, since without an enforcement structure the problem of first performance can not be solved.

authorizing of a particular person or persons to occupy the office of sovereign need not require anything more than a majority vote, since all the contractors have agreed to follow the decision of a majority of their members. This is due to the terms of the constitutional contract as well as to the conditions of authority themselves.

This division of the contract is never explicitly acknowledged by Hobbes in *Leviathan*. I have argued that the distinction is implicit if Hobbes is to be consistent in his contract doctrine. Whether the contract is explicitly divided, though, is not important to the general point I wish to make about the structure of Hobbes's arguments about contracting, to which I now turn.

IV. Conclusions

Hobbes's own concluding remarks at the end of *Leviathan* show the extent of his respect for the proper limits of right through the constitutional contract and for the constitutional limitations on sovereignty. For Hobbes, sovereignty is absolute in the sense that the sovereign does not have rights that have correlative duties to individual subjects or citizens. But there is a sense in which sovereignty is not absolute, since it is limited by the aims of the contract, most importantly by the idea that sovereigns are constituted only so as to provide for the safety of the people. And as we have seen, safety of the people is given a very broad construal by Hobbes. In a sense then, sovereignty is limited by the way sovereignty is generated, and most importantly, how it is instituted.[27] Those who occupy the office of sovereign commit themselves to various things, as can easily be seen in Chapter 30 of *Leviathan*.

When the sovereign is established by conquest, for instance, it is the contract and consent, not his naked power, which legitimates his authority. When this is not recognized by the conqueror, his sovereignty is jeopardized. Even conquerors cannot claim a right to rule that antedates this grant of right made by the people.[28] To claim otherwise is to risk rebellion. Thus,

---

[27] David Dyzenhaus has also explored this issue in Hobbes's works. See his essay, "Hobbes and the Legitimacy of Law," *Law and Philosophy*, vol. 20, no. 5, September 2001, pp. 461–498, especially pp. 490–491.

[28] EW III 706, Tuck 486.

for prudential as well as theoretical reasons, sovereigns must recognize that their authority is bestowed on them, and also limited, by a grant of right from their subjects.

Unlike most contract theorists, with the notable exception of Locke, Hobbes tackled the substantive questions of political obligation faced by politicians and citizens alike. In this sense Hobbes addressed straightforwardly questions of the institutional limits on sovereignty that will consume us over the next few chapters. Hobbes was not interested merely in abstract moral justification; he was also deeply concerned about the practical and institutional problems faced by grounding sovereign authority on the continued consent or agreement of the individual members of a society. Hobbes's contract theory thus serves two purposes—one ideological and one constitutional. The specific contract terms espoused by Hobbes are not terribly attractive to contemporary political theorists, since Hobbes's contract seemingly does not provide sufficient safeguards against the abuse of power by the sovereign. Nonetheless, the above examination of the structure of his contract theory could be instructive to political and legal theorists today who are becoming increasingly aware of the need to bridge the gulf between hypothetical justifications and real constitutional problems. In the next chapter I will explain how Hobbes's political philosophy should be read as more palatable than is normally thought.

One of the most important contributions of Hobbes's contract theory is that it sets the individual citizen, not the mass of citizens, as the most basic component in the establishment of political sovereignty. Hobbes's own account of the majoritarian constitutional scheme that corresponds to this emphasis on individual transfer of right is deserving of careful study. Viewing the sovereign as merely a beneficiary to a contract she has not made, of course, presents difficulties, most especially concerning the duties of that sovereign to her citizens. But there is no reason to think that this difficulty cannot be overcome and I will argue that Hobbes sought to overcome it with an ingenious understanding of the idea of equity.

3
Equity and Justice

Most contemporary readers of Hobbes's works are shocked by his seeming reduction of justice to mere legality. If we want to know if we have acted justly we need merely ask, 'have we obeyed the law?' This is shocking because it implies (and Hobbes elsewhere states explicitly) that there can be no unjust laws. If such a statement were made today we would be inclined to view the person making the statement as a strict legal positivist: namely, someone who believes that morality does not overlap with legality.[1] I shall argue that Hobbes is not such a strict legal positivist because he had a much narrower conception of justice than we have, but also a wide notion of equity or fairness which did provide for a moral basis of limiting law-making, and is perhaps closer to our notion of justice than what Hobbes called justice.

Further, I shall argue that equity, not justice, is the dominant moral category in Hobbes's political and legal philosophy. I will begin by analyzing a number of key passages in Hobbes's corpus, mainly from *Leviathan* and *A Dialogue Between a Philosopher and a Student of the Common Laws of England*, where both equity and justice are contrasted with one another. If Hobbes sees equity as the primary moral category limiting the political authority of the law-making sovereign, then if he is a positivist his positivism is less strict than is generally thought to be the case. At the end of this chapter I attempt to show some of the contemporary implications of Hobbes's views, interpreted in the light of his pronouncements on equity and natural law generally. I shall use Hobbes's later work to clarify his earlier work, and in this

---

[1] Various commentators have taken up the question of whether Hobbes really was a strict legal positivist. H.L.A. Hart criticizes various aspects of Hobbes's conception of law in his book, *The Concept of Law*, Oxford: Clarendon Press, 1960. Robert Ladenson has tried to show that Hart's objections can be rebutted by a Hobbesian. See his "In Defense of a Hobbesian Conception of Law," *Philosophy & Public Affairs*, vol. 9, no. 2, Winter 1980, pp. 134–159.

way seek to unite *Leviathan* and the *Dialogue* in ways that most interpreters of Hobbes have resisted or failed to consider.

I. The Earlier View

For Hobbes, there were two possible bases for limiting the sovereign law-making power. First, since the sovereign did not have any strictly "legal" duties imposed on him (because he was not a contracting party in the constitutional contract establishing sovereignty) his duties must in some sense or other be "natural" duties. In *De Cive* Hobbes clearly articulates what this means:

> Now all the duties of rulers are contained in this one sentence, *the safety of the people is the supreme law.*[2]

Hobbes then defines the term "safety" in its broadest sense to include considerations of enrichment, liberty, and happiness as well as the obvious considerations of defense. This duty is derived from the fact that the sovereign, by accepting his authority and power as a "free gift," assumes the responsibility of guaranteeing peace for his subjects (since this was the reason why the gift of sovereignty was bestowed in the first place). In the previous chapter I talked of this duty as a constitutional limitation, since when the sovereign fails to abide by it, the contract constituting the commonwealth can be dissolved.

The second limit on sovereign power stems from the dictates of reason (the laws of nature) that led men to submit to the ruler. Here, as we will see, the prime law of nature is that of equity, which places a limitation on the exercise of rulership instead of on the right of rulership. The sovereign is restricted from propounding laws that are unreasonable, superfluous, or arbitrary. The sovereign is thus bound by certain standards of fair proceedings which are firmly rooted in Hobbes's concept of civil morality. Equity seems to provide us with the moral wedge we can drive between Hobbes's seemingly severe terms of the constitutional contract. Merely because the sovereign's laws cannot be called unjust does not mean that they are immune

---

[2] EW II 166, ch. XIII, para. 2.

to all moral valuation. In what follows we will see to what extent Hobbes allows this moral wedge to be driven into his legal scheme.

Some commentators have recognized the importance of equity, but from A. E. Taylor's important essay onward, there has been little attention to seeing equity as a limit on law-making in Hobbes's system. Taylor said:

> Iniquity, which can exist in "the state of nature" or in the conduct of the sovereign, who, since he is not subject to his own command, cannot be guilty of injustice proper, is violation of the "natural law," which is also, according to Hobbes's repeated explanation, the *moral* law.[3]

Only very recently is there a recognition that Hobbes's concept of equity, as a limit on the sovereign, can have a procedural legal status.[4]

Before beginning the exegesis a few words should be said about the term "equity" itself. Aristotle employed the word to mean a particular type of justice, making corrections for the anomalies that arise when general rules are applied to unusual circumstances. The Roman use of the term started as an elaboration of Aristotle but later came to apply to any action properly brought before the *praetor*, and these were generally all procedural matters. In Tudor England, lawyers and philosophers began to ask

> whether equity is a principle of justice transcendent and distinct from the law (legal justice) or whether it is of the same substance as the positive one, but expresses the spirit rather than the letter of that particular law?[5]

In this way, equity came to be linked with procedural fairness.

By Hobbes's time, equity was given an increasingly wide scope such that many philosophers virtually equated justice and equity, often linking the two concepts together as an inseparable pair (this is still a common practice

---

[3] A.E. Taylor, "The Ethical Doctrine of Hobbes," *Philosophy*, vol. 13, no. 52, October 1938, p. 408. Howard Warrender also talks of moral limits of the sovereign but he does so in terms of God's law rather than civil law restraints. See Howard Warrender, *The Political Philosophy of Hobbes*, Oxford: Clarendon Press, 1957.

[4] Several essays in Dyzenhaus and Poole's anthology begin to see this point. See especially, Evan Fox-Decent, "Hobbes's Relational Theory: Beneath Power and Consent," in David Dyzenhaus and Thomas Poole, *Hobbes and the Law*, Cambridge: Cambridge University Press, 2012.

[5] Stuart E. Prall, "The Development of Equity in Tudor England," *The American Journal of Legal History*, vol. 8, no. 1, 1964, p. 1. Prall provides a truly excellent account of the debates on the meaning of equity just prior to Hobbes's time.

in contemporary Anglo-American jurisprudence). Further complicating the issue was the fact that the Lord Chancellor's courts of equity came to have such wide jurisdiction by the seventeenth century as to be virtually indistinguishable from the common-law courts. In the second part of this chapter I show how this confusion might have affected Hobbes's use of the term. It will be clear, though, that Hobbes did distinguish the domains of justice and equity, and in his legal philosophy made equity the primary consideration.

At the beginning of Chapter 15 of *Leviathan* Hobbes discusses the third law of nature: "*that men perform their covenants made.*"[6] This is the specific law of nature that led men out of the state of nature. It is also the basis for the very thin role of justice in civil society for Hobbes.

> And in this law of nature, consisteth the fountain and original of JUSTICE. For where no covenant hath preceded, there hath no right been transferred, and every man has a right to everything; and consequently no action can be unjust. But when a covenant is made, then to break it is *unjust*; and the definition of INJUSTICE, is no other than *the not performance of covenant.* And whatsoever is not unjust, is just.[7]

According to this definition, the actions of the sovereign law-maker can never be said to be unjust, for the sovereign made no covenant with any individual person. Since whatsoever is not unjust is just, it would seem that all the sovereign's actions, no matter how unfair, should always be called just.

But Hobbes does not claim that all of the sovereign's acts must be considered just; instead he says that

> before the names just, and unjust can have place, there must be some coercive power.[8]

Since there is no coercive power over the sovereign himself, his actions cannot be called unjust or just. The coercive power of the sovereign creates the situation where the terms "justice" and "injustice" can be applied; but since the sovereign stands outside this situation, the terms that he legitimizes

---

[6] EW III 130, Tuck 100.
[7] EW III 131, Tuck 100.
[8] EW III 131, Tuck 100.

cannot be used on himself. Thus, neither justice nor injustice properly applies to the sovereign law-maker who, by definition, stands outside the law.

There is, though, another and more subtle reason why the sovereign's actions are neither just nor unjust. The rule that we must perform our covenants is the rule of justice, according to Hobbes. This rule is derived from the general rule of reason stating that "we are forbidden to do anything which is destructive of our life." But the sovereign, in his capacity as an artificial person, does not make promises or covenants nor does he even have the kind of life that he must preserve by acting justly. It is true that he may be bound by these considerations in his capacity as a natural person, but that strictly does not concern him as a sovereign. Thus, in his sovereign (artificial) capacity he cannot be accounted just or unjust.

Subjects on the other hand are clearly bound by the dictates of the natural law concerning the performance of their covenants. In the sphere of civil society the boundaries to person's freedom are called laws. In vivid imagery Hobbes draws the analogy between natural chains and artificial chains which restrict free action.

> But as men, for the attaining of peace, and conservation of themselves thereby, have made an artificial man, which we call a commonwealth; so also have they made artificial chains, called *civil laws*, which they themselves, by mutual covenant, have fastened at one end, to the lips of that man, or assembly, to whom they have given the sovereign power; and at the other end to their own ears.[9]

The key here is that people have placed these chains upon themselves by their own acts. That is, they have chosen to restrict their own freedom by creating a sovereign for the express purpose of propounding these artificial "chains." These self-imposed chains in fact often conflict with a particular person's will to do something. But since we have voluntarily imposed these barriers upon our own actions, in most situations it makes no sense to claim that we should fight against them. Likewise, it would make no sense to say that any of these chains or laws are unjust.

Hobbes returns to the issue of justice when he seeks to establish the authority of the law-maker by reference to covenant. In promising to act in accordance with the laws propounded by the sovereign, we have declared

---

[9] EW III 198, Tuck 147.

that it is our will so to act. Barring any impediment (for instance an accident that makes us mentally incapable of obeying the laws) our actions should conform to what we have promised. It is thus reasonable to say that when our actions do not conform to what we have promised, we have acted unjustly. And when a habit of breaking our promises has been established, then it is reasonable to say that we are unjust.

At the end of Chapter 15 of *Leviathan* Hobbes gives one of the clearest articulations of his view of morality, of which the above "thin" theory of justice is a part.

> For moral philosophy is nothing else but the science of what is *good* and *evil*, in the conversation, and society of mankind. *Good*, and *evil*, are names which signify our appetites and aversions; which in different tempers, customs and doctrines of men are different.[10]

This claim that what is good changes from society to society distinguishes Hobbes from the philosophers of the natural law tradition. If, as Hobbes says, the natural law is "immutable" and "eternal," then what is good should also be unchanging if Hobbes were an adherent of natural law philosophy. But, of course, Hobbes does not draw this conclusion. Instead he asserts that the good, even though it is tied to the immutable natural law, is constantly changing "in the conversation, and society of mankind."[11]

Thus, while admitting the natural law advocates' premises, Hobbes refuses to admit their conclusion. The reason for this is that Hobbes, again and again, claims that the laws of nature, immutable and eternal though they are, are not properly laws.

> These dictates of reason men used to call by the name of laws, improperly: for they are but conclusions or theorems concerning what conduceth to the conservation and defense of themselves; whereas law, properly, is the word of him, that by right hath command over others.[12]

For Hobbes, moral philosophy is the science concerned with the changing notions of the good, which is relativized because the good merely stands

---

[10] EW III 146, Tuck 110.
[11] See Michael Oakeshott, *Hobbes on Civil Association*, Berkeley, CA: University of California Press, 1975.
[12] EW III 147, Tuck 111.

for what is the subject of our desire. Hobbes thus holds a subjective theory of the good.

Here we might first raise the question: are there any principles of natural morality that Hobbes carries over into his scheme of civil law? As initially formulated, equity is merely the dictate of reason stating that "*if a man be trusted to judge between man and man…he deal equally between them.*"[13] This is the eleventh law of nature, and its principle of equality of treatment is generally derived from the same source as the other laws of nature.[14] From this description one would think that this law of nature is no different from the others propounded by Hobbes. Yet, as we will see, this law is singled out and given a higher status than the others when Hobbes discusses the duties of the sovereign. The reason for this seems to be that equity, unlike all the other laws of nature, applies only to those men who are "trusted to judge between man and man." Already, the addition of the element of trust takes this law of nature out of the realm of the state of nature, or at least concerns the bridge between the state of nature and civil society. Hobbes makes this explicit when he adds that without this law "the controversies of man cannot be determined but by war."[15]

Since the state of nature is properly that realm where people are in a constant state of war and where no trust is even reasonable, this dictate of reason is not appropriate in that state. It is a law of nature that must await the institution of a judge and positive law before it is made effective. Thus it is a principle of morality that can be applicable only in civil society. It is also clearly addressed to a sovereign-like figure, "a judge," and therefore it is meant to be applied directly to a sovereign or sovereign representative and not to those natural men who are striving to find their way out of the state of constant war. For further substantiation of this point, let us turn briefly to that section of *Leviathan* where civil morality and equity are discussed.

---

[13] EW III 142, Tuck 108.

[14] In *The Elements of Law (De Corpore Politico)* Hobbes had seemingly given a narrow definition of equity: "And this it is men mean by *distributive justice*, and is properly termed *equity*. The breach of the law is that which the Greeks call *pleionexia*, which is commonly rendered covetousness, but seemeth to me more precisely expressed by the word *encroaching*" EW IV 104, ch. IV, para. 2. Here already, though, we can see the beginning appreciation of the wider notion of equity Hobbes develops in *Leviathan*, and then expands further in the *Dialogue*. If violations of equity are seen as encroachments one can see how a move toward more than a consideration of distributive justice is countenanced. As I argue throughout this book, equity is about limitations on sovereign law-making, where failing to stay within limits is an encroachment against the people. Note also that the reference to *pleionexia*, demanding too much, can be understood as failing to stay within the limits of legitimate law-making.

[15] *The Elements of Law (De Corpore Politico)* EW IV 104, Ch. IV, para. 2.

The centrality of equity to Hobbes's philosophy is shown already in Chapter 18 of *Leviathan* when Hobbes says:

> because every subject is by this institution author of all the actions and judgments of the sovereign instituted, it followeth that whatsoever he doth, it can be no injury of any of his subjects, nor ought he to be by any of them accused of injustice...It is true that they that have sovereign power may commit iniquity; but not injustice or injury in the proper signification.[16]

Iniquity is a violation of equity, and the way that sovereigns are bound by equity is not fully spelled out in *Leviathan*, but as we will see it is one of the main topics of the *Dialogue*.

At the end of Chapter 28 Hobbes says that he is next going to speak "of what laws of nature the sovereign is bound to obey." But Hobbes does not specifically address this issue until Chapter 30, when he says that the prime duty of the sovereign is the safety of the people. As in *De Cive*, Hobbes defines this duty in *Leviathan* in a very broad way:

> And this is intended should be done not by care applied to individuals, further than their protection from injuries, when they still complain; but by a general providence, contained in public instruction, both of doctrine and example; and in making and executing of good laws, to which individual persons may apply their own cases.[17]

Remember that Hobbes had previously said that the duties of the sovereign are all linked to the preservation of the "safety of the people," and later Hobbes was to say that the sovereign is not bound except by equity.

Hobbes links the safety of the people and equity in his analysis of why the sovereign should make and execute good laws.

> The safety of the people requireth further, from him or them that have the sovereign power that justice be equally administered to all degrees of people...for in this consisteth equity; to which being a precept of the law of reason a sovereign is as much subject, as any of the meanest of his people.[18]

Hobbes had previously shown that it was impossible that a legitimately propounded law could ever be called unjust, since the law defined what was

---

[16] EW III 163, Tuck 124.
[17] EW III 322–323, Tuck 231.
[18] EW III 332, Tuck 237.

just. But Hobbes went on to claim that a just law and a good law are not the same, for all laws are just but not all are good. "A good law is that which is *needful* for the *good of the people*."[19] Hobbes seems to understand "good law" in terms of the principles of equity, and carefully distinguishes it from just laws. Equity becomes the cornerstone for evaluating laws as good or bad, and is thus the prime natural law to bind the sovereign.

At one crucial point in *Leviathan*, Hobbes does show that he was already thinking about how there might be limits on the sovereign's power, although it is not until the *Dialogue* that we see this as clearly about equity. Here is the relevant and often overlooked passage:

> If a subject have a controversy with his sovereign, of debt, or of right of possession of lands, or goods, or concerning any service required of his hands, or concerning any penalty, corporal, or pecuniary, grounded on a precedent law; he hath the same liberty to sue for his right, as if it were against a subject, and before such judges as are appointed by the sovereign.[20]

This right to sue the sovereign is limited to matters that are based on application of law rather than based on the exercise of the sovereign power more directly. But already in *Leviathan* we can see that Hobbes contemplated that a subject could go before a court appointed by the sovereign to obtain a fair result. We will see next that in the *Dialogue* the court that Hobbes assigns the role of hearing such disputes is the Chancery Court, often simply called the Court of Equity. One of the central questions is whether the courts of equity set limits on sovereign law-making that are merely drawn in terms of procedural fairness in how laws are applied, or whether these courts can also impose substantive limits.

In general, Hobbes does not spell out how equity comes to be the primary law of nature in the civil morality of *Leviathan*. In *De Homine*, Hobbes presents further evidence of the centrality of equity, when he links equity with rationality and says that God "has inscribed it in all hearts."[21] But only in the *Dialogue*, much later in Hobbes's life, is equity explained in any

---

[19] EW III 335, Tuck 239.
[20] EW III 206–207; Tuck 152–153. For a very interesting discussion of this passage see Thomas Poole, "Hobbes on Law and Prerogative," in *Hobbes and the Law*, ed. David Dyzenhaus and Thomas Poole, Cambridge: Cambridge University Press, 2012, pp. 68–96.
[21] *De Homine*, Ch. 15; Bernard Gert, ed. *Man and Citizen*, 1991, p. 73. See a discussion of this passage in S.A. Lloyd's *Morality in the Philosophy of Thomas Hobbes: Cases in the Law of Nature*, New York: Cambridge University Press, 2009, pp. 276–277.

detail. I will explicate some of the views in the *Dialogue* in the next section, but leave to Chapter 4 a fuller treatment of the *Dialogue*—a vastly underappreciated work in Hobbes's corpus.

II. The Later View

At the end of his life, when he wrote the *Dialogue*, Hobbes rarely spoke of the state of nature and the corresponding notion of natural right. Instead, he spoke of civil right and law, with the singular exception that he continued to speak of certain natural law considerations, especially equity. In this work Hobbes continued his reduction of justice to legality: "A just action is that which is not against the law,"[22] but filled out his moral concepts by specifying more clearly the nature of equity. At the beginning of the *Dialogue* (which has only two participants: a Lawyer and a Philosopher) the "Lawyer" says that if statute law is taken away, all that would remain is "equity and reason, (laws Divine and eternal, which oblige all men at all times in all places)."[23] This reference by the "Lawyer" to the laws of nature is not meant to be interpreted necessarily as Hobbes's own position. Nonetheless, we can gain a sense for which terms are carried over from *Leviathan*, and how the context of discussing these terms comes to change.[24]

First, Hobbes is concerned only with the laws of nature relating specifically to law-making: that is, to equity and justice. Second, Hobbes discusses these subjects only in respect to actions not covered by the statute laws, or when the statute law did not exist (in times of civil war or international disputes). He is not concerned, as he was in *Leviathan*, to speak at length about the hypothetical state before humans entered society. Also, he is addressing himself not to natural lawyers but to common lawyers. This means that he is more concerned with the actual basis of limiting the law-making authority—for instance, through the courts—than with the strictly theoretical basis of limiting sovereignty *per se*.

---

[22] EW VI 29, Cropsey 72.

[23] EW VI 6, Cropsey 55–56.

[24] As the *Dialogue* opens, it is initially unclear which of the two participants in the *Dialogue*, the "philosopher" or the "lawyer" speaks for Hobbes. Soon it seems Hobbes speaks through the "philosopher" but a fourth of the way through the text the "lawyer" also speaks in a way that is consistent with Hobbes's own views in earlier works.

In this work, Hobbes makes his position on justice extremely clear when he has the "Philosopher" say

> it is manifest that before there was a law, there could be no injustice; and therefore laws are in their nature antecedent to justice and injustice.[25]

Since sovereignty is antecedent (or at very least contemporaneous) to the establishment of civil law, it follows from the above remark that sovereignty also must be antecedent to justice and injustice for Hobbes.

Hobbes also importantly clarifies the distinction between justice and equity in the *Dialogue*:

> the difference between injustice and iniquity is this; that injustice is the transgression of a statute-law, and iniquity the transgression of the law of reason.[26]

This conclusion follows from Hobbes's analysis of the different functions of the Courts of Justice and the Courts of Equity in English law. The Court of the King's Bench (one of the courts of justice) was the court where one brought a dispute on a matter covered by a particular statute. The Court of Chancery (one of the courts of equity), on the other hand, was a separate court to which one appealed if there was no statute or precedent case governing a disputed matter, or if the application of the relevant statute was thought to be inappropriate. Considerations of justice were matters of positive law proper, whereas considerations of equity were matters of "reason:" that is, matters of natural law.[27]

Before we examine what Hobbes meant by equity and reason in the *Dialogue*, let us turn briefly to see what one legal scholar, W. P. Baildon, said about the development of the Courts of Equity prior to Hobbes's time.

> The Court of Chancery became necessary because it was found that the Courts of Common Law were, from various causes, frequently unable to do justice[28] to

---

[25] EW VI 29, Cropsey 72–73.

[26] EW VI 25–26, Cropsey 70.

[27] In *Behemoth*, Hobbes says that "by the law of equity, which is the unalterable law of nature, a man that has the sovereign power, cannot, if he would, give away the right of anything which is necessary for him to retain for the good government of his subjects, unless he do it in express words, saying that he will have the sovereign power no longer. For the giving away that which by consequence only, draws the sovereignty along with it, is not, I think, a giving away of the sovereignty; but an error, such as works nothing but an invalidity of the grant itself." EW VI 310–311.

[28] Baildon is here using the term justice not in the narrow way that Hobbes used it but in a broader way.

suitors. This might result from two classes of reasons: (1) from the inelasticity of its principles and practice; or (2) from the peculiar situation of the parties in cases which could otherwise have been dealt with at Common Law.[29]

Equity courts and common law courts remained separated until the end of the nineteenth century.

Hobbes shows us that he was aware of some of these historical distinctions in the following exchange between the "Lawyer" and the "Philosopher."

> Lawyer. Seeing all judges in all courts ought to judge according to equity, which is the law of reason, a distinct court of equity seemeth to me to be unnecessary, and but a burthen to the people, since common-law and equity are the same law.
>
> Philosopher. It were so indeed, if judges could not err; and that the King is not bound to any law but that of equity, it belongs to him alone to give remedy to them that, by the ignorance or corruption of a judge, shall suffer damage.[30]

This exchange shows that Hobbes knew that there was a special function given to the courts of equity, and that the function was different from that of the standard common law courts. It also shows that Hobbes realized that equity placed a duty on the King to make sure that his laws were fairly administered and applied.

Since in *Leviathan* Hobbes had said that the sovereign was bound to provide for the safety of the people, we have here another indication that equity and provision of the safety of the people are linked for Hobbes. As I will point out several times in the chapters that follow, one reason for seeing the King or sovereign bound by equity as a matter of fairness was that when the sovereign does not treat the people fairly, sovereignty is weakened, making it more difficult for the sovereign to protect the people from both external as well as internal threats.

The Court of Chancery was the proper domain of the King's first minister, the Chancellor. When Hobbes's mentor, Francis Bacon, was Lord Chancellor he sought to establish the independent authority of the Court of Equity over the common-law courts. The Chief Justice of the

---

[29] W. P. Baildon (ed.), introductory notes, *The Publications of the Selden Society* (V896) Select Cases in Chancery 1364–1471 10, London, 1896, p. xxi.
[30] EW VI 26, Cropsey 70.

King's Bench, Edward Coke, fought a vehement struggle with Bacon on this issue, and ultimately lost the battle. In Hobbes's time the Court of Chancery was a very strong court that had unusual power, much like that of the old Court of Star Chamber, to be used for political purposes as well as for strictly judicial ones. Hobbes later suggests that the Court of Equity is the proper place to bring a complaint against the King's law and possibly even against the King himself. Since this court is administered by the King's own minister, it is questionable what efficacy such an action could have. Whether this is really what Hobbes had in mind is not terribly clear, as we shall see, but it is clear that Hobbes felt that the King was bound by equity in a way which he could not have been bound by justice.

At one point in the *Dialogue* Hobbes addresses the claim that equity entails "that a man's conscience should be allowed to prevail over the law" in certain cases.[31] It is claimed also that this is grounded in the stipulations of certain statutes. Hobbes has the "Philosopher" counter this claim by showing that these are statutes which do not set equity above the law nor the law above equity. Instead, these statutes merely showed how equity and law combine to set rules of proper legal pleading.[32] Once again Hobbes is primarily concerned with what might be called procedural due process here, although as is true today as well, there is sometimes a fine line between procedural due process and substantive due process, as when Hobbes argues that the innocent should not be punished.

Equity for Hobbes is the concept governing legal interpretations and judgment. Hobbes is particularly careful to distinguish between Edward Coke's view that equity could "cancel" the King's laws and Hobbes's own view that equity could only "correct" the meaning or grammar of the laws.

> It cannot be that a written law should be against reason; for nothing is more reasonable, than that every man should obey the law, which he hath himself assented to; but that is not always the law which is signified by *grammatical*

---

[31] On this point see Edward G. Andrew, "Hobbes on Conscience Within the Law and Without," *Canadian Journal of Political Science*, vol. 32, no. 2, June 1999, pp. 203–225. At one point Andrew argues that Hobbes can be read as supporting jury nullification, *Canadian Journal of Political Science*, p. 223.

[32] Cf. EW VI 49–51, Cropsey 86–88.

construction of the letter, but that which the legislature thereby intended should be in force; which intention, I confess, is a very hard matter many times to pick out of the words of the statute.[33]

One type of equity proceedings is then the reasonable review of a particular law in order to ascertain if the true intent of that law has been expressed properly in the opinion of a common law court. This is because

> there was a necessity of a higher Court of Equity than the Courts of Common-law, to remedy the errors in judgment given by the justices of inferior courts.[34]

After examining several statutes that concern jurisdictional disputes between courts of equity and courts of common law, Hobbes is led to conclude that equity also concerns those cases brought by people who claim to have been aggrieved by the courts of common law. But these equity proceedings are not properly brought against the law so much as for an elucidation of the law. The King appoints his Chancellor to hear these cases because it is the King, as maker of the law, who must be the one to interpret or change his own pronouncements:

> for no one can mend a law but he that can make it, and therefore I say [equity] amends not the law, but the judgments only when they are erroneous.[35]

Hobbes comes to the conclusion

> that justice fulfills the law, and equity interprets the law, and amends the judgments given upon the same law.[36]

Thus Hobbes has shown that justice applies to subjects and concerns whether they followed and thus fulfilled the law, and equity applies to the judges or kings and concerns whether they have correctly interpreted or applied the law.

---

[33] EW VI 64, Cropsey 97.
[34] EW VI, Cropsey 94–95.
[35] EW VI 68, Cropsey 101.
[36] EW VI 68, Cropsey 101.

We are now able to see why the actions of the law-maker can never be against justice but may be against equity. The sovereign's actions cannot be unjust, because justice concerns fulfilling the law, and the maker of the law cannot be said not to fulfill his own law, since she is not subject to it. On the other hand, the sovereign's actions may be against equity if she does not properly interpret her law in a manner consistent with the intent that was originally expressed through the law, or in a manner consistent with her duty to act for the good of the people, since that is what underlies all legitimate law-making.

Equity, as the primary law of reason binding the law-maker, also dictates that the sovereign law-maker must follow certain rules of fairness in administering and applying his laws. To act otherwise is to err, and the subject may then go to court to show that an error was made and should be corrected. This becomes the only legitimate means the subjects have of challenging the law-maker. They cannot challenge a law itself, because to do so would be to challenge the justness of the law, but they can challenge the interpretation, administration, or application of that law—that is, its equity—in their own case.

This curiously rigid use of the words "justice" and "equity" was certainly not common in Hobbes's time. Hobbes uses these words in this peculiar way because he wishes severely to limit the ability of the subject to challenge the law on moral grounds. His approach is to restrict the realm of morality that is applicable to the law-maker, by reducing moral challenges to questions of fair proceedings. But his purpose is not, as is sometimes said, to eliminate the possibility of any moral limitation of law. Indeed, Hobbes held the view that there are moral limits on legitimate law-making. And equity was the source of such limitations, as we will see in more detail in the next chapter.

III. Conclusions

Let us recall why Hobbes thought that people should submit to the law-maker to begin with. Hobbes tried to show that, starting from the goal of self-preservation, it is reasonable for people to accept the sovereign's authority and thus to limit their freedom if the sovereign can guarantee the kind of protection they could not get otherwise. The agreement to allow an entity to curtail our liberty continues to be reasonable unless our self-preservation is again threatened. Short of this, it is never reasonable to challenge the law-maker's authority, because such a challenge would undermine the law-maker's ability to provide the safety we seek. It was this consideration that caused Hobbes to say that all laws, properly propounded, are just. They are always just because their goal, the safety of the people, is always just.

On the other hand, we see in *Leviathan* an admission by Hobbes that laws are not always good ones. While it is not always reasonable to challenge the interpretation or even the existence of law, the judgment of the goodness of a law is based on a much wider standard than that of the justice of a law. Goodness of laws and of legal judgments is determined with reference to the moral standards of equity.

> The things that make a good judge, or good interpreter of the laws, are first *a right understanding* of that principal law of nature called *equity*, which depend[s]…on the goodness of a man's own natural reason, and meditation.[37]

A good law-maker is one who follows equity.

I believe that the texts we have considered support the conclusion that there are two types of moral limitations which the principle of equity places on law-makers. First, Hobbes explicitly states that the law-maker and the judge are restricted from interpreting laws in an inconsistent manner or from applying laws in an arbitrary or unequal way. This limitation, albeit a strictly formal limitation on the administration of the laws, is grounded in the natural law principle that judges (and law-makers) treat people equally, and then administer the laws in a manner that allows the people to know what they are required to do to act legally. Thus, the first limitation on law-making is a moral limitation in the sense that it emanates from Hobbes's general views on fairness. I will explain later how Hobbes's view here is similar to that of Lon Fuller, who also held that what appear to be procedural limits on law-making can also be understood as moral limits.

Second, Hobbes explicitly states in the *Dialogue* that laws cannot be unreasonable,[38] and implies that laws also cannot be capricious[39] or

---

[37] EW III 269, Tuck 195.
[38] EW VI, 134, Cropsey 150.
[39] EW VI 137–138, Cropsey 151–152.

superfluous.[40] It seems to me that these limitations, which are also said to follow from the principle of equity, especially against capricious law-making, verge into being substantive limitations on what the law-maker can declare to be law. These are again moral limitations of equity in the sense that the law-makers are restricted from acts that threaten the safety of the people and thus violate the law-maker's duty to provide security for the subjects who have sworn obedience to him. It is fairly clear that Hobbes saw this limitation as binding the law-maker in a moral way, at least in his conscience.

Thus, Hobbes did allow an important overlap of morality with legality. There was a clear moral restriction on the law-maker, and it concerned the fair administration of the law. Fairness itself (as many recent legal theorists have been quick to point out) cannot be inferred from a strictly positivistic account of law, yet most people would admit that a legal system must, above all else, remain fair. Hobbes recognized this problem and allowed the moral wedge of equity to be driven into his legal positivism. Without this natural-law principle, people would have no basis for settling disputes about interpretation of the laws (especially when these laws conflict). True to his blurring of morality and prudence, Hobbes could not allow this uncertainty because such disputes could jeopardize the acceptance of the whole legal order—which in turn might throw the people back into a state of war. The lawmaker's first duty is to prevent such a return to the state of nature.

Thus Hobbes came to link equity with the sovereign's duty to uphold the safety of the people, by among other things protecting the people from themselves. By implication, then, the law-maker could not even declare laws that might jeopardize that security. For Hobbes there is an important difference between those natural law principles that are necessary for civil law to function (such as equity), and those natural law principles that merely lead men toward civil society. Hobbes felt that his contemporaries were foolish in insisting that all aspects of liberty be safeguarded against the crown. "Safeguarding liberty" (in the name of natural justice), as it was defined in seventeenth-century England, was often inconsistent with securing safety against either foreign invasion or civil war. But this does not mean that the sovereign should be given absolute control over his subjects. For this would also risk civil war.

[40] EW VI 157, Cropsey 166.

There must be some visible limits to the sovereign's power in order that the subjects see the legal system as both

(a) necessary for their safety, and
(b) fair: that is, not arbitrary and not without appeal when the laws excessively interfere with the subject's liberty.

The principle of equity provided such a limitation on the authority of the sovereign law-maker. Attending to Hobbes's statements concerning equity will reward us with a picture of Hobbes much more palatable to our contemporary tastes and also much closer to the true picture of Hobbes himself.

4
Concept of Law

Many political philosophers have argued that Hobbes's conception of law is simple, and undeserving of critical attention. John Plamenatz stated what I take to be this dominant view when he said: "About Hobbes's conception of law there is no ambiguity, it may be inadequate but at least it is clear."[1] Nonetheless, I shall argue that Hobbes's conception of law is surprisingly subtle. I shall contend that Hobbes derives his most important political concepts from a legal model, the rudiments of which he had developed as early as *Leviathan*, but which was not completely spelled out until he wrote his dialogue on the laws at the end of his life. In this chapter I walk the reader through my interpretation of Hobbes's *Dialogue*, comparing it to Hobbes's earlier writings on the scope and nature of law as well as the main types of law that Hobbes felt to be not law properly so-called.

First, I will briefly discuss the format of Hobbes's *Dialogue*. Second, I will discuss Hobbes's views of how knowledge of the law is acquired. Third, I will discuss Hobbes's views of the origin and sources of law. Fourth, I will set out Hobbes's ideas concerning the nature of law, and especially how civil law differs from other forms of law. Fifth, I will provide specific treatment of Hobbes's typology of law, beginning with its overall form. Sixth, I discuss Hobbes's critique of custom in law. And then, in the seventh section, I conclude this chapter with a discussion of the important category of natural law as well as more of Hobbes's thoughts on equity, which I have already begun discussing in earlier chapters.

---

[1] John Plamenatz, *Man and Society*, 2 vols., New York: McGraw Hill, 1963, 1:138.

I. Hobbes's *Dialogue*

More than 350 years ago Thomas Hobbes wrote *A Dialogue Between a Philosopher and a Student of the Common Laws of England*.[2] Since the posthumous publication of this work in 1681, a curious scholarly literature has developed. For over a hundred years there was virtually no comment at all on this work, which is Hobbes's only work dealing specifically with law. There is one extraordinary exception to the scholarly silence on the *Dialogue*. Before the actual publication of the manuscript, Matthew Hale, Lord Chief Justice of the King's Bench in England, wrote a reply to Hobbes's *Dialogue*, apparently based on a copy of the *Dialogue* circulated shortly before Hobbes's death in 1679. Unfortunately, Hale's reply remained unpublished until 1921, when the English legal historians Pollock and Holdsworth discovered it among Hale's papers.[3] Joseph Cropsey published an edition of the *Dialogue* forty years ago, but there has been little critical commentary since then either.[4]

A new edition of the *Dialogue* was published by Alan Cromarie and Quentin Skinner in 2005. So far, this new edition has also not yet sparked a renewed interest in this work.[5] Cromarie's introduction sheds some new light on the *Dialogue*, such as his claim that Hobbes's book had practical political importance in that "It seems to have been shown to the senior judges" in Hobbes's time.[6] Cromarie devotes only three pages to the

---

[2] See Joseph Cropsey's excellent discussion of the authenticity of this manuscript and his argument for saying that 1675 was probably when Hobbes wrote it. *A Dialogue Between a Philosopher and a Student of the Common Laws of England*, ed. Joseph Cropsey, University of Chicago, 1971, pp. 1–8.

[3] See Frederick Pollock, "Reflections by the Lord Chief Justice Hale on Mr. Hobbes His Dialogue on the Laws," *The Law Quarterly Review*, 1921, pp. 274–303; and William S. Holdsworth, *The History of English Law*, 5 vols. London and Boston, MA: Metheun, 1924, 5: 499–513. It is of some interest that eighteenth- and nineteenth-century biographies of Hale make reference to his essay on Hobbes, but without comment. Why this essay was "lost" for 250 years remains a mystery.

[4] In the last fifty years, curiously little has been said about Hobbes's *Dialogue*. This has held true even though two new editions of his *English Works* have been published wherein his *Dialogue* holds a prominent place at the beginning of Volume VI (and had held that place since Molesworth first published the *English Works* in 1840). In 1971 Joseph Cropsey published a corrected edition of the *Dialogue* with an introduction and notes.

[5] See *Thomas Hobbes: Writings on Common Law and Hereditary Right*, ed. Alan Cromarie and Quentin Skinner, Oxford: Oxford University Press, 2005. In addition, as I was finishing the last draft of my book, I came into possession of a new collection of essays on Hobbes's legal theory edited by David Dyzenhaus and Thomas Poole, under the title, *Hobbes on Law*, due for publication in 2012 by Cambridge University Press. Several of these chapters refer to the *Dialogue*.

[6] *Thomas Hobbes: Writings on Common Law and Hereditary Right*, p. xvii.

concept of equity in the *Dialogue*, instead devoting by far the largest part of his commentary to what Hobbes says about why the crime of heresy should not carry the death penalty, which Hobbes himself feared at the end of his life.[7]

Hobbes's *Dialogue*, as the title indicates, is set in the form of a dialogue between a philosopher and a lawyer. Similar to most philosophical dialogues Hobbes somewhat misuses this format. There is no character development of the two participants in the work, nor is there any attempt to give a fair hearing to both speakers. By this vehicle, though, Hobbes juxtaposes his own views to those of Chief Justice Edward Coke, the greatest contemporary proponent of the common law tradition in early seventeenth-century England, and a mentor of Matthew Hale. Thus the format does provide the advantage, at least in the beginning stages of the *Dialogue*, of showing both Hobbes's views on the law and how he saw his views differing from those of contemporary jurists.

One indication of the focus of the *Dialogue* is that it opens with the following exchange, entitled "Of the Laws of Reason":

> Lawyer. What makes you say, that the study of the law is less rational, than the study of mathematics?
>
> Philosopher. I say not that; for all study is rational, or nothing worth: but I say that the great masters of the *mathematics* do not so often err as the great professors of the law.
>
> Lawyer. If you had applied your reason to the law, perhaps you would have been of another mind.[8]

From these first lines of the *Dialogue* it is clear that the "Philosopher" wishes to discuss the rationality of the jurists but not necessarily the rational basis of the law itself. In his other works, especially in the beginning of *Leviathan*, Hobbes started by comparing the theoretical bases of mathematics and politics. But in the *Dialogue*, Hobbes is interested more in the specific errors of the jurists, thus setting a substantially different tone from *Leviathan*.

---

[7] It is also unfortunate that Cromarie continues the tradition of discounting the importance of this work, especially by such remarks as "some allowance should be made for [Hobbes's] dwindling intellectual energies." *Writings on Common Law and Hereditary Right*, pp. xiv–xv.

[8] EW VI 3, Cropsey 53–54.

From these beginning lines it is not so evident which one of the two interlocutors (who are the only two participants in the entire *Dialogue*) speaks for Hobbes. As the *Dialogue* proceeds it seems as if the "Philosopher" defends Hobbes's positions and the "Lawyer" defends Edward Coke. About a fourth of the way through the dialogue the "Lawyer," seemingly convinced by the arguments of the "Philosopher," ceases to defend Coke and becomes merely the sounding board, and often the elaborator, of Hobbes's doctrines expressed in rudiment elsewhere.

Another important difference between *Leviathan* and the *Dialogue* is found in the first long speech by the "Philosopher":

> I…have looked over the titles of the statutes from Magna Charta downward to this present time. I left not one unread, which I thought might concern myself…But I did not much examine which of them was more, or less rational; because I read them not to dispute, but to obey them…"[9]

Twenty-five years earlier, Hobbes had written a chapter of *Leviathan* entitled "Of Civil Laws," which began thus:

> For the knowledge of particular laws belongeth to them, that profess the study of the laws of their several countries; but the knowledge of civil law, to any man…my design being not to show what is law here, and there; but what is law; as Plato, Aristotle, Cicero and diverse others have done, without taking upon them the profession of the study of the law.[10]

In *Leviathan* Hobbes did not, and could not, make the claim to have studied the laws of England (or the laws of any country, for that matter). He was simply explaining the grounding of law generally. In the *Dialogue*, Hobbes was on much different footing. Probably at the instigation of his now famous biographer, John Aubrey, Hobbes had undertaken a study of the laws of England which culminated in the writing of the *Dialogue*.[11] In this

---

[9] EW VI 3, Cropsey p. 54.
[10] E.W III 250–251, Tuck 183.
[11] "In 1664 I say'd to him 'Me thinkes 'tis pitty that you have such a cleare reason and working head did never take into consideration the learning of the lawes'; and I endeavored to perswade him to it…I than presented him the lord chancellor Bacon's Elements of the Lawe (a thin quarto) in order thereunto to draw him on…" *"Brief Lives" Chiefly of Contemporaries, set down by John Aubrey between the years 1669 and 1696.* ed. Andrew Clark, Oxford: Clarendon Press, 1898, 1: 341.

Dialogue Hobbes is still concerned (as he has the "Philosopher" say) with the general concept of law:

> Lawyer. You speak of the statute law, and I speak of the common law.
> Philosopher. I speak generally of law.[12]

But this general discussion of law is based not on deduction alone, but also on induction from Hobbes's recently completed study of all the relevant statutes since Magna Charta. Thus, the *Dialogue* is more than what Cropsey calls "in some respects an elaboration" of Chapter 26 of *Leviathan*.[13] It constitutes a full-blown treatise, which Hobbes himself had called "De Legibus"[14] (possibly, thus, giving it as much weight as the three parts of his philosophical system: De Corpore, De Homine, De Cive). It represents what one of the few sympathetic legal historians has called the mature Hobbes's "final thoughts on the nature of law and power."[15]

II. Knowledge of the Law

Hobbes begins his substantive critique of the dominant legal theory of his time by having the "Philosopher" set out several of the doctrines of Edward Coke, where he "found great subtilty, not of the law, but of inference from law, and especially from the law of human nature, which is the law of reason."[16] These doctrines are:

a) that argumentation and reasoning in the Law lead more quickly to knowledge of the law than do examination of the statutes;
b) that nothing is law that is against reason;
c) that reason is the life of the law (also that reason is the soul of the law);
d) that the Common law is nothing but reason;
e) that Equity is an unwritten law which is nothing but right reason.

---

[12] EW VI 5, Cropsey 55.
[13] EW VI, Cropsey 11.
[14] See the letter from Hobbes to Aubrey, 18 August 1679, cited in "*Brief Lives*," p. 342.
[15] D. E. C. Yale, "Hobbes and Hale on Law, Legislation, and the Sovereign," *Cambridge Law Journal*, vol. 31, no. 1, April 1972, 123.
[16] EW VI 3–4, Cropsey 54.

While the "Philosopher" says that he agrees with all these doctrines, he eventually refutes the first three. And even though the last two temporarily are left to stand, both the common law and equity are later shown not to be laws properly so called, though equity is given primacy over justice as a limit on law.

The refutation of Edward Coke's legal philosophy begins with a discussion of the following problem. If law is reason, as Coke claims, then man may justify his disobedience of a law by saying he found it against his reason. This possible argument would frustrate "all the laws in the world."[17] There is an obvious equivocation here in the use of the term "reason." The "Philosopher" is quick to point this out and show why reason cannot provide a proper basis for law. The "Lawyer" responds by saying that Coke meant "an artificial perfection of reason gotten by long study, observation, and experience, and not of every man's natural reason."[18]

The distinction between natural and artificial reason was one of Coke's most important conceptual contributions to legal theory. Artificial reason, for Coke, is the synthesis of the natural reasoning of many men on disparate questions. The synthesis represents that part of each individual's natural reasoning that most men come to accept as true. This does not mean that everything spoken by a judge must be taken for artificial reason. On the contrary, an individual judge, like any common person, possesses only natural reason. His dictates are regarded as artificial reason only insofar as they have been accepted over the ages. For Coke, unlike Aquinas and his followers (who also held that law was a product of reason), the test of reasonableness was an artificial one: namely, the ability of a law to stand the test of time.[19]

The "Philosopher" rejoins that this statement is "partly obscure, and partly untrue."[20] What is obscure, he says, is how knowledge of the law is gained through artificial rather than through natural reason. In the *Dialogue* Hobbes denies that there is any reason relevant to law other than human reason, which he equates then with natural reason. But this is possibly in tension with *Leviathan*. In its "Introduction," Hobbes had said that the State "is but an artificial man" and that "*equity*, and *laws*, [are] an

---

[17] EW VI 4, Cropsey 54.
[18] EW VI 4, Cropsey 55.
[19] Yale, "Hobbes and Hale on Law," p. 125.
[20] EW VI 5, Cropsey 55.

artificial *reason* and *will*" just as the original contract is an artificial act of creation.[21] Hobbes's notion of artificial reason was not the same as Coke's. In *Leviathan*, artificial reason, for Hobbes, was the reason of the sovereign as he ruled in respect to justice—that is, as he made decisions about what was to be called law proper in his commonwealth. Artificial reason, for Coke, was "custom."

Throughout his writings, Hobbes had consistently maintained that reason leads to true knowledge only of those bodies that we have generated.[22] Since the State is an artificial body that has been generated by the people, true knowledge of it is a possibility (just as true knowledge of the geometrical form of a triangle can be gained because we have constructed it). The laws, according to Hobbes, have also been created by the sovereign. Thus the sovereign must be able to acquire true knowledge of his own laws. But since the sovereign is an artificial person, the reason he employs to acquire this knowledge must be an artificial reason. Similarly, it can be argued (from essentially Hobbesian premises) that the people, having created the sovereign, must be able to acquire knowledge of what the sovereign creates—namely, of the laws. But this knowledge would not be gained by artificial reason, since, strictly speaking, natural persons are not capable of artificial reasoning. For Hobbes, the people could only acquire knowledge of the laws through natural reason.

Regardless of whether it is gained through artificial or natural reason, can this knowledge of the law be said to be gained, as Coke claimed, from custom? If "custom" means the synthesis from experience of what has been created by another, and not of what we ourselves have created, then Hobbes would say that "custom" could only lead to belief but never true knowledge. (In a different work Hobbes said that "*experience concludeth nothing universally.*"[23]) If, on the other hand, "custom" refers to the interpretation of laws, where the meaning of laws is created by the common acceptance of the meaning of legal words as commands, then custom, for Hobbes, could be the basis for knowledge of the laws. But, as we shall see, Hobbes denies that this is how laws come to gain meaning. Thus artificial reason is "obscure" to Hobbes not as a

---

[21] EW III ix–x, Tuck 9.
[22] See EW I 81–83. I will refer to the translation of *De Corpore* as reprinted in *The English Works of Thomas Hobbes*, ed. Sir William Molesworth, 11 vols. (London: John Bohn, 1839), vol. I.
[23] EW IV 18.

general concept, but only according to the specific application of the concept employed by Coke. Hobbes hints at this solution to the supposed "obscurity" when he says "but I suppose that he [Coke] means, that the reason of a judge, or of all the judges together without the King, is that *summa ratio*" which makes laws."[24] If this is indeed what Coke means, then Hobbes denies it, for he says, it "is not wisdom, but authority that makes a law."[25] I will return to this discussion of artificial reason in more detail in Chapter 6.

Hobbes here subtly shifts the argument from what constitutes knowledge of the law to what constitutes the law itself. The sovereign might be the one who makes the law, but this does not necessarily affect the judge's, or the ordinary person's, ability to know the law. When the "Philosopher" rejects Coke's claim "that the law hath been fined by grave and learned men, meaning the professors of the law,"[26] the "Lawyer," sensing some kind of shift in argument, comments "you speak of the statute law, and I speak of the common law."[27] The shift, though, is not from common law to statute law, but from knowledge of the law to the nature and origin of the law.

By so shifting the argument, Hobbes avoids an extended discussion of the role of the judge as interpreter of the law. The "Lawyer," having just espoused a conspicuously Thomistic notion of law, concedes that Coke should have included the King, along with the Justices, as makers of the law. But Hobbes will not allow even this concession to stand, and says that he himself can be as equipped as Judges to make law, after only two months of studying the law of the statutes. "But you will be an ill pleader" says the "Lawyer." And the "Philosopher" drives his point home by showing that neither he nor judges make the law. Either all judges are also ill pleaders, because they are just as knowledgeable as any layman like Hobbes, or they are deceivers in pretending to do more than just interpret the law. We next turn from questions that are largely abstract and epistemological to questions that are addressed primarily historically, although the overlap between these questions about knowledge and origins of law are intertwined, as we will see.

[24] EW VI 5, Cropsey 55.
[25] EW VI 5, Cropsey 55.
[26] EW VI 5, Cropsey 55.
[27] EW VI 5, Cropsey 55.

III. The Origin and Sources of Law

In this section I will provide an interpretation of the origin and sources of law in Hobbes's *Dialogue*. At a certain point the "Philosopher" asks:

> I pray tell me, to what end were statute laws ordained, seeing the law of reason ought to be applied to every controversy that can arise.[28]

To this the "Lawyer" replies:

> the laws of man, though they can punish the fruits of them, which are evil actions, yet they cannot pluck up the roots that are in the heart. How can a man be indicted of avarice, envy, hypocrisy, or other vicious habit, till it be declared by some action, which a witness may take notice of?[29]

The mention of the relation between "laws of man" and "laws of reason" leads the participants in the *Dialogue* in two directions, both of which are well-known Hobbesian themes: law between nations, and justice without law. I shall treat the first of these themes in a subsequent chapter.

The second area of interest concerning the relation of laws of men and laws of reason is the question of the status of "justice" in a setting where there is no human law:

> Lawyer. the scope of all human law is peace and justice...
>
> Philosopher. But what is justice?
>
> Lawyer. Justice is giving to every man his own.
>
> Lawyer. Seeing then without human law all things would be common...the same law of reason dictates to mankind, for their own preservation, a distribution of lands and goods, that each man may know what is proper to him...
>
> Philosopher. All this is very rational; but how can any laws secure one man from another...[when] the laws of themselves are but a dead letter, which of itself is not able to compel a man to do otherwise than himself pleaseth...[30]

The argument here seems to be, after we untwist the knot of statements above, that "distributive" justice requires an authority to declare who owns

---

[28] EW VI 7, Cropsey 57.
[29] EW VI 7, Cropsey 57, my italics.
[30] EW VI 8–10, Cropsey 57–59.

(or who is due) what. Without that authority, there is no good reason for anyone to honor the ownership claims of another. Thus justice requires a law-giver, and therefore does not exist in the state of nature, since by definition that is a state with neither law-giver nor law.

In *Leviathan* and *De Cive* Hobbes speaks of the hypothetical origin of law in protracted discussions of the state of nature. This treatment has led some scholars to conclude that Hobbes sought to base civil society and law on the natural laws of that state of nature. This conclusion, while debatable in regard to *Leviathan*, is unsupportable in respect to *A Dialogue*. Here Hobbes speaks of the historical origin of law. Beginning with Solon he analyzes the law-making authority of Alexander the Great, Justinian, William the Conqueror, and Magna Carta. Hobbes ends this historical discussion with a critique of the power of the present King of England to create laws levying taxes. Laced throughout the discussion is a second-level discussion of who *should* hold the sovereign power (which encompasses the power to declare laws): should it be retained in the hands of the people, or should it be held by the King exclusively as the single sovereign authority, or should it be by the King in Parliament?

The flavor of this discussion is set by the "Lawyer," who stipulates that "By the laws, I mean, law living and armed."[31] Thus law in the state of nature, which might be living but is definitely not armed, is excluded not by the "Philosopher" speaking for Hobbes, but by the "Lawyer." The exclusion of non-positive law from this discussion in the *Dialogue* is made even more explicit when the "Lawyer" next proclaims: "It is not therefore the word of the law, but the power of a man, that has the strength of a nation, that makes the laws effectual." This proclamation turns the discussion to how the laws were made effective, and by whom, throughout history.

Here we begin to get a sense of Hobbes's own substantive views on the origin and sources of law.

> Lawyer. It was not Solon that made Athenian Laws, though he devised them, but the supreme court of the people; nor the lawyers of Rome that made the imperial law in Justinian's time, but Justinian himself.
>
> Philosopher. We agree then in this, that in England it is the King that makes the laws, whosoever pens them…[32]

---

[31] EW VI 10, Cropsey 59.
[32] EW VI 10, Cropsey 59.

The difference between the person who makes the law and the person who pens the law is important. If a written set of imperatives becomes law simply upon being penned, then there could be innumerable codes of law existing simultaneously in the same society. Mere declaration of an imperative is not enough to constitute the origin of a law. A law begins to be called a law proper when there is a power that can enforce obedience to that law. Thus Solon did not make the law, he merely penned it. His dictates remained merely written documents until "the supreme court of the people" of Athens adopted these documents as their own laws and placed their own power and enforcement behind them. From this point, Hobbes developed his theory of law in the *Dialogue*.

The seeming commonsensical character of this argument may perhaps make us forget how novel and unpopular this was to the ears of seventeenth-century jurists. To say that positive law depended on the power to enforce it and not on agreement with the natural order or the divine will, was seen as both blasphemous and foolish. John Whitehall, a contemporary of Hobbes, and himself a lawyer, said that Hobbes's theory of the origin of law (as expressed in *Leviathan*),

> will destroy his country's law and make room for arbitrary power...'Tis true the law is a Politic thing that can act nothing of itself without something that is natural conjoined to it, but, notwithstanding, 'tis properly called the Action of Law, though the execution be by men's hands. Because it is the Authority of the law that empowers them, and through its efficacy they are justified in their actions.[33]

Whitehall recognized that Hobbes's doctrine of the origin of law would revolutionize both civil and constitutional law. In constitutional law, Hobbes's doctrine would lead to the destruction of the doctrine of the Divine Right of Kings. It would seemingly supplant this doctrine with what was thought to be an authoritarian view that was dangerous simply because of how strikingly appealing it was to common sense.

---

[33] Quoted in John Bowie, *Hobbes and His Critics: A Study in Seventeenth-Century Constitutionalism*, London: Jonathan Cape, 1951, pp. 180, 183, 184.

Hobbes seems to have been much more concerned with the pernicious doctrine advocated by Edward Coke than with criticisms like that of Whitehall. Coke traced the origin of the judiciary's law-making authority from the common law and Magna Carta: an obvious attempt to establish the judiciary's power as independent of, and as a countervailing force to, the power of the King. Like Hobbes, Coke argued from essentially common-sense premises. Throughout the *Dialogue*, Hobbes attempts to counter Coke's claims both by historical and theoretical arguments. His historical argument is posed as an alternative rather than as a refutation of Coke. Hobbes argues that all authority to make laws in England stems directly from William the Conqueror. William brought the people of England out of their miserable condition, and by the implicit transfer of right from these people after the conquest he gained the authority to declare laws. From William's time onward, "God made Kings for the people, and not the people for the King."[34] This is not, in my opinion, to mean that kings are a different kind of people who are born to rule over their herd-like subjects. Rather, Hobbes seeks to show that kings provide services to their subjects (protection from foreign invaders, protection from the malicious assaults by their fellow man, and so on), and hence do not rule merely by superior force.

Rousseau would criticize Hobbes in Chapter II of *The Social Contract* for saying that rulers were naturally superior to their subjects. He summarizes what he takes to be Hobbes' argument, as follows:

> As a shepherd is of a nature superior to that of his flock, the shepherds of men, i.e. their rulers, are of a nature superior to that of the people under them.[35]

But Hobbes does not argue that the conqueror has the power and authority to declare laws because he is naturally superior to the subjects. Rather, Hobbes argues that the subjects have tacitly agreed to let the conqueror protect them. Hobbes's doctrine of the institution of commonwealth by

---

[34] EW VI 13, Cropsey 61.

[35] Jean-Jacques Rousseau, *The Social Contract and Discourses*, translated by G. D. H. Cole, New York: Everyman Library, 1913, p. 5. Rousseau's remarks seem to miss the point of Hobbes's conception of sovereignty. I have quoted them here to show how badly Hobbes's doctrine has been misinterpreted.

acquisition holds that once a nation has been subjugated, the members of the nation recognize and then legitimate the power and authority of the conquering man or body of men, by accepting the protection of that conqueror. This problematical view of conquest will be examined shortly. Suffice it to say here that there seems to be an incongruity between the lawmaker's seemingly absolute power and his dependency on the consent of his subjects.

This complicated and elusive argument concerning the origin of English law is advanced by Hobbes to counter Coke's claim that judges have autonomous authority to make, interpret, and enforce the laws. Here it is quite clear that Coke is the object of the attack:

> Philosopher. Though it be true that no man is born with the use of reason, yet all men may grow up to it as well as lawyers; and when they have applied their reason to the laws (which were Laws before they studied them, or else it was not law they studied) may be as fit for, and capable of judicature as Sir Edw. Coke himself, who whether he had more or less use of Reason, was not thereby a judge, but because the King made him so…[36]

From here it is but a simple step to Hobbes's concluding assault on Coke's understanding of the origin of law.

> Philosopher. Unless you say otherwise, I say, that the King's reason, when it is publicly upon advice and deliberation declared, is that *anima legis*; and that *summa ratio* and that equity, which all agree to be the law of reason, is all that it is, or ever was law in England, since it became Christian, besides the Bible.[37]

All other sources of law (the "Canons of the Church," "the imperial law used in the Admiralty," "the customs of particular places," and even the "laws of the courts of judicature") are law only because they "were all constituted by the Kings of England."[38] And these Kings all derive their authority, through succession, from William the Conqueror.

---

[36] EW VI 14, Cropsey 62.
[37] EW VI 15, Cropsey 62.
[38] EW VI 15, Cropsey 62.

The next several pages of the *Dialogue* concern the causes of the Civil War in England. Hobbes held the jurists and clerics of his day responsible for the denigration of Charles I's authority and the ensuing war.[39] It is also clear that the Civil War was the major impetus for writing the *Dialogue*. Let us consider two important consequences of that war to this *Dialogue*. First, Hobbes witnessed that Charles I maintained that his accusers had no right to try him. Charles then attempted to strip them of their power to do so. Since Charles's argument was basically Hobbes's own, and since it was effectively rebutted by the decapitation of Charles, Hobbes was anxious to more firmly establish the legal and historical arguments for the power of the King to make and enforce the law. Secondly, the Civil War had also dealt a blow to the followers of Coke, who were now increasingly charged by the common people to have been traitors and revolutionaries. Thus, Sir Matthew Hale, one of Coke's successors to the role of Lord Chief Justice, was much less polemical in rebutting Hobbes in the 1670s than Coke was in rebutting Bacon (who had advanced many similar arguments to those of Hobbes) before the Civil War.

Hale (reversing the order and importance of Coke's arguments) argued that the sovereign power of making law resides in the King, not in an absolute but in a shared capacity:

> Itt is certain that the King without Consent of the Lordes and Comons in Parliament neither by Proclamation nor by Ordinance, Act of Council or Ordinance, cannot make a binding Law; and this is so known a truth that itt needs no Instances to confirme itt.[40]

Rather than criticizing the monarch, Hale spent most of his time trying to reinstate the idea of a divided sovereignty, which Cromwell had attempted to destroy. Among other things he sought to counter Hobbes's view of the origin of the law-making authority.

First, Hale argued that the "Originall Institution" or Authority was impossible to describe because a) it arose in prewritten history and thus there is no record of what transpired, and b) the Institution had changed over time according to the new "Emergencies, accidents and Capitulacions."

---

[39] See Hobbes's book-length indictment of those who were complicit in Charles's demise, *Behemoth: The History of the Causes of the Civil Wars of England*, EW VI 161–418.

[40] Pollock, "Reflections by the Lord Cheife Justice Hale on Mr. Hobbes," p. 298.

Secondly, he argued strongly against Hobbes's view of the role of William the Conqueror in the succession of authority in England.

> They that thinke King William the first gott this Kingdome by such a right of Conquest as abrogated all former rights of Government or gott such a Dominion over this Kingdome as absolute Conquerors obtaine are very mistaken.[41]

Hale realized that if Hobbes was allowed to trace the law-making authority to William, virtually no doctrine of divided sovereignty would ever stand. It is to Hale's credit that he alone saw the consequences of these historical arguments of Hobbes, and that he sought to refute them with much vigor.

Following Hale, it must be admitted that Hobbes was on very thin ice regarding the theory of the origin of English law. These historical arguments, by their dogmatic rather than scholarly tone, reveal that Hobbes was attempting to create a story about the origin of law to replace his myth of the state of nature which had been under intense scholarly political attack since the publication of *Leviathan*. Hobbes's doctrine that sovereign authority passed undivided from William to Charles was the first of his doctrines to fall, and justifiably so. This notwithstanding, the theory of law and authority that Hobbes built on his story of William's line of succession, but which was conceptually isolatable from it, has better stood the test of time.

IV. The Nature of Law

The conceptual core of Hobbes's *Dialogue*, as well as his legal philosophy in general, concerns the nature and definition of law.

> Philosopher. We have hitherto spoken of laws without considering any thing of the nature and essence of a law; and now unless we define the word *law*, we can go no farther without ambiguity, and fallacy, which will be but loss of time.. .
> Lawyer. I do not remember the definition of *law* in any statute.[42]

Hobbes, true to his nominalist sympathies, here begins to build his own theory of law from the meaning of the word "law." It is significant that

---

[41] "Reflections by the Lord Cheife Justice Hale on Mr. Hobbes," p. 295, Holdsworth adds the following note: "This was a question in which Hale was much interested, and upon which he wrote at some length in Chap. V. of his History of the Common Law."

[42] EW VI 24, Cropsey 69.

Hobbes has his "Lawyer" turn to the jurists and professors of the common law for a definition of law, while his "Philosopher" rejects this in favor of a definition drawn from the statutes. The common-law interpreters are said to be "mere" philosophers, whereas the writers of the statutes provide the only truly authoritative meanings, since these are based in the proclamations of those rulers who had the consent of the people to proclaim authoritatively.

At this juncture, the roles of the *Dialogue*'s participants have changed. "Statutes are not philosophy, as is the common law and other disputable arts," says the "Philosopher." Instead, statutes "are commands or prohibitions which ought to be obeyed, because assented to by submission made to the Conqueror here in England..."[43] If the common law is merely philosophy, then the "Lawyer," who is called "The Student of the Common Laws of England" (in the title of the *Dialogue*) is himself a student of mere philosophy. On the other hand, the "Philosopher," as a student of the statute law, is seen as better able to understand the nature of law than his "Lawyer" counterpart, and thus the "Philosopher" becomes the true lawyer. By this curious device, Hobbes demonstrates why the testimony of the "Philosopher" in the *Dialogue* is to be given more weight than that of the "Lawyer." This demonstration was prefigured in the opening remarks of the *Dialogue*. There the "Philosopher" had not stated that the study of law is less rational than other studies, but only that "the great masters of the mathematics do not so often err as the great professors of the law." It now seems that the purpose of the *Dialogue* is to correct the errors of the lawyers, and then to re-establish the study of law on a firm rational footing.

The most important error to be corrected concerns the definition of law, properly so called. Hobbes wants to demonstrate that "the positive laws of all places are Statutes," not common law. This correcting task begins with the statement of the error by the "Lawyer:"

> There is an accurate definition of law in Bracton, cited by Sir Edw. Coke *Lex est sanctio justa, jubens honesta,* et *prohibens contraria.*[44]

---

[43] EW VI 24, Cropsey 69.
[44] Hobbes has the "Philosopher" translate this in the following way: "Law is a just statute, commanding those things which are honest, and forbidding the contrary." EW VI 25, Cropsey 69.

To this the "Philosopher" replies:

> that which I most except against in this definition, is, that it supposes that a statute made by the sovereign power of a nation may be unjust. There may indeed in a statute-law, made by men be found iniquity, but not injustice.[45]

This criticism recalls Hobbes's doctrine that before there was the commonwealth, there was no justice. Justice is defined by Hobbes in *Leviathan* as "*the constant will of giving to every man his own.*"[46] Where there is not yet the notion of "own" there can be no justice or injustice. Likewise, since the sovereign defines what "own" means, he must also define what "justice" is. For, "before the names of just, and unjust, can have place, there must be some coercive power."[47] Hobbes then concludes that if the coercive power of the sovereign defines what actions are just and unjust, those same names cannot be assigned to the actions of the sovereign. But this conclusion does not readily follow from the above. There is a missing step needed, as we shall see.

If I define the term "longbow" to be any bow which I, and only I, judge to be "long," and if, for some very strange reason (possibly related to some people's desire to humor me), I am allowed to be the authoritative determiner of those bows that fall under the term "longbow," then it is true to say that the term "longbow" is *defined* by me. But this, of course, does not lead to the conclusion that my own bow cannot be called a "longbow." Here the definition of the term "longbow" has two criteria:

1) that I judge it to be of sufficient length to be called "long"; and
2) that my judgments are accepted as authoritative on this subject.

It can certainly be the case that I simply stipulate that my own bow meets criterion 1; but if I fail to meet criterion 2 (because, for instance, I refuse to humor myself and thus do not recognize myself as the authoritative determiner of the meaning of the term "longbow"), then truly the term cannot be assigned to my bow.

Likewise, in *Leviathan* Hobbes stipulates that sovereign action can never be unjust, because the sovereign can never meet the second criterion of

---

[45] EW VI 25, Cropsey 69.
[46] EW III 131, Tuck 101.
[47] EW III 131, Tuck 100.

justice: namely, he has not covenanted to accept himself as the definer of the term "justice" for himself. Yet there was a missing step: criterion 2. The two criteria are:

1. justice is what the sovereign defines it to be, [*and*]
2. only for those who have covenanted to accept the sovereign as the authoritative determiner of what actions are just and the punisher of those actions that are said by him to be unjust.

The reason the sovereign fails to meet criterion 2 is that he was not a party to the "original contract" between each man and every man to accept himself as the authoritative determiner of what is justice. Thus, in *Leviathan*, Hobbes says that the sovereign's actions can never be called unjust, or just, for that matter. We saw in earlier chapters that "justice" is strictly defined in procedural terms: a just action is one done in conformity with the rules of law, and an unjust action is one done contrary to the rules of the law. Since the sovereign is always outside the law, his actions also are always outside the realm of what is just and unjust. But the sovereign's conduct is not outside the realm of equity.

In the *Dialogue* Hobbes proceeds to the same conclusion about equity as that reached in *Leviathan* from analogy rather than from stipulation. His analysis begins with the following chain of analogies:

> Injustice is to the Court of Justice as Iniquity is to the Court of Equity; Court of Justice is to the Positive Law as Court of Equity is to the Law of Reason; Injustice is to the Positive Law as Iniquity is to the Law of Reason.

If these analogies make sense, then Injustice will entail a violation of the Positive Law. Since the sovereign has been said to have created the Positive Law, it would seem that his actions could not be called unjust. Hobbes draws essentially this conclusion when he says that "the King is not bound to any other law but that of equity."[48]

But again we are missing a step in the argument. We have not yet heard why the sovereign cannot make positive laws which he himself could violate and thus be called unjust. All we have heard is that the "Lawyer's" definition of law would

---

[48] EW VI 26, Cropsey 70.

lead to the possibility of calling the King unjust, and this, we are told, runs contrary to what we know of justice. It must be remembered that this argument was supported by analogy and not by normal argumentation. When Hobbes comes to argue more formally, below, we shall see that the missing step is supplied by the stipulation that a law must have a party commanding *and* a party receiving the commands. The two "parties" cannot be contained in the same person. Stated in a simpler fashion, one cannot issue laws to oneself. Thus, if the sovereign issues positive laws, he cannot be bound by them, and his own actions cannot be called unjust (where unjust simply means in violation of this positive law).

Let us now turn to Hobbes's formal treatment of the nature and definition of law as set out in the *Dialogue*.

> Lawyer. How would you have a law defined?
>
> Philosopher. Thus; a law is the command of him, or them, that have the sovereign power, given to those that be his or their subjects, declaring publicly, and plainly what every of them may do, and what they must forbear to do.[49]

This definition, already stated above, can be divided into its component parts and examined part by part. The parts are:

1) the command of him who has the sovereign power;
2) given to those that be his subjects;
3) declaring publicly; and
4) what they may do and forbear to do.

I shall discuss these parts as four criteria of the definition of law: 1) the Command criterion, 2) the Authority criterion, 3) the Promulgation criterion, and 4) the Prescription criterion.

The Command criterion is given the least amount of discussion of all the criteria in the *Dialogue*. This is probably somewhat due to the fact that Hobbes had devoted an entire chapter to this subject in *Leviathan* (Chapter 25). There, Hobbes defined a command as "where a man saith, *do this*, or *do not this*, without expecting other reason than the will of him that says it."[50] In the following chapter Hobbes proposed a definition of civil

---

[49] EW VI 26, Crospey 71.
[50] EW III 241, Tuck 176.

law quite consonant with the general definition of law in the *Dialogue*. It is significant that the definition in the *Dialogue* is not merely of Civil Law but of law in general, and this shows the wider scope which law came to have in Hobbes's later work. The difference between these two texts on this subject becomes clearer when Hobbes has the "Lawyer" ask the following question:

> It is true that the moral law is always a command or a prohibition, or at least implieth it; but in the Levitical law, where it is said: that he that stealeth a sheep shall restore four fold, what command or prohibition be in these words?[51]

From the answer to this question, and many other similar statements, it becomes clear that Hobbes feels he has provided a general definition of law that should hold good for civil law as well as for moral or Levitical law. This is a much bolder claim than the limited claim advanced in *Leviathan*.

The boldness of the *Dialogue* is due to Hobbes's earlier assertion that all law is law properly so called only when propounded and enforced by the sovereign. Thus the moral law and the Levitical law, when endorsed by the sovereign, are laws properly so called and must be shown to conform to the criteria established for all laws to be called laws. This is why the "Philosopher" does not cringe from the "Lawyer's" question above, but states: "Such sentences as that are not in themselves general, but judgments; nevertheless, there is in those words implied a commandment to the judge, to cause to be made a fourfold restitution."[52] The Command need not be explicit, as we here see. In fact, it need not even be in the imperative mood. But, above all else, it must be declared and enforced by the sovereign to be called a law. The command criterion thus has more to do with the speaker of the command than with the words he uses. This brings us to our second criterion: the authority of the speaker to be obeyed by those whom he commands.

In a long speech the "Philosopher" quotes Bracton and other jurists on the nature of authority. First he asks: "Can you be defended, or repaired, but by the strength, and authority of the King?"[53] He answers his own question by quoting Bracton as saying: "to make laws is to no purpose, unless

---

[51] EW VI 28, Cropsey 72.
[52] EW VI 28–29, Cropsey 72.
[53] EW VI 30, Cropsey 73.

there be somebody to make them obeyed."[54] In *Leviathan*, an entire chapter is devoted to the relation between authority and consent (Chapter 16). In the *Dialogue*, though, there are very few references to consent and covenant, since both ideas were seemingly out of place for Hobbes after he dropped the fiction of the state of nature and the notion of the "original contract." Yet there are still a few explicit as well as implicit references left. One example is the following:

> Philosopher. He that transfereth his power, hath deprived himself of it, but he that committeth it to another to be exercised in his name, and under him, is still in the possession of the same power.[55]

This remark concerns the King's delegation of power to his judges. But in the very next speech, Hobbes seems to link this idea (that was very important in *Leviathan* for the actual creation of the sovereign's power and authority) with the delegation of power in the King by the people.

> Philosopher. As for the statutes they are always law, and reason also; for they are made by the assent of all the kingdom...[56]

The references to the consent of the people are limited in number because Hobbes is mainly discussing commonwealth by acquisition, not commonwealth by institution (contract). Nonetheless, even the arguments resting the present King's authority on William's conquest imply an assent of the people to be ruled by William. It would have been unwise for Hobbes to dwell on this too much, since it seems to stand against his argument that individual subjects cannot themselves decide what laws are reasonable. A "strict" consent-based doctrine would encourage individuals selectively to withdraw their consent, if they disagreed with the rationality of a particular law. But a doctrine of "tacit" consent somewhat avoids this problem, because, since consent was never explicitly given, it is more difficult for it to be explicitly withdrawn. Authority based on tacit consent has serious consequences, though, which a strict consent-based authority does not have. Tacit consent can be used to legitimate the authority of any reigning ruler

---

[54] EW VI 31, Cropsey 74.
[55] EW VI 52, Cropsey 89.
[56] EW VI 53, Cropsey 89.

or group of rulers. If even successful usurpation, in the form of conquest, implies a tacit consent, then there is hardly any form of government, as long as it is relatively stable, which is not authorized. In other words, the very stability of a government implies the tacit acceptance by the people of that government, since they "choose" not to overthrow it.

There has been a scholarly debate about whether Hobbes supported a view at his time called the "*de facto*" theory. According to this view, whoever was able to be a *de facto* ruler had in some sense the right to rule. As far as I am aware, the participants in this debate have not availed themselves of the rich material on this topic in Hobbes's *Dialogue*. If they had, the view would attain more substantial support.[57]

The third criterion of law is Promulgation. The "Lawyer" challenges the appropriateness of this criterion in the following passage:

> Lawyer. Again, whereas you make it of the essence of a law to be publicly and plainly declared to the people, I see no necessity for that. Are not all subjects bound to take notice of all acts of Parliament, when no act can pass without their consent?
>
> Philosopher. If you had said that no act could pass without their knowledge, then indeed they had been bound to take notice of them.[58]

In consenting to the "law" in general, or even to laws in particular, it does not follow that each subject knows the law. Rather, Hobbes claims that the passing of an Act requires only that the members of Parliament know what the law means, and in some sense assent to it.

The consent implicit in the law-making authority is not sufficient to legitimate the authority of each law. In addition, it is necessary that the Act be "publicly declared." This requirement is not postulated in order to allow the subjects a greater opportunity to choose to disobey the law if they so desire. Rather, it is required so that each person "take notice of what they are obliged to; for otherwise it were impossible that they should be

---

[57] See Quentin Skinner, *Visions of Politics III: Hobbes and Civil Science*, Cambridge: Cambridge University Press, 2002, especially pp. 305–307; and Kinch Hoekstra, "The *de facto* Turn in Hobbes's Political Philosophy," in *Leviathan After 350 Years*, ed. Tom Sorell and Luc Foisneau, Oxford: Clarendon Press, 2004, pp. 33–73.

[58] EW VI 27, Cropsey 71.

obeyed."[59] The subject must be made aware of the sovereign's pronouncements because these are the only bases of law proper for Hobbes.

Hobbes sets it as a dictum that either "the knights of the shires should be bound to furnish people with a sufficient number of copies (at the people's charge) of the acts of Parliament at their return into the country...," or else those subjects must be excused from obligation.[60] Disobedience of laws is justified when those laws are not known (thus ignorance of the law is an excuse, for Hobbes). And here we can also refer to Hobbes's claims about *ex post facto* law in *Leviathan*, as well as later in the *Dialogue*, to which we will return.

Promulgation is necessary for obedience to be demanded, not so that one can intelligently choose between obedience and disobedience, but so that one can know what it is that one is obliged to do. Hobbes makes this stipulation even more severe in the following exchange:

> Philosopher. But what reason can you give me why there should not be as many copies abroad of the statutes, as there be of the Bible?
> Lawyer. I think it were well that every man that can read had a statute book.[61]

While mass distribution of the statutes is not required, it is certainly something desirable. What is required by this promulgation criterion is that the acts be made readily available for scrutiny by the people, without their having to "search for them at Westminster or at the Tower."[62] The promulgation requirement is stipulated to assure that the people can know what they are obliged to do. Without this requirement there would be no way to distinguish legitimate laws from *ex post facto* laws. This requirement sets the stage for seeing Hobbes as supporting something like a rudimentary rule of law, as I will argue later.

We come now to the last of the criteria: the Prescription criterion. Concerning this point, Hobbes again returns to the notion of justice. For the third time the same question is asked:

> Philosopher. Now define what justice is, and what actions, and men are to be called just.

---

[59] EW VI 27, Cropsey 71.
[60] EW VI 27, Cropsey 71.
[61] EW VI 28, Cropsey 72.
[62] EW VI 28, Cropsey 72.

> Lawyer. Justice is the constant will of giving to every man his own...A just action is that which is not against the law.[63]

The "Philosopher" follows up on this point by saying that, "it is manifest that before there was a law, there could be no injustice, and therefore laws are in their nature antecedent to justice and injustice."[64] Not only are laws antecedent to justice, but laws actually define justice by prescribing what men should and should not do. To make this point exceptionally clear, in a way not possible in *Leviathan* or *De Cive*, the "Lawyer" says that "when our laws were silenced by civil war, there was not a man, that of any goods could say assuredly they were his own."[65] This points again to Hobbes's later view of the origin of the laws. The origin of law is not from a hypothetical but an historical set of events, determining the transfer or succession of sovereign authority from ruler to ruler.

The definition of law, set out above, has been copied by many philosophers and jurists, but never has it had a clearer formulation than that provided by Hobbes himself. With equal clarity Hobbes sought to identify, define, and classify the various types of law spoken of by his contemporaries. I will subsequently argue that despite its similar structure, Hobbes is not providing the kind of positivist account of law that Austin and Bentham advocated. At least in part this is because of the role that Hobbes gives to equity. Before turning again to that topic, in the next section we will examine Hobbes's pronouncements on the proper application of the term "law" to the various kinds of rules and commands we encounter in nature and society.

V. Aquinas and Hobbes on the Typology of Law

Early in the *Dialogue* the "Lawyer" puts forth a statement quite reminiscent of Thomas Aquinas's conception of law.

> Lawyer...statute law taken away, there would be not left, either here, or any where, any law at all that would conduce to the peace of a nation; yet equity,

---

[63] EW VI 29, Cropsey 72.
[64] EW VI 29, Cropsey 72.
[65] EW VI 29, Cropsey 73.

and reason, laws divine and eternal, which oblige all men at all times, and in all places, would still remain, but be obeyed by few; and though the breach of them be not punished in this world, yet they will be punished sufficiently in the world to come.[66]

Here equity is not punished in this world, and, in light of our analysis of equity so far, the reason might be that no one has the right to punish the sovereign, qua sovereign, since the sovereign was not a party to the social contract. But it seems that certain court proceedings can be launched against the sovereign nonetheless in terms of violations of the natural law concept of equity.

Aquinas[67] had held that positive human law arose because "a man has a natural appetite for virtue; but the perfection of virtue must be acquired in man by means of some kind of training."[68] The eternal and natural laws are not sufficient to train men toward right action in their mundane affairs. These general laws, which nonetheless obligate men, need to be supplemented by more specific laws that guide and train men in respect to their particular actions.

> It is from the precepts of the natural law, as from the general and indemonstrable principles, that the human reason needs to proceed to the more particular determinations of certain matters…called human laws.[69]

For Aquinas, positive human laws are particularized instances of the natural laws (which in turn are particularizations of the eternal law of God) arrived at through the interpretation of higher law by the ruler. A political ruler, wishing that his subjects not be punished in the next world, issues and enforces laws that guide his subjects away from non-virtuous behavior. The ruler is able to interpret the eternal and natural laws for his subjects by his superior reason, and thus is able to promulgate positive laws which his subjects are obligated to obey.

---

[66] EW VI, Cropsey 55–56.
[67] Aquinas's *Summa Theologiae* will be cited both as to question and article, as well as to the paperback pagination of the edition of part of this work entitled *Thomas Aquinas: Treatise on Law*, Chicago: Henry Regnery Company, 1970.
[68] *Summa Theo*. I–II, q.95.a.1, Gateway 74.
[69] *Summa Theo*. I–II, q.91.a.3, Gateway 18.

It is in this way that positive law participates in the eternal law, and is enforced by the ruler acting as God's representative on earth. This, in brief, is one version of the so-called "natural law" theory of the derivation and obligation of the positive law. According to that theory, laws are identified and classified according to the degree to which they participate in the divine wisdom of God. Aquinas himself divided law into four classes: eternal law, natural law, and positive law—both human and divine (divine law is the revealed positive law of the Scriptures). These laws were said to be in a hierarchical order, whereby, as one moved from the eternal law downward, there was both a decreasing level of perfection and an increasing level of particularization. But importantly, at each level there was an autonomous authority, even though the lower level laws existed as laws, in the first place, only at the sufferance of God's will.

In Chapter 26 of *Leviathan*, Hobbes employs something similar to Aquinas's division of laws to illustrate his own notion of law. Two fundamental objections are raised to the Thomistic ideas outlined above. First, Hobbes asks how can the "authority of man to declare what be these positive laws of God" be known? Second, "*how can [one] be bound to obey them?*"[70] To the first question Hobbes suggests that the sovereign might derive his authority from revelation. But then only he who has the revelation knows that the sovereign has been authorized. For others to know of the sovereign's authority it is required that they also have a revelation to this effect. Barring the unlikely fact that all men have revealed knowledge of this kind, they can only have a *belief* that the authority has been vested in a particular man. Even the case of miracles will never reveal to all men the *knowledge* of who has authority from God, because:

> Miracles are marvelous works: but that which is marvelous to one may not be so to another…therefore, no man can infallibly know by natural reason, that another has had a supernatural revelation of God's will.[71]

Thus, revelation cannot provide grounding for the knowledge that the sovereign's authority stems from God. Since revelation is the only means by which knowledge of this sort could be gained, then we must fall back and say that this is only opinion, not knowledge.

[70] EW III 272, Tuck 198.
[71] EW III 273, Tuck 198.

Concerning the second question, Hobbes first asserts "that he who is to be obliged, [must] be assured of the authority of him that declareth it." Since the authority for deriving positive law from eternal or natural law can never be *known* by all but only *believed*, the obligation cannot stem from knowledge of God's will. Hobbes then cites two Biblical sources to support his position, and concludes:

> By which two places it sufficiently appeareth, that in a common-wealth, a subject that has no certain and assured revelation particularly to himself concerning the will of God, is to obey for such the command of the commonwealth.[72]

Because one lacks knowledge about who has the true revealed authority to interpret God's laws, the subjects must have some other basis for their obligation. One cannot know that positive law has eternal or natural law as its basis, in its particular manifestations. Instead, positive law must be obeyed because it is the command of the sovereign, who derives his authority from this-worldly, not other-worldly, sources. The subject can only *assume* that the sovereign's laws correspond with God's laws. Any laws of God which do not so correspond to the sovereign's commands cannot be known, and thus cannot be obligatory because the promulgation criterion has not been met.

Hobbes thus turns Aquinas's hierarchy of laws upside down. The eternal and natural laws are obligatory for subjects or citizens only when, and because, they are commanded by the sovereign. We have already seen Hobbes's clearest statement to this effect when in the *Dialogue* the "Philosopher" states that all laws in England have authority and obligation only when they are "constituted by the Kings of England." Eternal and natural laws, as well as common laws, are laws properly so called only when they are commanded and enforced by the sovereign. To obtain a clearer idea of this new order of laws, I will spend the remainder of this chapter in a particular investigation of what Hobbes says of common law and natural law, and their relation to statute law, which is the command of the sovereign.

Before beginning this task we can quickly dispense with canon laws based on what has just been said about Aquinas.

[72] EW III 274, Tuck 199.

> Lawyer. Are not the Canons of the Church part of the Law of England.
>
> Philosopher…such of them as we have retained, made by the Church of Rome, have been no law, nor of any force in England, since the beginning of Queen Elizabeth's reign, but by virtue of the great seal of England.[73]

Hobbes once again returns to history in the *Dialogue* to find evidence for his views. If canon law was law because it was revealed to be God's will, then the actions of Henry VIII and Elizabeth would have no effect on its status as law. But, for Hobbes, this is not the case. Henry VIII, as sovereign, had the power and authority to void the canon law as law in England. Elizabeth, as sovereign, had the authority and power to reinstate some of the canon laws as laws in England, not because canon laws were laws properly so called, but because she could make them so by placing the "great seal of England" upon them.

> Lawyer….For the Canon laws of the Church of Rome were no laws, neither here, nor anywhere else, without the Pope's temporal dominions, further than kings, and states, in their several dominions respectively did make them so.[74]

Hobbes's view is that the Pope could make laws in only two ways: a) in his capacity as sovereign ruler of his Papal States—that is, in his capacity as a temporal King—or b) when a sovereign has agreed to declare and enforce the Pope's proclamations as law in his own nation. The Pope has no power or authority to declare laws, properly so called, simply based on his role as the revealed interpreter of God's will. Canon law, by itself, is not law, because it fails to meet the *authority* criterion of Hobbes' definition of law. In *Leviathan*, Hobbes also states this quite clearly when he says that canon laws are merely "*rules propounded.*" The canon laws of the Church became "*rules commanded*"—that is, laws only when "the emperors themselves…were forced to let them pass for laws."[75]

In the first part of *Behemoth*—Hobbes's history of England—he also argued that one of the causes of the Civil War was that the Pope and his English Bishops claimed an obligation for their canon laws independent of the crown.[76] When such claims are given acceptance, then the crown ceases

---

[73] EW VI 15–16, Cropsey 63.
[74] EW VI 22, Cropsey 67.
[75] EW III 609, Tuck 421.
[76] Behemoth, EW VI 165–167.

to be sovereign, since there is a power recognized to be superior to the crown. At that point canon law effectively supersedes civil law, and the Pope or his Bishop should be recognized as the true King.

VI. Common Law

Hobbes examines many different possible groundings of the common law in the *Dialogue* before coming to the conclusion that the common law is not law properly so called. First, he examines the thesis that the common law is the law of reason. This was one of Coke's central doctrines, and it therefore receives special attention by Hobbes. In an important parenthetical remark Hobbes seems to agree with Coke that this is the true basis of the common law:

> Philosopher. (remember this, that I may not need again to put you in mind, that reason is the common law)[77]

Having accepted Coke's grounding of the common law does not mean, however, that Hobbes agrees with Coke regarding the legitimacy of calling it a law. Two pages earlier, Hobbes had criticized the law of reason and shown that it was not a firm grounding for law proper:

> Philosopher....for upon this ground any man of any law whatsoever, may say it is against reason, and thereupon make a pretense for his disobedience.

Accepting the law of reason as law would then come to "frustrate all the laws in the world."[78] If common law is the law of reason then this criticism can be applied equally to the common law. But before Hobbes draws this conclusion he examines some of the other possible groundings of the common law.

In response to a particularly Thomistic argument by the "Lawyer," the "Philosopher" sets up the second possible grounding of common law.

> Philosopher. It followeth then that which you call the common law, distinct from statute law, is nothing else, but the law of God.[79]

---

[77] EW VI 6, Cropsey 56.
[78] EW VI 4, Cropsey 54–55.
[79] EW VI 22, Cropsey 67.

But we have just seen that the law of God cannot be called law proper, since it cannot be known as an authoritative promulgation. Furthermore, in arguing that the sovereign is not bound by law, Hobbes argues that no one would

> be persuaded...that he who is subject to none but God, can make a law upon himself, which he cannot also as easily abrogate as he made it.[80]

In other words, the sovereign cannot be said to be strictly bound by the common law as God's law, because even though he must be accountable to God this would not prevent him from breaking that law as easily as he could make it, since God has no temporal power to punish the sovereign.

Next, Hobbes examines the thesis that the common law is custom. Hobbes first points out that not even Coke accepted this thesis, since he drew a careful line between what is merely custom and what is the common law of the land. But even if Coke was wrong in doing this, Hobbes says that custom cannot provide common law with a proper grounding.

> Philosopher. I deny that custom of its own nature can amount to the authority of a law. For if the custom be unreasonable, you must, with all other lawyers, confess that it is no law but ought to be abolished; and if custom be reasonable, it is not the custom but the equity that makes it law.[81]

Hobbes also rejects custom as the basis of the common law for historical reasons. He argues that before the time of Henry IV there was no custom in England (since it was Henry who first declared that custom be taken for law), yet after Henry IV, custom was law. It was not the fact of custom that made it law, but rather the declaration that it be so by Henry IV, acting in his capacity as sovereign law-maker.

What of precedent as the grounding for common law? Hobbes sees precedent as failing to meet the promulgation requirement of law, since there are often contradictory precedents. Any contradiction of this sort would make both precedents void, because no man could ascertain his correct obligation from reading them. Secondly, Hobbes says that precedent could never be the grounding for even common law because there have been so many

---

[80] EW VI 33, Cropsey 75–76.
[81] EW VI 62–63, Cropsey 96. Note that equity has this prominent role.

erroneous decisions over the years, for proof of which one need only note the large number of reversals of previous cases in the courts.

Having rejected all these as groundings of the common law, Hobbes concludes by implying that the common law is merely the opinion of judges. While discussing homicide, the "Lawyer" gives the famous dictum of Coke: "If the act that a man is doing, when he kills another man, be unlawful, then it is murder." The "Philosopher," who had been arguing for the importance of "intent," provides a very modern-sounding example to demolish what he calls "Coke's common law:"

> Philosopher. This is not distinguished by any statute, but is the *common-law* only of Sir Edward Coke. I believe not a word of it. If a boy be robbing an apple-tree, and falling thence upon a man that stands under it, and breaks his neck, but by the same chance saveth his own life, Sir Edward Coke, it seems, will have him hanged for it, as if he had fallen of prepensed malice.[82]

This example illustrates two of Hobbes's central theses: a) that lawyers more often err than men of science because they confound arguments from authority with arguments from common sense, and b) that the common law should not be granted the status of law proper, since it, more often than not, represents merely the bad reasoning of judges.

Common law not only fails to meet the authority and promulgation requirements, but it also fails to meet the other two criteria of the definition of law. As we saw earlier, Hobbes states that common law is mere philosophy, by which he means, mere ungrounded opinion. (In *Leviathan* Hobbes takes a much less cynical view of philosophy by saying that it produces true knowledge and by defining it as "*the knowledge acquired by reasoning from the manner of the generation of anything, to the properties; or from the properties, to some possible way of generation of the same.*"[83]) This is seen quite clearly when Hobbes defines Statute law.

> Philosopher....statutes were made by authority, and not drawn from any other principles than the care of the safety of the people. Statutes are not philosophy as is the common-law, and, other disputable arts, but are commands or prohibitions which ought to be obeyed...[84]

---

[82] EW VI 87, Cropsey 115.
[83] EW III 664, Tuck 458.
[84] EW VI 24, Cropsey 69.

Here we see that common law, for Hobbes, also fails to meet both the command and prescription criteria. That is, the common law is neither the command of him, or them, who are authorized to make binding declarations, nor the set of rules that stipulate clearly what should or should not be done.

Lord Chief Justice Hale responded to Hobbes's criticism of the common law not (as Coke did) by returning to reason, but by arguing from experience. For, he argues,

> those amendments and Supplements that through the various Experiences of wise and knowing men have been applyed to any Law must needs be better suited to the Convenience of Laws, than the best Invention of the most pregnant witts not ayded by such a Series and tract of Experience.[85]

Hale then concludes that

> the Production of Long and Itterated Experience…is the wisest Expedient among mankind, and discovers those defects and Supplys which no witt of Man could either at once foresee or aptly remedye.[86]

Thus Statute law must be complemented with the wisdom of experience provided by the common law.

While arguing in favor of the importance of the wisdom of experience, Hale also followed both Bacon and Hobbes in supporting a codification of the laws. Hale felt that it was possible to codify both statute *and* common law.

> Itt is one of the things of greatest moment in the profession of the Common Law to keep as neare as may be to the Certainty of the Law, and the consonance of it to it Selfe, that one age and one Tribunall may speake the Same things and carry on the Same thred of the Law in one Uniforme Rule as neare as is possible.[87]

Throughout Hale's reflections on Hobbes's *Dialogue*, the Lord Chief Justice is critical of most of Hobbes's legal philosophy. But Hale showed that he had learned from what Hobbes had said, particularly in respect to his criticism of the common law.

---

[85] Pollock, "Reflections by the Lord Chiefe Justice Hale," p. 291.
[86] Pollock, "Reflections by the Lord Chiefe Justice Hale," p. 291.
[87] Pollock, "Reflections by the Lord Chiefe Justice Hale," p. 291.

Hale felt that some, or most, of Hobbes's objections could be met by codification under a "Uniforme Rule" of law. Hale thus stands as a turning point in English legal history because he was one of the first jurists to begin the modern systematization of English law. In this he carried out the plan laid down by the former Lord Chancellor, Francis Bacon. But the impetus for this systematic effort may have come from Hobbes. It might be true, as some legal scholars now assert, that Hobbes failed to grasp fully the nature of the common law; but Hobbes's skepticism made jurists like Hale aware of the problems inherent in allowing a totally malleable common law to have equal status with potentially precise statute law. Today, criminal law is increasingly a matter of statute not of common law, and this change has occurred for many of the same reasons that Hobbes gave in his skepticism of criminal law based on the common law.

VII. Natural Law and Equity

We will later examine Hobbes's views of the law between nations, as they are set out in the *Dialogue*. Let us now turn to the other side of the question of law without sanction: the view that there is a higher law of nature or of reason to which all men owe obedience. In his later writings Hobbes was seemingly opposed to this latter view. From what has been said about the criteria for law, properly so called, it would seem on *prima facie* grounds that the law of nature does not meet these criteria and thus that it is not to be called "law." But if these laws of nature or reason are not laws, then what are they? In this section I propose to supply a provisional answer to this question.

Hobbes's most definitive statement in *Leviathan* concerning the laws of nature or reason was made when he wrote:

> These dictates of reason men used to call by the name laws, but improperly: for they are but conclusions, or theorems concerning what conduceth to the conservation and defence of themselves; whereas law, properly, is the word of him, that by right hath command over others. But yet if we consider the same theorems, as delivered in the word of God, that by right commandeth all things; then are they properly called laws.[88]

Seeing how remote this statement is from being definitive is already to point out the difficulty in the law of nature doctrine of *Leviathan*. The last

---

[88] EW III 147, Tuck 111.

sentence of the above statement, in effect, mitigates the thrust (and even the sense) of the preceding sentences of this paragraph. The laws of nature are at first said to be improperly named "laws." They are improperly so called because they fail to meet the command and authority criteria of the definition of law. Clearly this is consistent with all that Hobbes has argued in the *Dialogue*. But the last sentence presents an opening for a rather Thomistic view of God's role as creator of laws, thus granting someone other than the sovereign the role of law-giver. References like this one have led commentators such as Taylor, Warrender, and Hood[89] to conclude that Hobbes was in basic sympathy with the school of natural law philosophy.

The references to the laws of nature in the *Dialogue* would be hard to support in terms of the Taylor/Warrender/Hood conclusion. What in *Leviathan* was called God's "right to command all things" is shown to be an empty concept unless there is a "common power in *this world* to punish" disobedience of these laws.[90] The identification, in *Leviathan*, of laws of nature with dictates of reason is changed, in the *Dialogue*, to the identification of equity with these dictates of reason. This shift makes it possible for Hobbes to draw again on juridical analogies to make his point clearer.

We have already seen that equity is distinguished from both positive law in general and statute law in particular. Courts of justice deal with violations of positive statute law, whereas courts of equity deal with violations of the law of reason and fairness in application of law.

> Philosopher....the difference between injustice and iniquity is this; that injustice is the transgression of a statute-law; and iniquity the transgression of the law of reason.[91]

It is interesting to note that while Hobbes claims that equity is not law properly so called, he nonetheless says that equity is binding, particularly on the sovereign:

> the King is not bound to any other law but that of equity.[92]

---

[89] See Howard Warrender *The Political Philosophy of Thomas Hobbes*, Oxford: Clarendon Press, 1957; A. E. Taylor, "The Ethical Doctrine," in K. C. Brown, *Hobbes Studies*, Oxford: Basil Blackwell, 1965, pp. 35–55; and Francis C. Hood, *The Divine Politics of Thomas Hobbes*, Oxford: Oxford University Press, 1964.
[90] EW VI 8, Cropsey 57, my italics.
[91] EW VI 25–26, Cropsey 70.
[92] EW VI 26, Cropsey 70.

In words reminiscent of *Leviathan*, Hobbes had also said:

> the King is subject to the laws of God, both written and unwritten, and to no other…[93]

Thus Hobbes denies that God is a legislator who can declare laws properly so called, in the *Dialogue*, but asserts that God's dictates are binding on the King, and equates these dictates with what was commonly called equity in law.

How can these dictates of God be binding if they are not properly laws? Hobbes provides an answer that is quite subtle. He begins by again attempting to distinguish between justice and equity.

> Philosopher….justice fulfills the law, and equity interprets the law, and amends the judgments given upon the same law.[94]

People are thus bound to the dictates of equity insofar as, and because, equity interprets the statute law to which these people are already obligated. The laws of equity or of nature are binding because they are enforced by the sovereign. But how, then, can it be that the sovereign himself is also bound to obey these dictates, when he certainly is not coerced by his own power nor bound by his own statutes? Hobbes answers that the sovereign is bound here just as he is bound to preserve the safety of his subjects—namely, due to the structure of his sovereignty and authority.[95]

According to the structure of sovereignty, the sovereign is bound to interpret his own commands according to a rational interpretive principle. He must not propound contradictory laws nor interpret his own laws as requiring arbitrary, impossible, or contradictory actions by his subjects. The

---

[93] EW VI 21, Cropsey 67.
[94] EW VI 68, Crospey 101.
[95] My position here is somewhat different from those like Eleanor Curran, who interprets Hobbes as holding that the "sovereign has duties that exist simply as requirements of the office of sovereign." Eleanor Curran, *Reclaiming the Rights of the Hobbesian Subject*, New York: Plagrave Macmillan, 2007, p. 113. Curran connects these duties to the "right to full preservation" and connects equity also to this right, *Reclaiming the Rights of the Hobbesian Subject*, p. 110. I argue that the duties of the sovereign are entailed by the requirements of equity and the structure of sovereignty is undergirded by equity. But our positions are relatively close nonetheless. Alan Cromarie also tries to conceptualize the complex position that Hobbes takes in the *Dialogue* here. He says that in the *Dialogue* Hobbes "developed his theory about the rule of law—though it might be better to call it an ethics of the sovereign magistrate," Cromarie, *Thomas Hobbes: Writings on Common Law and Hereditary Right*, p. xlii.

sovereign cannot act in these ways because this would violate the promulgation criterion of law, and thus violate his own law-making authority. These actions would thus undermine the safety and stability of the commonwealth and therefore destroy his own sovereignty. The logic of sovereignty dictates that the King should act reasonably (according to certain principles or dictates of reason), not because his subjects have a right to demand it, but because to act otherwise would be destructive of his sovereignty. This argument, which is not explicitly articulated in the *Dialogue*, is implicit in Hobbes's stipulation that sovereigns must assure that their judges interpret not just the letter but the intent of the law by correcting the erroneous decisions of the courts of England.[96]

Since all laws must be interpreted to be meaningful, there is a sense in which all positive laws are subject to the laws of equity, seen now as principles of rational interpretation. Hobbes has his "Philosopher" say that statutes "are always law, and reason also."[97] The necessity that statutes always be both legitimate and reasonable is based on the implicit structure of sovereignty, and not as some commentators have suggested on a natural necessity stemming from a natural obligation. This logical necessity relates back to Hobbes's general criteria of promulgation and prescription. For legal obligation to exist, the subject must be able to have access to the statutes *and* she must be able to ascertain what actions are prohibited and allowed by interpreting these statutes. If the statutes do not provide the subjects with a clear idea of their prescribed duties under the law, they cannot be said to be obliged to obey these statutes. Thus the law-giver must define and interpret the statutes according to rules of reason which each subject can know.

We see here a possible gloss on one of Hobbes's most puzzling statements in *Leviathan*: namely, his claim that

> The law of nature and the civil law contain each other, and are of equal extent. For the laws of nature, which consist in equity [etc.]…are not properly laws, but qualities that dispose men to peace and obedience.[98]

Both subjects and sovereigns seek after peace and act toward this end. In *Leviathan* this is propounded as the most basic law of nature. In terms of the

---

[96] See the end of the section of the *Dialogue* on Courts.
[97] EW VI 53, Cropsey 89.
[98] EW III 253, Tuck 185.

Dialogue this law is seen as merely a rule or interpretive procedure which is necessary for law and sovereignty (the main means by which peace can be obtained) to be legitimate. Thus, although laws of reason or nature are not laws properly so called, they are obligatory in order for the third and fourth criteria of law to be met by any law that *is* law properly so called. It is in this way that laws of nature and positive laws contain each other.

It seems to me that natural law can have little relation to positive law except in procedural terms within this system. The content of the positive law must remain unchallenged in order for the sovereign law-maker to provide the peace and security for which we search. But the procedures by which this content is interpreted and applied is open to critique in terms of the natural law principle of equity. Equity constrains the law-maker. As David Dyzenhaus has argued, "the constraints on the sovereign are not the 'kick the bastards out' constraints which Locke envisages, but the constraints that necessarily attend the exercise of power through law."[99]

In my view, Hobbes's discussion of the natural law limits on positive law is similar to Lon Fuller's view in *The Morality of Law*. Fuller famously argued against legal positivists of his day that law must have a purpose if it is to be deserving of respect.[100] Fuller calls for recognition of "a procedural, as distinguished from a substantive natural law." The "procedural version of natural law" is concerned "not with the substantive aims of legal rules, but with the ways in which a system of rules for governing human conduct must be constructed and administered if it is to be efficacious and at the same time remain what it purports to be." Fuller calls these procedural limits on law-making "the internal morality of law."[101] It is my view that Hobbes can be seen to embrace a similar view in how he understands equity, as we will see in more detail in the next two chapters.

---

[99] David Dyzenhaus, "Hobbes and the Legitimacy of Law," *Law and Philosophy*, vol. 20, no. 5, September 2001, p. 498.
[100] Lon Fuller, *The Morality of Law*, New Haven, CT: Yale University Press, 1964, p. 150.
[101] *The Morality of Law*, pp. 96–97.

5
Fidelity to Law

I ended the previous chapter by suggesting that Hobbes should be understood as supporting a position similar to that of Lon Fuller. Now, in discussing Hobbes on fidelity to law that connection to Fuller will be made closer yet. I will attempt to explicate Hobbes's conception of legal obligation by trying to understand what factors would lead people, on his view, to agree to obey a legal authority as well as to accept a legal system as deserving of respect. I am mainly concerned to understand Hobbes's curious claims that those who have been legitimately condemned to death and those who have been legitimately commanded to serve in combat situations may nonetheless justifiably disobey the law. Such claims seem to undermine fidelity to law, at least as that concept was understood by Plato in *The Crito*, and also by such contemporary legal theorists as Lon Fuller. As a result, it might appear that Hobbes provides too simplistic a view of legal obligation. On the contrary, I will argue that Hobbes supports quite a plausible and subtle view of legal obligation that has several advantages over various other views of legal obligation, and can be understood to be a precursor of Lon Fuller's view.

I. Obligation to Obey the Law

Hobbes is often portrayed as a proponent of the extreme view that a person must always obey the law. Certain passages in *Leviathan* are often cited in support of this claim. In Chapter 26, Hobbes says:

> For justice, that is to say, performance of covenant, and giving to every man his own, is a dictate of the law of nature. But every subject in a commonwealth, hath covenanted to obey the civil law…and therefore obedience to the civil law is part also of the law of nature.[1]

[1] EW III 254, Tuck 185.

Since the laws of nature, for Hobbes, seem to be coextensive with the principles of morality, passages like this one seemingly tell us that we are morally obligated to do whatever the civil law dictates. Somewhat later in the same chapter, Hobbes indicates that people are not merely bound to obey what has been written and promulgated as civil law, but their obligations go further. Reason dictates that people attempt to act in the interest of their sovereigns, and that such "fidelity" to the sovereign is also a "branch of natural justice."[2] Hobbes discusses this in reference to the obedience owed by ministers and representatives to the sovereign. The implication of this discussion is that at least some members of a commonwealth are obligated to do more than what is merely required by black-letter law. The point seems to be that all citizens should show obedience to law, and some citizens (due to their special positions in society) should also show fidelity to the sovereign. I will discuss this idea of role obligation at the end of this chapter.

Fidelity means more than merely displaying obedience; it also involves a positive moral attitude (normally that of respect) toward the law. The first reason for thinking that Hobbes supports the claim that all citizens should display fidelity to law is that he regards all obedience to law to be rationally compelling in addition to being morally obligatory. But it is important to ascertain what is rationally compelling about legal systems and even particular laws in order to see whether Hobbes did indeed hold that people should not only obey the law (perhaps out of fear) but also respect the law.

Hobbes holds that a given legal system should be supported because it is both consented to by all of the people and is also necessary for the maintenance of peace.

> But every subject in a commonwealth, hath covenanted to obey the civil law…the end of making laws, is no other, but such restraint; without the which there cannot possibly be any peace. And law was brought into the world for nothing else, but to limit natural liberty of particular men, in such manner, as they might not hurt, but assist one another, and join together against a common enemy.[3]

Since we all have strong reasons to form positive attitudes toward peace, it is not difficult to see that we would also have strong reasons to form positive

---

[2] EW III 259, Tuck 188.
[3] EW III 254, Tuck 185.

attitudes toward a given legal system (perhaps any legal system that was not completely destructive of individual liberty).[4] Legal systems are the only constraint that will be effective against the unbridled natural right which characterized the state of nature. It is for this reason that people should support such legal systems, and, Hobbes believes, it is for this reason that people do support them.

As long as a system of laws has been promulgated by a duly authorized sovereign, and also meets the other criteria of a valid law, such law is deserving of obedience. These same reasons might be marshaled to show that we should also have the attitude of fidelity to law. This is best seen in the passages where Hobbes argues against those people who hold their private consciences to be the final determiner of whether any given law or legal system should not be obeyed. He contends that such an attitude—we might call this the attitude of selective conscientious objection to laws—is imprudent, and is ultimately contrary to the laws of nature. Those who hold conscience to be above the law are not to be trusted to do that which all members of society should be trusted to do—namely, maintain the peace above all else. Selective conscientious objection to law will run the risk of undermining the authority of the law-giver, or of causing sedition within a given domain.[5] This will occur because, as we will see later, the sovereign's chief duty is to maintain the peace, and this requires the habitual obedience of the citizenry. Hence, individuals who have this attitude, instead of the attitudes associated with fidelity to law, act contrary to the laws of nature which all incline toward peace as the primary good.

The second reason for thinking that Hobbes supports fidelity to law is that he believes that we all should form negative attitudes toward selective conscientious objection to law. That this is Hobbes's view is clear from the following lengthy passage from the *Elements of Law* (*De Corpore Politico*):

> There are two things that may trouble his mind...For the first, it consisteth in this, that a subject may no more govern his own actions according to his own discretion and judgment, or, which is all one, conscience, as the present occasion

---

[4] This again seems to support the idea that Hobbes is one of the *de facto* theorists, arguing that whatever power can protect us is deserving of our allegiance. See Kinch Hoekstra "The *de facto* Turn in Hobbes's Political Philosophy," in *Leviathan After 350 Years*, ed. Tom Sorell and Luc Foisneau, Oxford: Clarendon Press, 2004, pp. 33–73.

[5] On this point see the first section of C. A. J. Coady, "Objecting Morally," *The Journal of Ethics*, vol. 1, no. 4, 1997, pp. 375–397, especially pp. 376–378.

from time to time shall dictate to him; but must be tied to do according to that will only, which once for all he had long ago laid up, and involved in the wills of the major part of an assembly, or in the will of some one man. But this is no real inconvenience. For, as it hath been showed before, it is the only means, by which we have any possibility of preserving ourselves. For if every man were allowed the liberty of following his conscience, in such difference of consciences, they would not live together in peace an hour.[6]

And part of the fuller explanation of this position given in subsequent discussions includes the observation (anticipating the contemporary problem of the free rider) that where one person has the attitude I am calling selective conscientious objection, and the rest do not, in such a society that person has "government" unto himself or herself and is not under the same government as the rest.[7] Such a situation is divisive and ultimately seditious.

So we have seen that it is plausible to attribute to Hobbes a strong concept of fidelity to law. First, he finds obedience to law to be obligatory not just out of fear of punishment, but also because the law is generally rationally compelling. Second, Hobbes opposes selective conscientious objection to law. Both of these factors point to a strong concept of respect for a legal system which is the hallmark of fidelity to law. In the next section I will examine some of Hobbes's limitations on legal obligation in order to set the stage for understanding how he can support a strong concept of fidelity to law and yet say that it is right for a person to attempt to kill his or her executioner even if the execution sentence is otherwise legally valid.

II. Limits on Legal Authority

It seems clear, as we have seen in previous chapters, that Hobbes recognizes various limitations on the exercise of sovereignty. I will here only mention the limitations that are most relevant for our purposes concerning fidelity to law. Although the sovereign is not a party to the social contract, Hobbes does recognize that the sovereign has duties to the people.

---

[6] EW IV 163–164.
[7] See EW IV 164.

> Now all the duties of rulers are contained in this one sentence, *the safety of the people is the supreme law.*[8]

Hobbes defines the principle of the people's safety in a very broad way in *De Cive*:

> But by *safety* must be understood, not the sole preservation of life in what condition soever, but in order to its happiness.[9]

Hobbes then states that there are four distinct conditions of happiness derived from this principle of safety.

1. That they be defended against foreign enemies.
2. That peace be preserved at home.
3. That they be enriched, as much as may consist with public security.
4. That they enjoy a harmless liberty.[10]

The first condition sets out one of the general parts of the first law of nature, for which people initially decided to leave the state of nature. The second condition is also derived from the first law of nature: "*seek peace, and follow it.*"[11] But conditions three and four are not so clearly linked with the first law of nature. For that law of nature is based on the "general rule of reason, that *every man, ought to endeavor peace, as far as he has hope of obtaining it.*"[12] This law of nature seems to imply that a person should use all means to obtain peace, not that such a person should retain natural liberty when it seems to be harmless. Such restraint in the cause of peace seems not to be rational.

But in fact, Hobbes does not think that just any state of peace is to be preferred to a state of anarchy. The peace that all people seek is not mere lack of war but includes commodious living involving various liberties.[13] In *Leviathan*, Hobbes says that if a given sovereign tries to pass bad laws—that is, laws that

---

[8] EW II 166, ch. XIII, para. 1.
[9] EW II 167, ch. XIII, para. 4.
[10] EW II 169, ch. XIII, para. 6.
[11] EW III 117, Tuck 92.
[12] EW III 117, Tuck 92.
[13] On Hobbes conception of liberty see David van Mill, *Liberty, Rationality, and Agency in Hobbes's Leviathan*, Albany, NY: State University of New York, 2001; and Quentin Skinner, *Hobbes and Republican Liberty*, Cambridge: Cambridge University Press, 2008.

are not "*needful*, for the *good of the people*"[14] and which unnecessarily restrict liberty—the sovereign acts wrongly by risking the loss of the people's trust. It may then not be contrary to the laws of nature for people to reject these laws and even the law-maker's authority when their own peace and safety, broadly conceived, are not being advanced by that sovereign.

The claim that it is the duty of the sovereign to provide that people "enjoy a harmless liberty" sets an important limit on legal authority for Hobbes.[15] If laws are passed in otherwise legitimate ways, but are not necessary for preventing citizens from harming one another or the commonwealth in general, then these laws do not deserve our respect. Indeed, it is tempting to say that such laws are, strictly speaking, not valid, though Hobbes does not go so far in any of his texts. This is because obedience may be owed, in certain cases, even if respect for these laws is not owed.

In trying to determine whether the violation of a particular law will risk harm to the commonwealth, it is important to ascertain what the intention was of the person who violates the law. If our intention is to harm the commonwealth, then, regardless of whether our act does harm, our state of mind can be seen to undermine the law in any event. This is why, as we will next see, Hobbes often puts great stress on the intention of the person who disobeys the law. To acquire a better understanding of the limits on legal obligation for Hobbes, let us examine, in some detail, the two cases of justified disobedience that Hobbes himself spends the most time analyzing in *Leviathan*.

III. The Soldier and the Condemned Man

Hobbes states that covenants in general may be voided if it happens that the covenant commits me "not to defend myself from force, by force."[16] There are two classes of law that Hobbes discusses that may have this effect: laws that require people to serve in battlefield situations, and laws that impose the death penalty for certain types of offense. These cases are not completely parallel, since in the former case it is not clear that the soldier is being commanded not to defend herself. Indeed, if one is sent into battle with arms

---

[14] EW III 335, Tuck 239.
[15] As with most of Hobbes's writings where normative limits are discussed, it is not completely clear whether these limits are moral or prudential. A foolish sovereign can perhaps pass valid laws that limit harmless liberty, but this would be so imprudent, and so contrary to the main duty of the sovereign to secure the peace, that sovereigns should not do so.
[16] EW III 127, Tuck 98.

then one is given the opportunity to defend oneself, even though the need for such defense arises from the conscription law itself. Nonetheless, these cases are parallel in that disobedience is justified even though the law is valid.

Hobbes made it clear that disobedience could be justified when the sovereign was not protecting the people. In "A Review and Conclusion" at the end of *Leviathan*, Hobbes writes:

> And thus I have brought to an end my Discourse of Civil and Ecclesiastical Government, occasioned by the disorders of the present time, without partiality, without application, and without other design than to set before men's eyes the mutual relation between protection and obedience.[17]

The final message of *Leviathan* is thus that disobedience can be justified in certain cases—that is, when protection is not effected.

Concerning laws that command citizens to become soldiers and command these soldiers to "fight against the enemy," Hobbes claims that it may be legitimate to refuse to obey this type of law. Even though the sovereign has a right to make such laws, and to punish a person's disobedience with death, it is not always unjust for a person to disobey in such situations. There are two types of case in which such disobedience may be justified. First, Hobbes claims that if a citizen "substitute a sufficient soldier in his place" such an act of disobedience of the conscription laws may not be unjust, since "in this case he deserteth not the service of the commonwealth." Here, Hobbes seems to hold the view that unless disobedience risks harm to the commonwealth, it may be justified to break the law. But such a view seems to run contrary to his very strong statements about what I have called selective conscientious objection to law. I shall have more to say about this later.

The second case in which disobedience to the conscription laws may not be unjust concerns a person who is naturally timorous. If persons (either women or men of "feminine courage") run away from battle "not out of treachery, but fear, they are not to do it unjustly, but dishonorably."[18] Hobbes qualifies these remarks with the claim that if a soldier has already accepted money in exchange for promised service then the excuse of cowardice will

---

[17] EW III 713, Tuck 491. On the controversy of how to understand the centrality of this comment, see Kinch Hoekstra, "The *de facto* Turn in Hobbes's Political Philosophy," *Leviathan After 350 Years*, ed. Tom Sorrel and Luc Foisneau, Oxford: Clarendon Press, 2004, pp. 35–48.

[18] EW III 205, Tuck 151–152.

not relieve him of his obligation to obey the conscription laws. Similarly, in the first case, if the defense of the commonwealth requires immediate bearing of arms, it is unjust for a person to decline merely with the hope of finding someone else to serve in his stead.

The conscription cases provide a number of important clues about Hobbes's conception of fidelity to law. People need not be faithful to particular laws but only to the legal system, and their fidelity must take the form of not intentionally risking harm to that system. If there are ways of meeting the needs of the commonwealth for defense and yet avoiding conscription for oneself, then this may be justified. It is interesting to speculate about a reckless sovereign who wages a hopelessly self-destructive war. At what point does such a war undermine the reckless sovereign's legitimacy to require obedience to his or her laws? It seems to be Hobbes's view that in this case disobedience would also be justified, since such a system of law was no longer deserving of respect. Fidelity to law is owed only to systems of law that protect the peace. I return to this point in Chapter 8.

Let us turn to the second set of cases: namely, where laws impose the death penalty for certain offenses. Hobbes is quite clear in saying that a person is not bound to follow such laws.

> If the sovereign command a man, though justly condemned, to kill, wound, or maim himself; or not to resist those that assault him; or to abstain from the use of food, air, medicine, or any other thing, without which he cannot live; yet hath that man the liberty to disobey.[19]

The reason for this is that no "man is bound by the words themselves, either to kill himself, or any other man."[20] And this claim is supported, a few pages later, by the following principle:

> The obligation of subjects to the sovereign, is understood to last as long, and no longer, than the power lasteth, by which he is able to protect them.[21]

Thus any law that calls for a person to jeopardize her self-defense is not a law which people are obligated to obey.

---

[19] EW III 204, Tuck 151.
[20] EW III 204, Tuck 151.
[21] EW III 208, Tuck 153.

The question to be asked is this: Do such laws fail to obligate because they are invalid or for some other reason? The answer to this question will help us decide whether Hobbes's remarks on execution sentences are inconsistent with his position concerning fidelity to law. Notice, initially, though, that the above quoted claim is that the person has the liberty to disobey, even "though justly condemned." This claim provides an initial reason for thinking that the lack of obligation is not based on the invalidity of the law.

The most plausible view is that Hobbes holds that there is a sense in which even the condemned man owes obedience; but it is the fidelity to law which is called into question in this example. The law which grants the sovereign the discretion to sentence a citizen to death may remain a valid law. Indeed, the sovereign may still legitimately put fear into the hearts of these subjects, even as the subjects also fear for their lives from the death sentence itself. But these people are not obligated to obey, because the law, even though in a sense legitimately requiring obedience, is not deserving of respect.

In *Leviathan* Hobbes offers quite a clear statement concerning the rationale behind his disposition of the cases we have just considered.

> No man is bound by the words themselves, either to kill himself, or any other man; and consequently, that the obligation a man may sometimes have, upon the command of the sovereign to execute any dangerous, or dishonorable office, dependeth not on the words of our submission; but on the intention, which is to be understood by the end thereof. When therefore our refusal to obey, frustrates the end for which sovereignty was ordained, then there is no liberty to refuse: otherwise there is.[22]

This statement seems to indicate that only if disobedience jeopardizes the peace of the commonwealth is it clear that such disobedience is intended to undermine the law. If disobedience does not jeopardize peace, then it may be justified.

In those cases where personal safety is at stake, it is not clear that the individual person always has a compelling reason to obey the law. Remember that if the sovereign will no longer protect the subjects, then the subjects are no longer obligated to obey the sovereign. From this it would seem to follow

[22] EW III 204–205, Tuck 151.

that a person is never obligated to obey the sovereign's capital punishment decrees or conscription edicts. Yet this is not Hobbes's view. If the violation of these laws "frustrates the end for which the sovereignty was ordained,"[23] then a person is still obligated to obey them out of respect for the system of laws. Hobbes seems to be stuck in a serious difficulty: we are obligated to do that which supports the proper functioning of the commonwealth, yet we are also obligated to do that which supports our own self-defense. In the laws we have been considering there is a conflict between these respective obligations, and it is not clear whether Hobbes is entitled, on his own principles, to resolve the matter in the way that he has indicated in these passages from *Leviathan*.

Indeed, David Gauthier has argued that Hobbes has simply changed his view here when compared with what he said earlier about authorization. Gauthier argues that since each person authorizes all that the sovereign does, in the earlier passages in *Leviathan*, then it should be that we can never violate the law without violating our own words. To remove Hobbes from the difficulty in which he seems to be concerning the cases we have been considering from Chapter 21 of *Leviathan*, Gauthier proposes a clever strategy. He proposes that we distinguish between authorization of law and authorization of punishment.[24] While every person authorizes (indirectly) each law, only those who have not broken the law authorize the punishment of the law-breakers. Thus it would turn out that Hobbes can say that the convicted criminal does not engage in injustice by avoiding his capital sentence.

Unfortunately, Gauthier's strategy for saving Hobbes from inconsistency only helps with one of our two sets of cases, and only with part of what Hobbes says about that set of cases. Gauthier is able to provide an interesting explanation of why some condemned criminals can justifiably avoid their sentences, if it is true that they have not authorized this particular punishment, but he is not able to explain why some other condemned criminals who have authorized the punishment cannot also justifiably break the law. And Gauthier is not able to explain at all why the conscripted soldier can sometimes justifiably avoid serving in battle, for the commands to the soldier are not punishments. Rather, they resemble quite closely the valid laws

---

[23] EW III 205, Tuck 151.
[24] David Gauthier, *The Logic of Leviathan*, Oxford: Clarendon Press, 1969, 1979, p. 148.

which the representatives of the sovereign issue to the citizenry. We are still in need of an explanation of these passages that accounts for both of Hobbes's examples.

IV. Mere Obedience versus Fidelity to Law

I propose to resolve this difficulty for Hobbes by distinguishing between mere obedience to law and fidelity to law. Fidelity to law involves the type of respect for law that helps us explain why Hobbes thinks that some people are still obligated to obey laws that run contrary to their self-preservation. Fidelity to law would also help us explain why Hobbes is against selective conscientious objection to law. If a person not merely obeys the law but respects the law, then such an individual would not pick and choose which laws to obey. Rather, such a person would feel committed to obey the law except in rare and extreme cases. But would a person who displays fidelity to law feel bound to obey laws even when those laws jeopardize personal safety? Would the attitude of fidelity to law, in some cases, even override our strong instincts of self-preservation?

Fidelity to law does not explain why a person might sacrifice self-preservation, but it does explain the glue of the commonwealth. If the only reason that people obeyed the law was fear of the sovereign power, then there would not be anything like a habit of obedience within a commonwealth. Yet without such a habit, the sovereign would have to win anew each day the obedience to law that was necessary for the law's continued legitimacy. Instead, though, Hobbes believed that people should develop the habit of obedience that would be so strong that a sovereign would not have to worry from day to day about the continued support of his or her subjects. In *The Elements of Law* (*De Corpore Politico*), Hobbes writes:

> Reason therefore, and the laws of nature over and above all these particular laws...constantly requireth no more but the desire and constant attention to endeavor and be ready to observe them.[25]

For the same reason that Hobbes argues for the development of the pro-attitudes toward peace in general, he also argues for the development of the

[25] EW IV 108.

attitude of respect for law in general. Such attitudes counteract the natural egoistic desires that result in decisions based solely on short-term gain.[26]

The attitude of fidelity to law is thus a necessary feature of any relatively stable system of law. But such an attitude does not exclude all disobedience toward specific laws. Only disobedience that would threaten the legal order itself is ruled out. Short of such a threat to the legal system itself, fidelity to law is consistent with disobedience of a particular law to avoid great personal risk. If I am right about this, then we would have an explanation for Hobbes's claim that the soldier may justly disobey the conscription law unless violating that law jeopardizes the peace of the society as a whole.

That this is Hobbes's position can be gleaned from several of his remarks. In *The Elements of Law (De Corpore Politico)* he explains that an obligation to obey a law, while different from an obligation to keep a promise, nonetheless rests on a promise or covenant. As a result of this, a person is obliged to obedience "before what he is to do be known."[27] This passage shows that people should develop the habit of fidelity to law whereby they come to feel bound to follow the law even before they know what, specifically, the law requires of them. Also, in *De Homine* Hobbes links such habits with virtue in civil society.

> Dispositions, when they are so strengthened by habit that they beget their action with ease and with reason unresisting, are called manners. Moreover, manners, if they be good, are called virtues, if evil, vices.[28]

The disposition or attitude of fidelity to law is the basis of civic virtues for Hobbes, as his subsequent discussion in *De Homine* makes clear, especially when he writes: "For whatsoever the laws are, not to violate them is always and everywhere held to be a virtue in citizens, and to neglect them is held to be a vice."[29]

If I am right that Hobbes supports the attitude of fidelity to law, then we can make sense of the otherwise puzzling passages about the obligation

---

[26] See Chapter 10 of this book.
[27] EW IV 222.
[28] De Homine, ch. XIII, para. 8, *Man and Citizen*, ed. by B. Gert, Garden City, NY: Anchor Books, p. 68.
[29] De Homine, ch. XIII, para. 9, *Man and Citizen*, ed. by B. Gert, Garden City, NY: Anchor Books, p. 69.

or lack of obligation of the soldier and the condemned man. In both cases, the law may be broken without giving up the attitude of fidelity to law as long as the system of law is not thereby jeopardized. Hobbes is able to preserve respect for law, even as he puts so much stress on individual self-preservation, by only granting the legitimacy of self-defensive acts against the sovereign when such acts do not threaten the commonwealth itself.

Hobbes's view is much more subtle and defensible than is normally acknowledged. As I reconstruct his view, fidelity to law is not an absolute, but is based on the reasonable principle that people should not disobey the law if such disobedience would threaten the stability of the system of law. Hence, fidelity to law is based on a respect for institutions, not for particular laws. Respect for a given legal institution remains in place until that institution can no longer provide for the common peace. But if disobedience does not threaten the stability of the legal order, then it may be justified to break even valid laws.

Unlike the position attributed to Socrates in *Crito*, Hobbes does not think that any violation of the law runs the risk of threatening this stability. And importantly for the topics we have been considering, Hobbes would think that Socrates could have justifiably avoided his death sentence as long as avoiding that sentence truly did not threaten the legal order. It should also be pointed out, though, that Hobbes does not say that it is justifiable to break any law the breaking of which would not threaten the legal order. Rather, he holds the much more restricted and reasonable view that this is true only in cases of peril to self. So, on my reconstruction of Hobbes's views, he does not support selective conscientious objection to law. His exception to the principle that a person ought to obey valid laws is not that a person should do so unless his or her conscience is opposed to the law, but rather that a person should do so unless his or her survival is clearly threatened (and then, not even in every case).

There is a potentially serious problem for my interpretation so far. In the previous section I argued that the sovereign has a duty to allow people to engage in harmless liberties. But now it appears that people can legitimately break the law only if obeying that law jeopardizes this person's survival. The simple answer to this difficulty is to point out that the duties of the sovereign and the rights of the citizens are not correlative for Hobbes. It does not follow from the fact that the sovereign has a duty to allow people to engage in harmless liberties that the citizens have a right to disobey any law that restricts their harmless liberties. As we will see later, the lack of attention to the rights of subjects and citizens is a major problem for the contemporary plausibility of Hobbes's views, but perhaps not as big a problem as some of Hobbes's critics have indicated.

V. Conclusions

While Hobbes sometimes says that the obligation to obey the law is simply based on fear of punishment,[30] the more defensible Hobbesian position is the one I have outlined previously. There the emphasis is not on fear of punishment but on the reasonableness of developing the habit of obedience to law along with a respect for the legal institutions. Hobbes's very subtle position on the justifiability of disobeying the law is important, I believe, in the contemporary controversy about obedience and fidelity to law.

Hobbes's conception of legal obligation has the advantage of providing a conative as well as a cognitive dimension to fidelity to law. Cognitively, fidelity to law calls for a critical attitude toward legal systems, where one comes to a belief of the reasonableness of a particular legal order. Conatively, fidelity to law is linked with the desire for peace that lies at the heart of the concept of legal obligation for Hobbes. Laws are to be respected based on the dual features of belief and desire. The conative dimension explains why people not only believe in the reasonableness of legal systems, but why they feel bound to adhere to them even in cases where their short-term self-interest will not be advanced.

Let us return to Hobbes's general statement of his position on disobedience to law. Hobbes says:

> When therefore our refusal to obey, frustrates the end for which the sovereignty was ordained; then there is no liberty to refuse: otherwise there is.[31]

Since it is sometimes hard to tell what will be the result of a particular act of disobedience, Hobbes seems to be committed to regarding the intention of the person at the time of disobedience as the key. For example, to return to Plato's *Crito*, as long as Socrates' intention was not to frustrate

---

[30] See the footnote added to an important discussion in *De Cive*, EW II 185, ch. XIV, note to para. 2.
[31] EW III 205, Tuck 151.

the end for which sovereignty was established, then his act of disobedience may be justified. And what is the end of sovereignty? In all of Hobbes's writings, the end of sovereignty is peace. So, unless Socrates' act of disobedience was intended to frustrate the end of peace in Athenian society, his act may be justified. If, in addition, it can be shown that Socrates was under no special obligation to obey this specific law, and that the sovereign was clearly not trying to protect Socrates, then it is justified for him to disobey.

This way of understanding Hobbes's position sees justification to disobey the law involving three criteria:

(1) that there is a threat to the livelihood or liberty of a citizen by a law of the sovereign (such as when the sovereign puts the citizen's life at risk);
(2) that there are no special obligations to obey a particular law (such as money paid to a soldier in exchange for a promise to obey particular commands of a military leader standing in for the sovereign); and
(3) that there is no intent, by engaging in the act of disobedience, to frustrate overall peace.[32]

These necessary conditions for justified disobedience may seem quite harsh, but in fact they leave the citizen with quite a bit more room for disobedience than was generally allowed by those philosophers like Plato who wrote on this subject prior to Hobbes. Most importantly, these criteria make it possible for Hobbes to accept some legitimate disobedience to law while still affirming a very strong conception of fidelity to law.

The limits on fidelity to law are clearly delineated by Hobbes. People should generally not only obey the law but see the law as deserving of respect. The law is not deserving of respect when the promise of peace has been broken. The promise of peace is not just an egoistic concern in Hobbes's account, but it clearly concerns the overall peace of the whole society. And since the striving for peace—for a person's society not just

---

[32] There is a difference between frustrating overall peace and supporting rebellion. In some limited cases, supporting rebellion may actually advance overall peace as in the case where a great many people are already, or on the verge of, rebelling, it may make sense to support the rebellion. Hobbes addresses such a case in *Leviathan*, where he says that even though it may be unlawful, acting with a great many others in self-defense can be allowed. See EW III 206, Tuck 152.

for himself or herself—is the key ingredient in Hobbes's reconstruction of natural law, it is easy to see that fidelity to law is a subtle and quite defensible notion in his scheme.[33]

There is an interpretive concern that remains. If Hobbes focuses on the peace of the society and not on the life of the subject, then what becomes of all of the passages that seem to put self-defense and self-preservation as the most important concern for the subjects? I will address this issue in detail in later chapters. Here I can say that in terms of disobedience it is the protection of the people that is crucial. But since Hobbes is a nominalist, the people are almost always understood as the aggregate of individual persons.[34]

Hobbes's position on disobedience to law is also quite subtle, though not as defensible as his view of fidelity to law. What Hobbes was beginning to struggle with was the conflict that sometimes arises between a person's obligation to pursue peace as a societal good versus the need to pursue safety as an individual good. Given the way that Hobbes is normally portrayed, it is interesting that he generally comes down on the side of societal peace. But in so doing he does not give enough attention to the class of disobedience to law that meets condition (3) above but which is not based on self-protection. There are cases in which selective conscientious objection to a law is seen as necessary to change the attitudes of the citizenry or the sovereign toward a potentially harmful practice. Many contemporary liberal theorists have recognized this type of legitimate civil disobedience. That Hobbes did not recognize this basis for legitimate disobedience shows that he was only a precursor of modern liberalism, not yet a member of that school of thought.

Lon Fuller held the view that we should not confuse "respect for constituted authority" with "fidelity to law," arguing that constituted authorities could fail to make law and then there would be no law to be faithful to. And Fuller also said that if a legal system is bad enough, as was true of Nazi law, "a citizen…has to decide for himself whether to stay with the system."[35]

---

[33] S. A. Lloyd has a somewhat different although related view of the natural law restraints on legality in Hobbes. She says that Hobbes's "theory turns out to be in practical terms indistinguishable from legal positivism. Yet at the level of theory it runs afoul of a defining positivist commitment to the separation of law and morals, insisting as it does that no command it would be immoral to obey could count as a law." See S. A. Lloyd, *Morality in the Philosophy of Thomas Hobbes: Cases in the Law of Nature*, New York: Cambridge University Press, 2009, p. 266.

[34] See Susanne Sreedhar, *Hobbes on Resistance: Defying the Leviathan*, New York: Cambridge University Press, 2011, esp. ch. 2.

[35] Lon Fuller, *The Morality of Law*, New Haven, CT: Yale University Press, 1964, p. 41. See also Lon Fuller, "Positivism and Fidelity to Law," *Harvard Law Review*, vol. 71, 1958, pp. 648–657.

Hobbes was very reluctant to urge citizens to opt for "the general revolution" that Fuller spoke of, but Hobbes showed that he was certainly aware of this problem for citizens faced with law that fails in various procedural ways to be a system that is deserving of our fidelity. As I indicated earlier, Hobbes also saw that a person's obligation to obey the law can turn on whether the person has assumed a special role in the State, which is another similarity with Fuller's views.

Hobbes's remarks on the importance of fidelity to law, and of the consistency of some forms of disobedience with fidelity to law, are important contributions to this debate. At the center of his discussion of these issues is the most important moral task of any age: a concern for instilling the attitudes that "conduceth toward peace." In the next chapters I will connect fidelity to law with how Hobbes's ideas on representation commit people to obey and respect law as if it were made by all those subject to the law. I will also examine Hobbes's conception of sovereignty, and I am especially interested in the role that he assigned to those who voluntarily assume the role of judges, as was true also in earlier chapters, in securing a minimal rule of law.

6

Sovereignty and Artificial Reason

Hobbes seems to have changed some of his ideas between the time he wrote *Leviathan* and when he composed his *Dialogue Between a Philosopher and a Student of the Common Laws of England*. In particular, he seems to have somewhat softened his view about who is best considered the sovereign, and perhaps indicated a support for a minimal rule of law. There has been much speculation that this was based in his considering what took place politically in England, especially the regicide and the Long Parliament. But it also seems likely that he was influenced by the writing of judicial theorists in his time, especially Edward Coke and Matthew Hale, which was already previewed in Chapter 4. Whatever the cause, it is interesting to examine in more detail the "debate" that ensued between Hobbes and the jurists of his day on how best to understand sovereignty and especially how to evaluate the claims that jurists were well placed to understand and interpret the law given their special skill in the type of artificial reason that is the hallmark of the study of law. In this chapter I will use, as my point of departure, Bernard Gert's excellent book on Hobbes.

This chapter proceeds as follows. I will examine first the Hobbes of the *Leviathan* and use Gert's sage adjudication of Hobbes's views about sovereignty and reason in *Leviathan* as a springboard. Then I will discuss the views of Edward Coke, the most important jurist of Hobbes's day, and will follow this with a discussion of Hobbes's *Dialogue*, in which Hobbes attempts to refute Coke. I will then turn to a piece by Matthew Hale, who followed Coke as Lord Chief Justice, which tried to defend Coke from Hobbes's criticisms in the *Dialogue*. I will then end with some remarks on these debates, especially on the idea of artificial reason and the role of the common law in questions about sovereignty as well as on the rule of law in light of remarks once again by Lon Fuller.

I. Natural Reason and Sovereignty in *Leviathan*

In Chapter 19 of *Leviathan*, Hobbes points out that the sovereign power can reside "either in one man, or in an assembly of more than one; and into that assembly either every man hath right to enter, or not every one." Hence, "there can be but three kinds of commonwealth": monarchy, democracy, and aristocracy.[1] He then argues that "where the public and private interest are most closely united, there is the public most advanced. Now in monarchy, the private interest is the same with the public."[2] Hobbes thus comes to support the idea that sovereignty is better lodged in a monarchy than in a democracy or an aristocracy. He does not rule out the possibility that sovereignty can be lodged in aristocracies or democracies, but only that as far as he can see, monarchy is the best.

Hobbes also famously argues in *Leviathan* against the idea that sovereignty should be divided:

> Therefore where there is already erected a sovereign power, there can be no other representative of the same people...For that were to erect two sovereigns; and every man to have his person represented by two actors, that by opposing one another, must needs divide that power, which (if men will live in peace) is indivisible; and thereby reduce the multitude into the condition of war, contrary to the end for which all sovereignty is instituted.[3]

When sovereignty is divided, according to Hobbes in the *Leviathan*, lasting peace and security cannot be achieved. Since monarchy is the epitome of undivided sovereignty, it is the best form of government for what people most desire of their governments.

In commenting on such passages in *Leviathan*, Bernard Gert rightly says:

> The religious disputes in the time of Hobbes coincided with disagreements between those who clamed sovereignty for the king and those who claimed sovereignty for the Parliament. Hobbes championed the claim of sovereignty for the king, but on the basis of his own view of how sovereignty is achieved

---

[1] EW III 171, Tuck 129.
[2] EW III 173–174, Tuck 131.
[3] EW III 172, Tuck 130.

not on grounds of the divine right of kings that others who championed the claim of sovereignty for the king championed.[4]

Gert contends that Hobbes's preference for monarchy has to do with his judgment that peace and security of the people is more easily achieved through monarchy.[5] We need absolute sovereigns to settle disputes most clearly. And it happens that monarchy is the most easily understandable and workable as an absolute sovereign. Gert then goes on to say that Hobbes took this view largely because he could not conceive of the kind of divided sovereignty that the United States would develop a century after he had died.

In a later section I will attempt to show that Hobbes came to understand what Gert is getting at during Hobbes's own lifetime, when he came to write his *Dialogue*. Before doing so, I want to examine briefly some of the ideas in legal theory in Hobbes's time, especially by Edward Coke, who was a champion of the idea of a divided sovereignty. For Coke, divided sovereignty made sense at least in part because there was such a thing as artificial reason, which has to do with developed expertise in reasoning in a specialized field due to long experience in dealing with the special problems of interpretive inquiry into the law. And in this sense we will come to see that disputes about the nature and types of reason dovetail with disputes about sovereignty.

One of the reasons for thinking that monarchs are especially apt to be good sovereigns, in Hobbes's view, is that the monarch will be most likely to advance a "rational" plan for governing rather than a plan that opposes the public interest, because the monarch sees most clearly that acting in the public's interest is also acting in the monarch's private interest. This is one kind of rationality—that is, acting so as to advance one's own interest. But as Gert shows, Hobbes is at least as interested in acting for the good of others, and hence is no strong egoist.

For Hobbes, reason is a natural faculty that all people have in roughly the same amount and with roughly the same competence. So, there is no basis for thinking that a given person can claim sovereignty on the grounds of being a more rational person.[6] Natural reason is so equally distributed

---

[4] Bernard Gert, *Hobbes: Prince of Peace*, Cambridge: Polity Press, 2010, p. 130.
[5] *Hobbes: Prince of Peace*, p. 127.
[6] *Hobbes: Prince of Peace*, p. 46.

that finding a supremely rational person, who is much more rational than everyone else, is a non-starter for Hobbes. But there are considerations of self-interest that might lead one kind of political leader to act reasonably for the common good better than would other political leaders.

For Hobbes, natural reason is a faculty of all humans that is partially encompassed by what we would today call "means–ends reasoning," whereby a person calculates the means that will best lead to a certain end. Gert correctly interprets Hobbes to hold that not all ends that are naturally desired are egoistic ones. Indeed, Hobbes quite clearly countenances natural desires for ends that relate to the interests of others. And Hobbes also speaks of reasoning about ends, as we saw earlier, ruling out some ends, such as seeking self-destruction, as clearly irrational and unnatural. And there are ends that advance the interests of others—what might be called altruistic ends—that Hobbes clearly also acknowledges as rational.[7]

One of the things with which Hobbes will disagree with the jurists is how experience connects to reasoning. Hobbes understood that people can have different sets of experience, and insofar as reason works with experience, people will have different reasons for acting. Yet, as Gert shows, concerning natural reason about politics Hobbes thinks that each of us has enough common experience to know what form of government is best.[8] This is ultimately used as a basis for thinking that expertise is not needed in political affairs. As we will see, this is one of the main points of contention between Hobbes and the jurists of his day.

II. Edward Coke on Artificial Reason

In the *Prohibitions del Roy*, Coke purports to record a meeting he had with King James about the extent of the King's ability to override the decisions of the courts. Here is the most famous part of the exchange:

> Then the King said, that he thought the Law was founded upon reason, and that he and others had reason, as well as the Judges: To which it was answered by me, that it was, that God had endowed his Majesty with excellent Science,

---

[7] *Hobbes: Prince of Peace*, p. 37, Gert refers us to Hobbes's definition of benevolence as "Desire of good to another," from chapter 6 of *Leviathan*.

[8] *Hobbes: Prince of Peace*, p. 47.

and great endowments of nature; but his Majesty was not learned in the Lawes of his Realm of England, and causes which concern the life or inheritance, or goods, or fortunes of his Subjects; they are not to be decided by naturall reason but by artificial reason and judgment of Law, which Law is an act which requires long study and experience, before that a man can attain to the cognizance of it; And that the Law was the Golden metwand and measure to try the Causes of the Subjects; and which protected his Majesty in safety and peace: With which the King was greatly offended, and said, that then he should be under the Law, which was Treason to affirm, as he said; To which I said that Bracton saith, *Quod Rex non debet esse sub homine, sed sub Deo et Lege* [The King ought not to be under any man, but under God and the Law].[9]

James I, portrayed here by Coke, was a strong advocate of the divine right of kings, and did not seem to understand how he could be subject to the law. In this view the courts and judges served the interests of the King, which of course were indistinguishable from the interests of the people, since the King was authorized by God to act in the people's interest.

Note how for Coke it is important that the King not be under any man but still be under the laws. This is an interesting way to allow for the King to be sovereign in the sense that no one else is above him and yet still leave open a kind of divided sovereignty insofar as the laws could be above the King. If the quotation means that those who interpret and apply the law cannot be overruled by the King, as seems to be Coke's view, then there is a sense in which, for a certain realm of affairs, the jurists are above the King, and for other matters the King is above the jurists. The different functions can be assigned different parts of the divided sovereignty based on different forms of expertise, for instance. But the more plausible way to read the quotation from Coke is that the laws are above the King, not that the judges are above the King. So, while the jurists' opinions may, in a sense, be over the King, it is not really true that the judges themselves are over the King in terms of sovereignty. The laws may be sovereign, but so is the King. This appears to be Coke's view.

What is of special importance to the themes of this chapter is the distinction that Coke draws between the natural reason of the King and the artificial reason of judges and lawyers. Coke would agree with James that natural

[9] Edward Coke, *Prohibitions del Roy*.

reason is something that all natural persons have, and that jurists do not have any greater claim to be experts at this kind of reason than anyone else. But Coke's point is that the jurists have a special kind of reason—an artificial reason concerning the laws of a particular region, which is not shared with everyone else. This artificial reason, like any other expert reason, comes only after long study. When a ruling is rendered on the basis of artificial reason by a judge, the only person who potentially could overrule this decision on grounds of reason would be another more learned judge. Coke thus comes to the potentially treasonous view that "the King in his own person cannot adjudge any case, either criminal, as Treason, Felony, &c., or betwixt any party, concerning his Inheritance, Chattels, or Goods, &c. but this ought to be determined and adjudged in some Court of Justice."

Coke does allow that there is a certain sense in which "the King is called the chief Justice" but only insofar as the King can reverse lower court rulings "with the assent of the Lords Spirituall and Temporall." The King is the embodiment of sovereignty for Coke, but that does not mean that the King can overrule the courts unilaterally. The King was under the natural law, and the natural law was indeed merely reason. But in England that reason was steeped in the experience of how Englishmen had come to see their legal status. And to understand properly what that experience meant required specialized reasoning. While the King was accepted to be a naturally good reasoner at understanding the general provision of natural law, the King had no special claim to be able to reason about what Coke and others were calling the "common law" of England.[10]

Coke was the first to develop systematically the idea that the common law—the body of precedents and customs developed over the centuries in England—was the proper purview of the courts. Only the lawyers and jurists, by dint of their training in a specialized artificial reason, were able to interpret and apply the common law. Even the King needed to consult and rely on the jurists in order to rule England effectively, since so much of what was law in England was derived from the common law. One could not understand the historical doctrines that had developed and received recognition through thousands of court cases without reading the cases

---

[10] See Harold J. Berman, *Law and Revolution*, vol. II, Cambridge, MA: Harvard University Press, 2003, pp. 238–245.

and having the specialized training to be able to distill from these cases that aspect of the law that was "common" throughout England.

One of the main aspects of the common law that Coke and his allies strongly advocated was that there were certain rights of Englishmen that the King could not abrogate, because these rights were grounded in principles that were ancient and foundational. Indeed, Coke elevated Magna Carta to near mythic proportions as he sought to ground the rights of Englishmen in ancient documents and judgments. In Coke's *Institutes of the Laws of England*, he devotes large portions of volume 3 to a line-by-line commentary on Magna Carta. Here is some of what Coke says about the famous Chapter 29 of the Great Charter: "the common lawes of the realme should by no means be delayed, for the law is the surest sanctuary, that a man can take, and the strongest fortresse to protect the weakest of all."[11] And in discussing the particular rights that Magna Carta enshrined, Coke comments that "the King cannot send any subject of England against his will to serve him out of this realme, for that would be an exile" that is expressly ruled out by Magna Carta's words "No man exiled." In general, Coke says that Magna Carta "signifieth the freedoms that the subjects of England have."[12]

One of the most significant provisions of Magna Carta is that liberty cannot be taken from an Englishmen, even by acts of the King, "unlesse it be by indictment or presentment of good and lawful men, where such deeds be done."[13] Here is where the courts come to have their main power over the King, especially concerning the protection of the liberties of Englishmen against the possible arbitrary exercise of the sovereign power of the King. Coke does not explicitly endorse a robust notion of divided sovereignty, but it is my view that this idea is clearly implied in his discussion of artificial reason and especially in his claim that juries uphold the great liberties of the citizenry and cannot be overruled by the King.

Coke's championing of Magna Carta was a way to indicate that the King had once actually recognized and memorialized the rights of citizens, and had even accepted the role of courts, especially through juries, to be the final arbiters of disputes about the liberties of citizenship. Coke then catalogued the number of times that subsequent kings and parliaments had

---

[11] Edward Coke, *Institutes of the Laws of England*, London: J. & W. T. Clarke, 1823, vol. 2, p. 56.
[12] *Institutes of the Laws of England*, vol. 2, p. 47.
[13] *Institutes of the Laws of England*, vol. 2, p. 46.

reaffirmed Magna Carta over four centuries as a way to indicate that Magna Carta was now a foundational document that stood the laws in good stead and placed these laws above the King, even though the King was certainly still sovereign over all other matters. This doctrine was similar to the idea of judicial review in the American system of jurisprudence, and hence also a recognition that not all of sovereignty resided in the King.

III. Artificial Reason and Sovereignty in the *Dialogue*

At a crucial point in his *Dialogue*, which was clearly aimed at many of Coke's doctrines, Hobbes puts into the mouth of his Philosopher these words:

> Though it be true that no man is born with the use of reason, yet all men may grow up to it as well as lawyers…Sir Edward Coke himself, who whether he had more or less use of reason, was not thereby a judge, but because the King made him so…[14]

Here Hobbes clearly has set himself the task of refuting Coke, and doing so by name.

But along the way, Hobbes seems to step back from some of the doctrines of *Leviathan*. Of note is the following passage, also on artificial reason:

> Philosopher. This does not clear the place, as being partly obscure, and partly untrue. That the reason which is the life of the law, should be not natural, but artificial I cannot conceive. I understand well enough, that the knowledge of the law is gotten by much study, as all other sciences are, which when they are studied and obtained, it is still done by natural, and not artificial reason…It is not wisdom, but authority that makes a law…That the law hath been fined by grave and learned men, meaning the professors of the law is manifestly untrue, for all the laws of England were made by the Kings of England, consulting with the nobility and commons in parliament, of which not one of twenty was a learned lawyer.[15]

Here we see Hobbes seemingly having the Philosopher admit that it is the King in Parliament who makes the laws.

---

[14] EW VI 14–15, Cropsey 62.
[15] EW VI 5, Cropsey 55.

I say that this is how it seems for three reasons. First, the text is somewhat ambiguous in that the phrase "King in Parliament" is not used, but rather the more convoluted phrase "Kings of England, consulting with the nobility and commons in parliament." And then there is also the matter of whether it is indeed Hobbes who speaks through the "Philosopher." At other points in the text it seems that not all the Philosopher says is to be treated as Hobbes's own views. And in addition, Hobbes seems to blunt the thrust of what he has just said, at the very end, when he points out that lawyers are not well represented in the group "nobility and commons in parliament." This third point may have been aimed also at Coke to show that even if one accepts the view of the "King in Parliament" this need not be a restriction on the King by jurists. Nonetheless, such consultation by the nobles and commons was required, and placed some limits on the King's exercise of sovereignty.

The doctrine of the King in Parliament, as lawmaker, had emerged after the Long Parliament and the defeat of Cromwell. And this doctrine is in keeping with the supporters of the return of the King as the supreme ruler in England. But the idea of the King in Parliament is not the same as the King as sole law-maker. Hobbes does not fully embrace this idea, since he thinks that Parliament has largely a consultative role to play in law-making. But it is my view that this is a shift nonetheless from Hobbes previous denigration of Parliament and support for a more traditional monarchy in *Leviathan*. We can see the shift even more clearly when Hobbes has the Philosopher say: "the King in Parliament if you will, but not the King and Parliament."[16] Here, Hobbes, at least through the Philosopher, opposes truly divided sovereignty, where both the King and Parliament share sovereignty, for the King is clearly above the Parliament. But in accepting the idea of the King in Parliament Hobbes does seem to acknowledge what the Long Parliament sought to achieve—even as Hobbes accuses the Long Parliament leaders of replacing the abuses of the King with those of Parliament.[17]

Hobbes does deny more clearly the doctrine of Coke that custom is one clear source of law. For Hobbes, this was a more pernicious view than that the Parliament or even the courts could place limits on what the King does. And here we return to the idea of artificial and natural reason discussed

[16] EW VI 34, Cropsey 76.
[17] EW VI 21, Cropsey 66.

in Chapter 4. Hobbes contends that customs can be either good or bad. If custom embodies reason it can do so only through good customs.[18] Hobbes cleverly picks on one of the most notorious of customs, which still can be found in American criminal law, that if a person kills while committing another felony such as robbery, then that person is also guilty of murder. This, the Philosopher says, is unreasonable in that the person engaging in the felony should not have the sole blame for an act that was caused accidentally.[19] Hobbes makes the position crystal clear when he has the Philosopher say:

> I deny that any custom of its own nature, can amount to the authority of law. For if the custom be unreasonable, you must, with all other lawyers, confess that it is no law, but ought to be abolished; and if the custom be reasonable, it is not the custom, but the equity that makes it law."[20]

Here again we see Hobbes assigning to equity the role of limiting unreasonable and unfair law-making.

Concerning the idea that precedents are a source of law, Hobbes is as equally skeptical as he was concerning custom. The Philosopher says: "but precedents prove only what was done, and not what was well done."[21] Hobbes's view of the authority of judges to make law is quite straightforward. Judges make law through the auspices of the King. The King has committed his power to the judges to act on his behalf. And yet this is not to say that the King has given up this power permanently. As Hobbes says, one needs to distinguish "between committing and transferring. He that tranferreth his power, hath deprived himself of it, but he that committeth it to another to be exercised in his name, and under him, is still in the possession of the same."[22] And Hobbes rejects what he takes to be Coke's view that Magna Carta somehow permanently transferred the power to decide about the liberties of subjects from the King to the courts.[23]

So, we see that Hobbes replies to Coke by denying that there is a significant role for artificial reason in making law and reasserting that it is the

---

[18] EW VI 134–135, Cropsey 149–150.
[19] EW VI, 132–133, Cropsey 147–148 and also 115–116.
[20] EW VI 62–63, Cropsey 96.
[21] EW VI 106, Cropsey 129.
[22] EW VI 52, Cropsey 89.
[23] EW VI 43, Cropsey 82.

power of the sovereign that makes law. What we have seen is that Hobbes seems to make a change in how he understands sovereignty in England—probably as a result of the Long Parliament having taken place between the time of the publication of *Leviathan* and that of the *Dialogue*. I shall now examine one more part of this debate, where Matthew Hale rises to defend Coke, before making some general observations about the idea of divided sovereignty.

IV. Matthew Hale's Defense of Artificial Reason

Hale takes as his task to defend his friend and mentor, Coke, from the sorts of charges we have just seen Hobbes to have laid at Coke's feet. Here is one of Hale's responses to Hobbes:

> Now if any of the most refined Braine under heaven would goe about to Enquire by Speculation, or by reading of Plato or Aristotle, or by Considering the Laws of the Jewes, or other Nations, to find out how Landes descend in England, or how Estates are there transferred, or transmitted among us, he wou'd lose his Labour and Spend his Notions in vaine, til he acquainted himselfe with the Lawes of England, and the reason is because they are Institutions introduced by the will and Consent of others implicitly by Custome and usage, or Explicitly by written Lawes or Acts of Parlem't.[24]

Hobbes had put into the mouth of the Philosopher in his *Dialogue* the idea of referring to Plato and Aristotle to understand the laws that Hale here derides.

Hale then provides several reasons for thinking that law is best interpreted and applied by lawyers rather than non-lawyers, even the King. In Hale's view, "the Certainty of the Law and the Consonance of it to it Selfe" is the key to what was emerging as the idea of the rule of law. Here there needs to be the idea of a "Uniforme Rule" that over time speaks the same and carries the same thread.[25] Hale then explicitly defends a divided sovereignty, where "one part of the Soveraigne Power is in one p't of the Governm't an other part in another."

---

[24] Frederick Pollock, "Reflections by the Lord Chief Justice Hale on Mr. Hobbes His Dialogue on the Laws," *The Law Quarterly Review* (1921), pp. 274–303, 292.
[25] *The Law Quarterly Review*, 293.

At this point, when Hale is writing at the end of the seventeenth century, the King cannot make law without first taking the "advice and consent of the 2 houses of Parlem't, without which no Law can be made. And therefore Proclamations cannot make Law."[26] Here is a straightforward attempt to defend the emerging idea that sovereignty in England resided in the "King in Parliament." Hale then stresses the prudential reasons for Kings to accept this limitation of their power, and in words very similar to those used by Hobbes argues that it is in the King's "Interest to use that Power of the Prince to the benefit and not to the Detrimen't of his Subjects, to keepe them Rich and thereby make them obedient."[27] Sovereignty became divided in England, says Hale, due to "Reciprocall Contract & Stipulacon between the King and his subjects."[28] He concludes that this arrangement has been true for "500 yeares."[29]

What Hale is best known for is his defense of the common law and the artificial reason upon which the common law is supposed to be based. At one point, Hale draws an analogy between mathematical reasoning and legal reasoning.

> Itt were ridiculous to expect that a Man that hath either onely the advantage of his owne materiall Ingenij, or hath spent a Month in readeing Some of the Rudim'ts of Geometrie Should be as good a Master in Mathematicks as he that had made it a Study of his life, and yet it is apparent that the Positions and Conclusions in the Mathematicks have more Evidence in them, and are more Naturally Seated in the minde than Institutions of Laws, w'ch in a great measure depend upon Consent and appointm't of the first Institut'rs.[30]

Such long study of the laws, like that of mathematics, affords one "Considerable advantages to render them fitter Judges and Interpret'rs of the Lawes of this Kingdome then any other whose Studyes and Education were entirely applyd to the Study of Philosophy or Mathematics or other Studyes."[31] Hale admits that those who have long study of the laws may have only the same natural reason as those who do not. But they will not

---

[26] *The Law Quarterly Review*, 297.
[27] *The Law Quarterly Review*, 302.
[28] *The Law Quarterly Review*, 300.
[29] *The Law Quarterly Review*, 303.
[30] *The Law Quarterly Review*, 293.
[31] *The Law Quarterly Review*, 293.

be equal in the specific form of artificial reason gained by such study of the laws.

Hale's support for the superior role of lawyers as interpreters and appliers of the law leads him to the idea that sovereignty is to be split between various branches of government based on what function the sovereign is asked to assume. The connections here are not as clear cut as one would like, either as a matter of textual exegesis or as a matter of conceptual clarity. The chief reasons that Hale provides seem to be analogical on the one hand and customary on the other. I have explored the analogical side of Hale's argument, so let us end this section with just a few words about the customary side of Hale's argument for divided sovereignty. Here it is interesting that he seems to rely on an actual consent model, ultimately, like Coke, going back to Magna Carta to show that both King and people agreed to a form of divided rule. This is to place enormous weight on what was then a contested interpretation of an event 450 years earlier at Runnymede, where King and barons agreed to Magna Carta. And it should be no surprise that Hale, like Coke, championed an interpretation of this document that undercut the King's claim to rule England as an absolute monarch.

V. Divided Sovereignty and the Rule of Law

As a conceptual matter one could hold that lawyers, and legislators, have a special role to play in government and yet still not admit that they can make or interpret law outside the authority of the King or other sovereign rulers. But the idea that sovereign authority is established by some kind of contract does make this task somewhat harder. Indeed, it is difficult to argue for absolute monarchy if it is assumed that sovereignty originally resided in the people and only by a granting act did sovereignty devolve to one person or a group of people. In *Leviathan*, Hobbes is justly famous, or infamous, for seeming to argue that it would only make sense for people to consent to be governed by an absolute sovereign if sovereignty were to be lodged in just one institution or office of government, since only such a sovereign could guarantee the people's safety. In this final section I will return to the arguments of *Leviathan* and contrast them to arguments in the *Dialogue* as I attempt to draw out some conclusions.

Despite the way Hobbes is often interpreted, in *Leviathan* he does not argue that monarchy is the only form of government that can secure the peace. And he does not even think that an absolute monarch can guarantee the peace either. In *Leviathan* it is more of a probabilistic claim—a monarch is more likely to quell dissent and maintain the peace than other types of sovereignty. Other forms of government are less likely than monarchy to be able to secure the peace. Similar arguments also occur in the *Dialogue*. Hobbes does come to recognize that in England the King has granted to the courts the right to exercise power on their own in judicial matters. He claims merely that this was not a permanent transfer of power. Yet even this admission seems to allow for a kind of, perhaps temporary, divided sovereignty.

Hobbes does not claim that the sovereign is possessed of superior reason, either natural or artificial.[32] This is not the reason why he should be an absolute sovereign. Rather, the reason is to solve a coordination problem—we cannot allow each person to exercise his or her private judgment about political or moral matters and still have a stable society. But what Hobbes ignored was that a stable modern society needed to exemplify a robust rule of law, not necessarily the rule of the people. And to accomplish this there must be some separation of sovereign power. This is perhaps what Hobbes saw in his later works but could not fully articulate. But he did not support the kind of tripartite sovereignty made famous by the American Constitution. Instead, judges needed to be seen as independent but in a very limited sphere.

Hale contends that there must be some significant separation within the sovereign powers for there to be a proper rule of law. I wish to focus on this claim in what follows, while I assess Hobbes's positions on sovereignty and artificial reason. To achieve the rule of law, one does not have to embrace a strong role for an independent judiciary. But it is the expertise, the artificial reason, of the judges that is important for seeing why things should not be overturned quickly but that gradual change is the best. And so kings and other sovereigns should not be allowed to overturn judicial rulings, especially those that draw on longstanding precedent.

It is this system of checks and balances that Hobbes is only gesturing toward in his qualified support for the "King in Parliament" view of sovereignty. Hobbes came to recognize that there is an important role that jurists and

---

[32] See Richard Tuck, *Philosophy and Government 1572–1651*, Cambridge: Cambridge University Press, 1993, p. 346.

courts played in providing advice to the sovereign about specific areas of his rule, and he even seems to recognize that the King should not meddle much with judicial and legislative matters. The rule of law, rather than the rule by a man or several men, also requires that the making, interpreting, and application of the law is not subject to a kind of personal veto by any man or men, lest it be a rule by these men rather than by law. This is not the same as the issue concerning conscientious objection to obeying the law, discussed in Chapter 5.

So, in my view it is not, as Gert asserted, that Hobbes did not have a model of divided sovereignty on which to draw, whether it is the one of the eighteenth-century Founding Fathers of the US Constitution, or its seventeenth-century variants espoused by Coke and Hale. Rather, the problem was that Hobbes was not fully committed to the idea of the rule of law and did not place value on the need for the law to be above the rule of men. If he had valued the rule of law he would have explored more straightforward ways to ensure that kings and other sovereigns were never above the law.

One last text to examine—probably the last that Hobbes wrote before he died—could shed some additional light on this issue. Quentin Skinner has discovered a very short tract written by Hobbes that addresses the question of whether the King could name his own successor. Hobbes supports the view that the King governs not from divine right but from his protection of the people. Hobbes is then asked what he thinks of a situation where "a Successor to a crown, be for some reason or other which is notorious, incapable to protect the people."[33] Hobbes responds that the King has no right to appoint a successor in this case, since the King does not have "any inheritance to give away."[34] Hobbes then ends by saying that "the King dying is *ipso facto* dissolved." While this text is far from crystal clear, Hobbes seems to support here the idea that there are limits on the sovereign, mainly in terms of being required to protect the people. And the people are not required to accept an heir to the throne who cannot or will not protect them. I will have more to say on this issue in subsequent chapters. Here I only wish to point out another source of the limits on sovereignty that Hobbes addressed right up to his last days.

---

[33] "Questions Relative to Hereditary Right," in *Thomas Hobbes: Writings on Common Law and Hereditary Right*, ed. Alan Cromarie and Quentin Skinner, Oxford: Clarendon Press, 2005, p. 177.
[34] *Thomas Hobbes: Writings on Common Law and Hereditary Right*.

It may be possible to strike middle ground between Hobbes on the one side and Coke and Hale on the other. A limited role for an independent judiciary is necessary for the rule of law which is itself necessary for long-run stability of States in the modern age. This is to say that one can become committed to the rule of law out of prudential considerations as well as more robustly normative reasons. Societies that are governed by the rule of law are simply much more likely to be stable than societies that are not. But the extent that one has to support divided sovereignty to achieve the rule of law is fairly minimalist. The monarch, or other sovereign, can indeed delegate to, not permanently grant away, authority to the courts or Parliament, as long as this particular monarch does not retain the power to overrule and hence potentially personalize the rulings of the courts.

Let me end this chapter by once again turning to Lon Fuller. Fuller quotes Coke's judgment in Bonham's case, where the court was asked to rule on whether the King in Parliament could create "a 'court' of physicians for judging infringements of their own monopoly and collecting half the fines for themselves." Coke says that this act of Parliament "was utterly void...[as] against common right and reason." Fuller interprets Coke's pronouncements not as grounded in a robust, and naïve, natural law position, but one that was closer to Fuller's own view that emphasized "procedures and institutional practices."[35] Fuller then suggests that Coke's view is fairly close to that of the Founding Fathers of the American Constitution. When courts overrule legislatures, it is more palatable, says Fuller, if the courts appeal to procedural rather than substantive natural law.[36] And in my view, this is just the kind of middle position that Coke espoused but that Hobbes was not able to support, even though Hobbes had the resources to do so.

In previous chapters I have stressed the moral and procedural limitations on sovereign law-making. Hobbes clearly recognized that law-making must be public and perspicuous, that there were no retrospective laws, and that harmless liberty not be infringed. But Hobbes never put

---

[35] Lon Fuller, *The Morality of Law*, New Haven, CT: Yale University Press, 1964, pp. 100–101.
[36] *The Morality of Law*, p. 102.

these pieces together into a robust doctrine of the rule of law. Perhaps there is a minimalist notion of the rule of law that Hobbes embraces but never fully articulates. In the next chapter I examine in more detail Hobbes's concept of authorization, which is crucial for his account of sovereignty, especially as it relates to the legitimacy and efficacy of institutions of various types.

7
Authorization, Joint Action, and Representation

In the previous chapter I examined issues concerning the sovereign and artificial reason. In this chapter I will look at Hobbes's ideas of authority as well as artificial actors and agency—especially the kind of mass action taken by collective agents that does not seem to result from organized decision or by explicit authorization. I am also interested in extending Hobbes's discussion of how a multitude becomes unified to set the stage for answering questions about how sovereign States should interact with groups. I will approach this topic by reviewing some of the ideas expressed primarily by Hobbes but also by other seventeenth-century thinkers, in an attempt to construct a Hobbesian view of authority in various types of group. The central problem is that to constitute a collectivity that can act there needs to be something that organizes the individual acts of the members of a collectivity. In the case of States this condition is easily met by the group's structure, and yet in the case of mass action this seems to be missing. And yet mass uprisings, such as the storming of the Bastille, have sometimes been able to accomplish greater joint actions than highly organized ones. Such examples of joint action are not organized, and there seems to be no explicit act of authorization. So, the simplest ways to explain the constitution of an artificial collective agent that can be responsible for joint acts seem not to work well in such cases.

I begin by explicating some of Grotius's views on collectivities, and attempt to build a Grotian account of collective agency and responsibility. Second, I turn to Hobbes's ideas about artificial persons and responsibility as set out in Chapter 16 of *Leviathan*. Third, I discuss an especially difficult problem for Hobbes that affects his view: namely, how we are to understand authorial intent, especially in cases involving what he calls "a multitude."

And I end by trying to develop a Hobbesian account of collective agency that may be able to deal with mass-action cases.[1] Eventually, it will emerge that a Hobbesian account of collective action is a concept that is limited in a variety of ways. In Chapter 8 I will build on the current chapter's account of limited authorization to explain how this affects a Hobbesian account of the international order.

I. Grotius's Consent Principle

Hugo Grotius seems to have had a strong influence on the character of various debates about collective agency in the early seventeenth century. Grotius is one of the first to have developed an individualistic theory of groups. In two long chapters in his *De Jure Belli ac Pacis* (1625), Grotius presents the case for thinking that people should generally not be punished for what others have done. Grotius is generally opposed to holding individuals responsible for what groups have done, as well as holding groups responsible for what individuals have done. As we will see, the exception to this view occurs when individuals have consented to what others are doing. In that case, it is legitimate to punish or hold responsible some for what others have done, or what a group has done.

In his chapter on the sharing of punishment, Grotius talks of potentially punishing all the members of a group for what one member has done. He says:

> No civil Society, or other publick Body, is accountable for the Faults of its particular Members, unless it has concurred with them, or has been negligent in attending to its Charge."[2]

This concurrence can take the form of implicit as well as explicit consent, as we see when Grotius says that "Toleration and Protection" make "Governors accomplices" and "Author" of the crimes of individual members.[3] In

---

[1] In this chapter I revisit issues I first considered in my book *The Morality of Groups*, University of Notre Dame Press, 1987.
[2] Hugo Grotius, *De Jure Belli Ac Pacis* (On the Rights of War and Peace) (1625), ed. Richard Tuck, Indianapolis, IN: Liberty Fund, 2005, p. 1055.
[3] *De Jure Belli Ac Pacis*, p. 1056. Of course, Hobbes also employs this talk of authorship to explain political authority.

addition, he says that two conditions must be met for such ascription of collective accountability: "to make a man accountable for another's Fault, there ought to be a Concurrence of Knowledge and Permission...founded on natural Equity."[4] It is not merely some coincidence of individual acts, but fairness calls for more than this. Explicit acts of individuals are interpretable as providing their consent to what other members are doing, or that an individual explicitly chooses to fail to act, when that person knows that a group is going to act, and also that individual has "sufficient Power to prevent it."[5] Grotius summarizes his view in the following terms: "Knowledge without Authority will not amount to Guilt."[6]

Concerning the ascription of accountability to a person for what others have done, Grotius is concerned first with groups of people organized into communities. His general position here is similar to the concurrence view described in the previous paragraph. He holds that persons should not be punished for a crime unless "they have consented to it."[7] According to Grotius, responsibility arises because of the acts that result from the will, yet a community is "destitute" of such a "physical will."[8] And here is the general argument he gives:

> Guilt must of Necessity be personal, because it results from our Will, than which nothing can be said to be more strictly ours, and it is therefore styled *autexousion, something entirely at our own Disposal.*[9]

Grotius ends this discussion by quoting "the Christian Emperors" who said: "Let every man be answerable for his own sins."[10]

On this Grotian account, the individual is held accountable for what that individual did. So, if a person authorizes another person to act on his or her behalf, this act of authorizing (or of consenting to let the person act in this way) links the acts of others to the one to be attributed with the responsibility. We hold the person authorizing responsible for what the authorized did, but the reason for this is not something about the acts of the represented but

---

[4] *De Jure Belli Ac Pacis*, p. 1058.
[5] *De Jure Belli Ac Pacis*, p. 1057.
[6] *De Jure Belli Ac Pacis*, p. 1058.
[7] *De Jure Belli Ac Pacis*, p. 1093.
[8] *De Jure Belli Ac Pacis*, p. 1078.
[9] *De Jure Belli Ac Pacis*, p. 1084.
[10] *De Jure Belli Ac Pacis*, p. 1085.

of the one who is representing. In this way, Grotius's view is clearly similar to that of Hobbes, which we will discuss later.

In discussing groups, Grotius offers an important insight that is consistent with the Hobbesian position:

> It cannot be denied that a people may cease to exist. The extinction of a people may be brought about in two ways: either by the destruction of the body, or by the destruction of that form or spirit which I have mentioned. A body perishes if the parts without which the body cannot exist have at the same time been destroyed or if the corporate bond of union has been destroyed...A people's form of organization is lost when its entire or full enjoyment of common rights has been taken away.[11]

Here the emphasis is on the form of organization—seemingly leaving open the question of how little organization is needed for a group to be held accountable, as well as whether it is necessary that groups have an explicit decision-making procedure for the group to be attributed agency or responsibility.

At the beginning of his discussion of this issue, Grotius says that we punish accomplices not "for other Mens faults" but for "their own."[12] He seems to take a similar view of all responsibility and punishment that we attribute to one person for what another has done. As was also true for Hobbes, the key seems to be whether an act of authorization, or some other showing of consent, has occurred. Grotius does not develop this idea any more than the quotations I have rehearsed so far would indicate. But it is of interest that Grotius precedes Hobbes in focusing on just this feature of a person's acts that would allow for the attribution of guilt to this person for the acts of others. And so it is a mistake to think that Hobbes's individualistic position was radically different from others in the seventeenth century. As we will see, Hobbes also holds a similar view to that of Grotius in denying the independent existence of collectivities.

---

[11] Hugo Grotius, *De Jure Belli ac Pacis* (On the Law of War and Peace) (1625), translated by Francis W. Kelsey: Oxford: Clarendon Press, 1925, pp. 312–313. I prefer Kelsey's translation of this particular passage.
[12] Tuck, 2005, p. 1053.

II. Hobbes on Artificial Persons and Authority

Hobbes develops a full-blown theory of authorization as a way to account both for how groups can act and how responsibility can be attributed to individuals for the acts of others. The cornerstone of Hobbes's view is that acts of authorization can constitute an artificial person. And the artificial person can unite many natural persons, who each delegate to the artificial person to act on behalf of the natural persons. It is in this way that a group can become unified and can act, even though the action of the group is not actually constituted by the aggregated acts of the persons who make up the multitude. Like Grotius, it is the act of authorization that warrants the acts of the representer to be called those of the represented, and thereby unifies them in a way that we can talk of a collective action for which responsibility or punishment could be assigned.

Here is what Hobbes says about how the acts of natural persons can create artificial persons:

> A PERSON, is he, whose words are considered, either as his own or as representing the words or actions of another man, or of any other thing to whom they are attributed, whether truly or by fiction
>
> When they are considered as his own, then is he called a *natural person*: and when they are considered as representing the words and actions of another, then he is a *feigned* or *artificial person*.[13]

In this account, Hobbes says that he uses the term "person" quite intentionally to mean an actor. He makes reference to the Latin origin of the term: "*persona* in Latin signifies the *disguise*, or *outward appearance* of a man, counterfeited on the stage." Hobbes then goes on to give this analogy to the theatre:

> So that a *person*, is the same that an *actor* is, both on the stage, and in common conversation; and to *personate*, is to *act*, or *represent* himself, or another; and he that acteth another, is said to bear his person, or act in his name.[14]

---

[13] EW III 147, Tuck 111.
[14] EW III 148, Tuck 112.

And then Hobbes gives his well-known account of authority:

> Of persons artificial, some have their words and actions *owned* by those whom they represent. And then the person is the *actor*, and he that owneth his words and actions is the AUTHOR: In which case the actor acteth by authority.[15]

This is the account of authority that Hobbes constructed from the analogy of the relationship between author and actor in a stage-play.

On the basis of his account of authority, Hobbes derives the idea of a kind of transfer of rights, whereby one person gives to another the right to act on his or her behalf:

> the right of doing any action, is called AUTHORITY and sometimes warrant. So that by authority is always understood a right of doing any act; and *done by authority*, done by commission, or licence from him whose right it is.[16]

If an actor and author covenant or contract, whereby the author gives to the actor the right of speaking his words, whatever words the actor speaks are attributed to the author as the word's owner. Hobbes goes on to say that the type of author he is describing here is he "that owneth an Action of another."

Yet up to this point Hobbes's analogy is a little curious. Normally, the actor's words are attributed to the author only in the case where the actor adheres closely to the script that the author has written, this being the terms of their agreement. Hobbes is apparently thinking of situations where the author of the play gives the actor the right to speak any words he or she likes while in the role created by the author. In Greek or Latin drama there may have been such an arrangement, but from what I can tell this would have been an odd arrangement even in those ancient times, and certainly so in contemporary times. One clue we have is that Hobbes makes reference to actors wearing "a mask or visard" by which the actor is disguised, thereby seeming to imply that the actor is not his own person but by wearing the mask becomes an artificial person created by the author. Even so, in a stage-play it would still be odd to have the actor speaking any lines he or she liked and having them attributed to the author as their owner. But

---

[15] EW III 148, Tuck 112.
[16] EW III 148, Tuck 112.

Hobbes's point seems to be that the terms of the relationship determine to what extent the actor's words and actions are owned by the author. This will be important later, when we discuss whether the people who are assaulted by their sovereign need to feel that they are bound not to rebel.

Perhaps the best way to think of this issue is in terms of authorial intent. The author can be seen as owning the actor's words and actions not merely on the basis of checking the script, if there is one, but as trying to ascertain what were the intentions of the author when the role was developed that the actor is now assuming. Hobbes does not talk in these terms in the *Leviathan* Chapter 16 passages we have considered so far, but there are later passages that could lead us to think that that is indeed what he might have had in mind in the passages I have just rehearsed.

First, we should note that Hobbes says that the intent of the law-maker is the key to the interpretation of law:

> For it is not the letter, but the intendment, or meaning; that is to say, the authentic interpretation of the law (which is the sense of the legislator), in which the nature of law consisteth.[17]

So at very least we can say that Hobbes is aware of the problem of establishing intent in interpreting what the sovereign says through the laws that the sovereign propounds. My point is that it also matters what was the intent of those who established the sovereign's authority.

Second, Hobbes goes on to say that understanding the intention of the legislator is crucial for understanding how to interpret laws also when those laws are confusing or silent:

> the intention of the legislator is always supposed to be equity: for it were a great contumely for a judge to think otherwise of the sovereign. He ought therefore if the word of the law do not fully authorize a reasonable sentence, to supply it with the law of nature, or if the case be difficult, to respite judgment until he have received more ample authority.[18]

Again, this is a recognition that intention matters in determining the meaning of the law.

---

[17] EW III 261–262, Tuck 190.
[18] EW III 267, Tuck 194.

Third, Hobbes explicitly recognizes the point about authorial intent in terms of limits on the sovereign's authority, though here the term "intent" does not occur:

> In a body politic, if the representative be one man, whatsoever he does in the person of the body, which is not warranted in his letters, nor by the laws, is his own act and not the act of the body, nor of any member thereof besides himselfe.[19]

Here is the most explicit acknowledgment of the idea that authorial intent matters in determining what the representative can legitimately do in order to claim to own the words and acts of the represented. And here we also obtain an explicit indication that the representative can be limited by the terms of the authorizing act of those who are then represented. One question—taken up at length in the next chapter—is whether the sovereign is authorized to attack, or leave undefended, the people he represents.

III. The Multitudes

Less controversial, and no less original, is what Hobbes says about the way that his conception of authority will allow us to make sense of how a multitude of people could be said to act as one person.

> A multitude of men, are made *one* person, when they are by one man, or one person, represented; so that it be done with the consent of every one of that multitude in particular. For it is the *unity* of the representer, not the *unity* of the represented, that maketh the person *one*.[20]

Hobbes further explains that a multitude "naturally is not *one*, but *many*." And of interest to the issue raised in the previous section, Hobbes then adds:

> they cannot be understood for one, but many authors of everything their representative saith, or doth in their name; every man giving their common representer, authority from himself in particular; and owning all the actions the representer doth, in case they give him authority without stint: otherwise, when

---

[19] EW III 212, Tuck 156.
[20] EW III 151, Tuck 114.

they limit him in what, and how far he shall represent them, none of them owneth more than they gave him commission to act.[21]

Here we have Hobbes explicitly endorsing the idea that for the multitude to be author of all the sovereign does, the multitude must grant the sovereign authority "without stint."

This passage is very clear, and it is interesting that Hobbes himself seemingly buried it in Chapter 16. The "without stint" qualification is related to his earlier discussion of authority and the analogy with stage-actors and their authors. It is only when the multitude of people has indeed authorized a representative "without stint"—that is, without limit—that the representative can claim to do and speak in the name of the multitude, regardless of what the representative has said or done. Otherwise, the problem of the representative speaking *ultra vires*—beyond the life or role that has been established for the representative—remains of central importance, and should ultimately affect the status of the sovereign's own right to speak and act for the people. The same will be true of any other artificial person or collectivity created by consent.

At this point it is good to recall the quotation from *De Cive* that is the epigram of my book:

> Most men grant, that a government ought not to be divided; but they would have it moderated and bounded by some limits. Truly it is very reasonable it should be so...for my part, I wish that not only kings, but all other persons, endued with supreme authority, would so temper themselves...within the limits of natural and divine law.[22]

Hobbes says that sovereigns should limit themselves within the confines of the natural law. In the present chapter I am interested in limitations that might be placed on the sovereign due to the terms of the authorizing acts. Some of these limitations may come from a combination of natural-law considerations such as concerning self-preservation and peace in combination with explicit limits in terms of the authorization acts of the people.

---

[21] EW III 151, Tuck 114.
[22] EW II 96 note, ch. VII, note to para. 4.

In addition, we might ask the question of how to think about collectivities that do not have explicit mechanisms whereby individuals can give consent to be represented. On Hobbes's account, can a multitude act without having an explicit procedure of authorization? Hobbes seems not to be aware of this problem in the central places where he would be expected to be aware of the problem. Indeed, he merely talks of "every man giving their common representer, authority from himself in particular."[23] One of the few clues he provides for cases where there is not a single leader who is the representer is when he says "if the representative consist of many men, the voice of the greater number, must be considered the voice of them all."[24] Hobbes does not seem to see that there is a problem in deciding whether the multitude is indeed united by the voice of the majority, or that it is merely those in the majority that have so united. Again the question is how to ascertain what the "letters" of authorization are, to use Hobbes's terminology.[25]

Hobbes is generally so focused on monarchy that he fails to heed his own remarks about how this is only one of three main forms of government. And so there is a distinct possibility that a group of people, a multitude, can be represented by another group of people—either a small group of people (an aristocracy) or possibly a very large (democratic) assembly.[26] In this case, we might wonder quite what it means when Hobbes, as well as Grotius, says that the unity of a multitude is seen only in the unity of the representative. Unless Hobbes were to rule out these two other group representatives he needs to explain how a multitude can be unified by another multitude that could be exactly the same size as the original multitude, as in the case of a direct democracy. Indeed, the members of the multitude may be the same persons as the members of an assembly.

The standard Hobbesian reply is to rely on the distinction between the natural persons who grant authorization and the artificial persons who are the representers, so that the very same people could be both represented and representer. An example of this could be the New England Town Meeting

---

[23] EW III 151, Tuck 114.
[24] EW III 151, Tuck 114.
[25] Philip Pettit also points out that Hobbes was seemingly unaware that majorities do not always represent the will of the collectivity, see his book, *Made with Words*, Princeton: Princeton University Press, 2008, pp. 82–83.
[26] Pettit says: "Clearly, the personator group associated with democracy would be a different sort of person [than]…in a monarchy," *Made with Words*, p. 80.

where once or twice a year all the people in a village gather in a particular hall to create laws for the town's citizens. Once the natural persons who are these citizens enter the town hall on a specified day, they temporarily become the artificial persons who represent the natural persons as citizens. When they leave the hall they become merely natural persons again. Of course, it may be that these people will actually vote differently as members of the assembly than if they were only individual citizens, perhaps being more open to proposals for the common good than they would otherwise be. On this Hobbesian story a large group can represent a multitude and give it unity, even though the assembly exists only once in a while.

Another possibility worth considering, and which Hobbes also brings up, as does Locke,[27] is that the act of authorization may be by tacit rather than explicit consent. A crucial question then becomes what form tacit consent can take and what the signs of such consent may be, especially in cases where the representative is a group. If there is an explicit decision-making procedure, such as a system of majority rule, then whenever the people are gathered in assembly the policy or action that gains the majority of votes is the one that is attributable to the whole group.

But if there is no explicit process by which authorization takes place, we must turn to implicit forms of consent. And in this respect it is common to think of how a single representative, a monarch, could be seen as representing a multitude if the members of the multitude had not expressly agreed to such representation. It seems to be in keeping with the tradition that includes Grotius, Hobbes, and Locke to look at what is natural to infer from people's actions and general behavior. If people routinely obey the commands of someone, even if they have not expressly consented to be ruled by him or her, such consent can be implied from their behavior. And following Socrates in the *Crito* we can look at a whole range of actions and behavior over the course of a natural person's life to determine whether there is an implied consent to be governed and represented by a particular artificial person or persons, and what limitations there are on such authorization.

One other suggestion that I will explore in the next section is that perhaps authorization can be implied when people act as a unified group by following certain members of the group. Think of a spontaneous uprising,

---

[27] See John Locke, *Second Treatise of Government*, Chapter VIII, paragraph 119, ed. C. B. Macpherson, Indianapolis, IN: Hackett Publishing Co., 1980, p. 63.

such as occurred in Egypt in late January and early February 2011. In this kind of case it is possible for a group to become unified sufficiently to act as one, even though the leader can shift from one short period of time to the next. What binds the people together is perhaps their solidarity, their sense of common interest and objectives, which gives them a sense of shared identity and allows them to be able to act together.

IV. A Hobbesian Account of Mass Action

I would next like to proceed in a Hobbesian vein to see what can be made of collectivities that do not have decision procedures, but seemingly are able to unite and act because of a sense of solidarity. There is a strong temptation to say simply that we are now talking about something very different from a Grotian or Hobbesian form of representation. In this section I will argue that the Hobbesian group-representation model can help us in understanding mass action, and the first task is to say a little about an expanded notion of authorization.

When a group of previously unorganized people—a "multitude," as Hobbes called them—is moved to act together, it is normally that they somehow "choose to decide" to follow a certain person or persons. And the people that they follow are often those who instil a sense of purpose in the group. Some of these emerging leaders may speak passionately in terms that capture the spirit of the people or inspire the people to see themselves as occupying a common situation or having a common goal. If a group of people select a leader, even if there has been no formal decision procedure by which this has occurred, there is a sense that the group has authorized someone to act on their behalf, or at least to be someone whose instructions they will follow as if the instructions were of their own making.

A Hobbesian account that takes seriously the idea that the intention of the authorizers matters will have to look to more than just the behavior of the members.[28] It will also be necessary to try to glean from their behavior what their intentions were in acting as they did. This task is especially difficult when there is no decision-making procedure that can be examined. Perhaps one strategy will be to ascertain the attitudes of the people before

---

[28] I am grateful to Paul Morrow for pressing me on this point.

and during their joining together. In Chapter 10 I will have much more to say about a Hobbesian account of attitudes. Suffice it to say here that if we can discern the attitudes of the members we will often be able to see what their intentions were in joining into collectivities.

The problem is that mass action sometimes seems to arise spontaneously, with no clear leaders at all. Despite the lack of clear leaders, people seem to form a unit and act to accomplish a common objective. An example I have used in previous writings on this topic is the storming of the Bastille in 1789. Over several days, a large group of people were able to accomplish something—breaching the walls of a great prison—which enemy armies had not been able to breach before. The group of people found themselves in the streets of Paris and then recognized their common interests and somehow translated that into mass action. I have suggested that it was the emerging solidarity that was responsible for these people being able to act as a group in what seemed to be a coordinated fashion.[29] Hobbesian authorization can make sense of such phenomena.

In the cases such as the one we have just investigated, there is a sense that there is mass action without a representative actor. Or, perhaps what we have is the kind of representation that occurs when a large multitude is represented by an equally large assembly. If we take this second option, then the issue of representation arises again. Let us think about the tacit consent that members of a multitude show toward having some kind of explicit decision-procedure like that of the Town Hall yearly meeting. People in effect show their attitude of consent by voting with their feet. Insofar as the people continue to show up to pass laws at the Town Hall for the yearly meeting and behave as members of the assembly on those occasions, they authorize this process and the assembly that is so generated. Perhaps, in a similar way, the members of a multitude that starts out as a mob may display its tacit consent to engage in collective action by also voting with their feet—by showing up and doing the tasks that are needed to be done in order to accomplish the goal of bringing down the Bastille, for instance.

Notice that in tacit consent cases, to be represented by an assembly, more is needed than merely each person authorizing her or him to vote once a year. There is also a more general tacit consent on the part of each

---

[29] See Larry May, *The Morality of Groups*, pp. 33–41.

person to be represented by the assembly. Similarly, one could think of the kind of representation that occurs in mass action by such groups as mobs as also involving a kind of representation or delegation of each to the whole group. In this way one can begin to see what solidarity amounts to: an attitude of mutual support that results in giving up to the group some control that the individual had completely to himself or herself before.

Hobbes says that the representer unifies the multitude, but in the case of the mob it is as if this is reversed, so that the individual who tacitly authorizes the group has supplied the unification to the mob, allowing it to act in a somewhat coordinated fashion. One way to think of this is in the idea that the wills of the individuals in the street have been partially merged in the mob. But in mob action there is not a unification so much as a confluence of individual wills, all working toward a common end. The single-mindedness of the individuals is what gives unity to the multitude.

While Hobbes did say that the unity of the representer gives unity to the multitude, he was speaking of a monarch as the representer. In the case of an assembly as representer, a different kind of unification is inevitably going on. It could still be said that the unity of the assembly—where the assembly is able to take action because of its group-decision structure—unifies the multitude. And I suppose the same thing could be said of my example of mob action. But this is at least somewhat misleading, since the multitude is made able to act because of what the individual members of the multitude are doing, such as linking with each other in solidarity, rather than something about the structure of the mob itself.

Perhaps the unity of the mob is more properly said to arise as a result of the shared sense of solidarity that has affected all the members of the multitude, where part of the sense of solidarity comes from the realization of being able, through joint action, to accomplish objectives that are seen as important to each member. The process of coming to a sense of solidarity is a two-way process, whereby a person first sees some common objectives and a loose common identity with others and is then reinforced in the sense that there is a solidarity by finding that fellow members are now able to work together jointly where they were not able to do so before. Mass action, on a Hobbesian account, is facilitated by something like authorization occurring tacitly among people who join themselves together once they recognize that they have common attitudes and interests.

V. Objections

I will now respond to a few objections. The first objection to what I have set out above is that it would be much simpler to omit the authorization element from the account of collective agency and mass action. When people come together under a common interest they do not normally, in addition, decide to let someone or some small subset represent the whole group. And even stranger would be to think that these people authorize themselves, as if they were now an assembly. Assemblies have decision-making structures—something that mobs seem to lack altogether.

My response to this first objection is to point out that mobs do act, and so there is a need to present an account of how this happens. The kind of coordination that some mobs display does not allow for their actions to be merely the result of sympathetic reaction or some other mass hypnosis or hysteria. The methodical way that the Bastille was stormed in 1789 is merely one of the best known historical examples of this sort. So, while there are no explicit decision-making procedures, there must be some mechanism by which decisions in the mob are made, and made in a way that is endorsed by the members of the group. Perhaps authorization does not seem to be the correct category to mark what happens in every case where a multitude congeals in a way that makes the members feel part of a collective project, but I think there is this one component in common in most cases that is important: the people come to feel as if they own what their fellow group members are doing in ways that were not true before the congealing. Sartre calls the stage where a multitude comes together in a way that allows them to engage in joint action the moment when the group fuses.[30] This is what I have been trying to emphasize, and Hobbes's approach to multitudes and collective agency seems to me to help in understanding that process. So, while it is true that mobs lack decision-making structures, normally a component of assemblies, there is something that allows the mob to act as if it had a decision-making structure that can be somewhat assimilated to the Grotian and Hobbesian idea of representation.

A second objection is that solidarity does not have the right elements to fit into the Hobbesian scheme for understanding collective agency. For

---

[30] See Jean-Paul Sartre, *Critique of Dialectical Reason* (1960), translated by Alan Sheridan-Smith, London: Verso/NLB Press, 1976, pp. 351–357.

Hobbes, when an assembly represents a multitude it is really the majority of the assembly that does the representing, not the "committee of the whole." Hobbes has allowed for the possibility of the representative being the "committee of the whole," but he never really takes this option seriously. In his earlier works, before *Leviathan*, Hobbes said that the assembly was only an intermediate stage prior to the formation of monarchy or aristocracy.[31]

My response to the second objection is to acknowledge that assemblies operate by vesting in the majority a further representative authority. But this is also somewhat misleading, since who is in the majority typically shifts quite radically over time, and even during the same time, concerning different issues. It is not as if there is a permanent majority that represents the assembly. Rather, on any given issue it is the will of the majority, not the will of all of the members of the assembly, that represents the multitude.

A third objection is that groups rarely obtain sufficient stability to act unless there is a single natural person who leads or acts for them. Indeed, the idea that there are leaderless mobs is a misnomer, there is almost always some individual person or small number of persons who actually act for the group. Consider the case of the people in Cairo's Tahrir Square in Egypt in early 2011 who were able eventually to topple the thirty-year reign of Hosni Mubarak. It turns out that there were leaders of even this reputed "leaderless revolution."

I have previously followed Hobbes in arguing that there are a variety of mechanisms by which a multitude can come to act, and in some cases it can be accomplished without settled leaders. In the most plausible case there will be leaders "of the moment," but not leaders that are voted upon and in some sense "permanent." So, it is true that there really are no totally leaderless groups that can act in a coordinated way. But the example of the mob is very interesting for showing that groups can reach decisions without explicit decision-making structures, and can act together even when there is no leader who is chosen by vote.

Finally, it could be objected that it is nearly impossible to ascertain authorial intent in situations where a solidified multitude represents the previously disparate multitude. There will thus be no way to determine when the representer acts *ultra vires* and hence when the original multitude is not

---

[31] See Philip Pettit, *Made With Words: Hobbes on Language, Mind, and Politics*, Princeton, NJ: Princeton University Press, 2008, chapter 5.

properly said to own the words and acts of the fused multitude. Without a clear way to establish authorial intent, once again it makes little sense to talk of a process of authorization having occurred. This problem then calls into question the whole Hobbesian project.

My response to this objection is to admit that authorial intent becomes much murkier the more we head down the path I have indicated in this chapter, especially when considering mob action. Yet it is also true that phenomenological reports indicate that the members of some mobs have a sense of group identity and even of what are group acts—ones that are in keeping with the identity of the group. But I must admit that whenever the authorizing acts are clouded, the authorial intent is also difficult to discern. This is why it has been easier to co-opt groups like mobs than groups like majority-rule assemblies.

Throughout this chapter I have argued that a Hobbesian approach to authorization and collective agency can make sense of much of mass action, even in some cases of action by mobs that appear to be leaderless. Multitudes in the streets of Paris in 1789 and in the squares of Cairo in 2011 pose an especially difficult problem for those who wish to have a coherent account of mass action. Focusing on authorization as Grotius and Hobbes did can be one of the best ways to proceed, even as we must somewhat stretch the idea of authorization to fit the difficult cases. People are often enabled to act jointly because they in effect authorize others to act on their behalf.

The next set of chapters examines international affairs—especially international institutions—and attempts to construct a Hobbesian approach. International institutions as well as the international community are collectivities, and so a Hobbesian understanding of collectivities will be useful as we proceed toward our next topic. In past chapters it has been shown that Hobbes's conceptions of law, sovereignty, and authority are much more subtle than often suggested by commentators. In the following chapters it will also be shown that Hobbes's conceptions of international institutions and practices are considerably more subtle than most interpreters have acknowledged. In all these cases I will continue to stress the limitations on States and other collective entities on which my interpretation of Hobbes turns.

8

Crimes and the International Order

In this chapter I argue that Hobbes's ideas can supply us with support for the idea that sovereignty can be legitimately abrogated when security is jeopardized by the sovereign, thereby also providing partial support for international criminal law. Many theorists would consider such a proposal odd, since Hobbes is normally portrayed as the great defender of the position that moral laws are not laws properly so called, and "states could be bound by no higher law."[1] Yet, as we will see, Hobbes nonetheless sets the stage for a contemporary defense of international law, and even for the International Criminal Court. As with my other interpretations of Hobbes's views, I will provide a non-standard interpretation of Hobbes in this chapter, but not one that is without textual support.

Hobbes is not, in my view, the person that realists and other theorists of international relations would like to think. He is not someone who believes that during war moral considerations are irrelevant, and he does not think that international affairs are always a state of war where no agreements are possible. Indeed, Hobbes would most probably think of the relations among States as he thought about the relations among individuals in a pre-civil situation. In previous chapters I have presented evidence for thinking of Hobbes as closer to Fuller in many ways than is normally allowed, and in this chapter I will offer evidence for thinking that Hobbes is definitely not the *bête noire* of international relations.

The strategy of this chapter is to determine how civil law arises out of the state of nature scenario as a model for how international law could emerge out of the international state of nature. In addition, I will argue that when a State sovereign is not protecting, or is actively oppressing, his subjects,

[1] Anthony Clark Arend and Robert J. Beck, *International Law and the Use of Force*, New York: Routledge, 1993, p. 16.

this opens the door for the possibility that another State or international institution could intervene to protect these people who are not having their security protected. In general, I argue that all should seek peace on a Hobbesian construal of legal and political philosophy. And it turns out that pursuing peace often means forming alliances and agreements that will lead to the establishment of a society that creates laws that are obeyed. Hobbes is quite explicit in allowing for just this possibility, and given that this is true, as I will show, one wonders why Hobbes has been misunderstood for so long. The uncharitable explanation is that some theorists have seized on one quotation (which I will examine in detail) and largely taken it out of context. The famous passage in *Leviathan* about states being like gladiators is very vivid, but it simply does not mean what realists and others have taken it to mean.

I will begin by surveying some of the leading theorists of international relations who have portrayed Hobbes as providing grounds for rejecting anything like an international order. In the second section I begin my reply by rehearsing Hobbes's well-known views from *Leviathan* on the problem of the first performer and on why trust is hard to achieve in the state of nature. In the third section I will provide an interpretation of Hobbes's few comments on the condition in which States find themselves, and on the possible formation of a civil society of States, similar to the formation of a civil society among individuals in a single State. In the fourth section I look to Immanuel Kant, who had views on these matters quite similar to those of Hobbes. In the fifth section I will speculate on what Hobbes might have said about the idea of international criminal law—especially of international institutions that could prosecute State leaders. And in the last section I will respond to several objections to what I have argued. Throughout this chapter I will attempt to present a plausible Hobbesian defense of international institutions today.

I. Hobbes and International Relations Theory

In this brief section I will provide a flavor of the dominant view of Hobbes in the fields of international relations and international law today. The view is that Hobbes is one of the most important theorists to have undermined any sense of international law or even of an international order that is anything other than one of anarchy. Indeed, Hobbes is thought to be something like the patron saint of realists in international relations who deny that morality has any influence in the international sphere and hold that power is the only value understood in this domain. I will begin with one of the best known attempts to use Hobbes as a proxy for the contemporary realist tradition in international relations, provided by Charles Beitz.

Beitz uses Hobbes as a foil in his book, *Political Theory and International Relations*, published in 1979 and reissued with a new postscript in 1999. The argument allegedly found in Hobbes's writings, and identified by Beitz as "the Hobbesian argument," has two premises:

> The first is the empirical claim that the international state of nature is a state of war, in which no state has an overriding interest in following moral rules that restrain the pursuit of more immediate interests. The second is the theoretical claim that moral principles must be justified by showing that following them promotes long-range interests of each agent to whom they apply.[2]

Beitz structures his argument against realism by refuting both of these "Hobbesian" claims.

Concerning the first premise, Beitz argues that "Hobbes thinks that a common power is needed to assure each person that everyone else will follow the laws of nature. The dilemma is that creating a common power in international relations seems to require cooperation in the state of nature, but cooperation, on Hobbes's account, would be irrational there."[3] On Beitz's reading of Hobbes, obligations are grounded only in prudence, and such obligations are not strong enough to move people in the state of nature to get them out of the dilemma.[4]

Concerning the second premise, Beitz argues that "Hobbes defines the state of nature so that both conformity to the laws of nature and action to escape the state of nature are equally irrational."[5] So, there is both this theoretical argument and the earlier empirical argument that leads Hobbes to think, on Beitz's interpretation, that only overwhelming power can provide

---

[2] Charles Beitz, *Political Theory and International Relations*, Princeton, NJ: Princeton University Press, 1979, 1999, p. 14.
[3] *Political Theory and International Relations*, p. 30.
[4] *Political Theory and International Relations*, p. 34.
[5] *Political Theory and International Relations*, pp. 40–41.

security, and yet in the state of nature that characterizes international relations there is only rough equality of power. The conclusion of this argument is that Hobbes sees no way out of the dilemma and is hence incapable of providing support for robust international relations and an international rule of law. Instead, argues Beitz, we need to see that international relations are not best understood either on the model of the state of nature or the model of domestic society, but on something between.[6]

Another major theorist of international relations who sees Hobbes as providing support for realism is Hans Morgenthau, in his celebrated book, *Politics Among Nations*, published in 1948. Morgenthau sees Hobbes as a defender of the theory of unlimited imperialism that Morgenthau contrasts to his own version of realism.

> The outstanding historical examples of unlimited imperialism are the expansionist policies of Alexander the Great, Rome, the Arabs of the seventh and eighth centuries, Napoleon I, and Hitler. They all have in common an urge toward expansion which knows no rational limits, feeds on its own successes and, if not stopped by a superior force will go on to the confines of the political world.

In note 16 that follows this passage, Morgenthau says that "Hobbes has given the classical analysis of the unlimited desire for power in *Leviathan*, Ch. XI."[7]

And then, later in his book, Morgenthau gives the reasons for holding that Hobbes believes that international relations are simply the war of every man against every man:

> the international scene would indeed resemble the state of nature described by Hobbes as the "war of every man against every man." International politics would be governed exclusively by those considerations of political expediency…In such a world, the weak would be at the mercy of the strong. Might would indeed make right.[8]

In Morgenthau's view, Hobbes is the *bête noire* of international relations and international law.

---

[6] *Political Theory and International Relations*, p. 50.
[7] Hans Morgenthau, *Politics Among Nations*, New York: McGraw Hill, 1948, p. 67.
[8] *Politics Among Nations*, p. 219.

Another important theorist to consider is Hedley Bull. In his book, *The Anarchical Society*, Bull criticizes "the doctrine of Hobbes and his successors that law necessarily involves sanctions, force and coercion." Bull then argues that for Hobbes, international law, which lacks sanctions, force, and coercion, is not "truly 'law.'"[9] Bull believed that the global situation was indeed an anarchical society, and so in this sense agreed with Hobbes, as he interpreted him. But Bull also believed that a society of States was consistent with this anarchical world order, contrary to what he believed to be Hobbes's view.

Finally, there are the views of Cherif Bassiouni, one of the preeminent contemporary international law scholars. Bassiouni has defended "a higher body politic" with a "collective social bond" which contains a robust conception of international law.

> Against this vision stands the Hobbesian state of nature, in which each state pursues its own interests, defines its own goals, follows its own path...a collective Hobbesian state of nature where the powerful and wealthy nations dominate the community's collective processes and arrogate to themselves the prerogative of exceptionalism.

In such a Hobbesian world there is no "international rule of law."[10] Bassiouni says that a Hobbesian view of international law calls for "equal sovereignty of States" and "only voluntary acceptance of international obligations with no external coercion or enforcement and no intervention into the domestic affairs of any State."[11]

In Bassiouni's view, the model of realpolitik is best understood as a Hobbesian model that has no room for international law—especially international criminal law. He thus follows in a long line of theorists of international relations and international law who see Hobbes as holding the most extreme version of realism. In what follows I will challenge this dominant image of Hobbes's view of international order and law, and I will be concerned especially to show that Hobbes could support something like the kind of international criminal law that currently exists after the passage of the Rome Treaty establishing the International Criminal Court.

---

[9] Hedley Bull, *The Anarchical Society*, New York: Columbia University Press, 1977, p. 127.

[10] M. Cherif Bassiouni, "The Perennial Conflict between International Criminal Justice and Realpolitik," *Georgia State Law Review*, vol. 22, 2006, pp. 544–545.

[11] "The Perennial Conflict between International Criminal Justice and Realpolitik," p. 547.

II. Trust and the First Performer

I begin with Hobbes's claim that the relationship among States in international affairs is like the relationship among people in the state of nature, where the natural human condition can be described as the "war of every man against every man."[12] As Hobbes says at the end of Chapter 30 of *Leviathan*:

> the law of nations and the law of nature, is the same thing. And every sovereign hath the same right, in procuring the safety of his people, that any particular man can have, in procuring the safety of his own body.[13]

Many who have interpreted this passage contend that Hobbes is the great defender of the use of violence, especially in situations where there is no sovereign, and most especially in the relations between States.

It is often forgotten, though, that in the very paragraph where Hobbes speaks of the war that exists in any state of nature, he also declares that the first branch of the "first, and fundamental law of nature" is "to *seek peace and follow it*."[14] The more Hobbesian-sounding law of nature, "*by all means we can, defend ourselves*," is said to be only the second branch of the first law of nature.[15] Hobbes has often been characterized unfairly as the defender of the right of States to use any means, including violence, in their relations with one another and with their own subjects. This is because in the state of nature, while individual persons have the right to do everything, this is not a reasonable position in which to remain.[16] Indeed, it is the equal rights of all to everything that creates the impossible situation where life is "solitary, poor, nasty, brutish, and short."[17]

Hobbes is also often portrayed as the main critic of a strong domain of international law. This is because Hobbes seemingly argues that it is irrational for any person to initiate trust in others to sustain peace unless that person has a guarantee that others will also act peacefully. Such a guarantee

---

[12] EW III 115, Tuck 90.   [13] EW III 342, Tuck 244.
[14] EW III 117, Tuck 91.   [15] EW III 117, Tuck 91.
[16] See Chapter 10 of my book.   [17] EW III 113, Tuck 89.

comes from having a sovereign power that keeps all subjects in awe by instilling fear into their hearts. In international relations, no such sovereign exists, and so no guarantee of the peacefulness of another sovereign exists. Hence, there seems to be no reason for States to act peacefully.

But Hobbes's argument is more subtle than this. In the state of nature, all people are roughly equal. Even the strongest must sleep, and then even the weakest can drive a knife into the back of the strongest. All people fear this loss of life, and any sign of weakness in the state of nature will risk such a loss of life. If two people make an agreement to trust each other, and not to use violence against each other, then each person renders himself or herself vulnerable to the other. Yet, by rendering oneself vulnerable, one risks that loss of life that is most feared. Hobbes's position takes on a subtlety, though, when he admits that it is just this sense of trust that is absolutely crucial for cooperation and commerce, and that trust is also crucial for overcoming the miserable conditions of the state of nature. For this reason, while it is always unreasonable to be a first performer of the social covenant, it is also unreasonable not to want to join cooperative associations that could protect us.[18]

It seems reasonable to argue that if Hobbes rejects the desirability of first performance to the social contract, he should also be opposed to the attitudes of cooperation and trust that are essential to an international rule of law. Yet, in Chapter 14 of *Leviathan*, Hobbes indicates that the first performance of contracts is only conditionally irrational in the state of nature—that is, only when cooperation jeopardizes self-defense.[19] Hobbes also counsels that we should always pursue peace over war, and that it is reasonable to go to great lengths to create a situation in which people feel bound to keep their promises and contracts. Indeed, Hobbes defines the law of nature as a dictate of right reason that counsels against the use of force and violence.[20] Civil society, along with the domestic rule of law, is created so as to provide just the sort of mutual enforcement of agreements that will make first performance reasonable.

The first performer is faced with a dilemma. She desperately wants the commerce and cooperation of her fellows, and yet she also fears that they will try to overwhelm her at the first sign of weakness on her part. This first

---

[18] See Larry May, "Hobbes on Fidelity to Law," *Hobbes Studies*, vol. 5, 1992, pp. 77–89.
[19] EW III 124–125, Tuck 96.
[20] EW III 116–117, Tuck 91.

performer is driven by self-interest, but self-interest pulls in two opposing directions. The state of nature, because of everyone's right to use violence, is "solitary, poor, nasty, brutish, and short"[21]—hardly the position that anyone would prefer from the standpoint of self-interest. Yet in order to get out of the state of nature, she needs to give a sign that she is trustworthy and not likely to engage in violence against her fellows. But, as soon as she would give such signs of cooperativeness in order to entice others into cooperation with her, she risks a great loss. Any showing of cooperation on her part risks an act of violence, resulting in loss of liberty, or even loss of life, at the hands of others who will see her weakness as a basis for their own gains. Hence, the first performer is paralyzed—pulled in different directions by two equally strong motivations, both connected to self-interest.

And yet Hobbes is clear on one thing: a person should seize on any reasonable plan that will allow for people to trust one another and form themselves into societies that can act for their mutual defense. As we will see, this is as true in the state of nature where individual humans are guided by the strong counsel to seek peace, as it is where States are similarly counseled to seek peace as well. Nonetheless, Hobbes regards the problem of first performance as a real problem that needs to be solved in order for people to be able to achieve their top priorities: peace and security.

III. International Civil Society

We can view Hobbes's parable about the first performer in the state of nature as a model for States that resist forming agreements in international law that would limit their sovereignty, or that would not recognize the right of international criminal tribunals. International civil society, with its corresponding international rule of law, seems initially just as fraught with insoluble problems of first performance as that of the state of nature that individual persons face. As the events of September 11, 2001 have shown, even the most powerful member of the world community, the United States, can be harmed by one of the weakest members, a small band of Muslim militants. When the United States slept, the weakest were able to drive a knife into its back. On Hobbesian grounds, the United States would clearly

[21] EW III 113, Tuck 89.

gain from being a party to a multilateral treaty that would force its enemies to restrain themselves, just as individuals gain by entering society where a State sovereign maintains and mandates peace.[22]

Hobbes recognized that it would be rational for States to form themselves into associations. In Chapter 22 of *Leviathan* he says:

> For a league being a connexion of men by covenants, if there be no power given to any one man, or assembly, as in the condition of mere nature, to compel them to performance, is so long only valid, as there ariseth no just cause of distrust: and therefore Leagues between commonwealths, over whom there is no human power established, to keep them all in awe, are not only lawful, but also profitable for the time they last.[23]

Here Hobbes seems to accept the possibility of leagues of States, and also to regard them as profitable and in some sense legal.

It is interesting that Hobbes thinks that it is prudential for States to form associations, but only in the situation where there is no sovereign ruler over these States—as is, of course, true today as well. In *Leviathan*, Hobbes opposed divided sovereignty, although in *De Cive* he strongly supported limitations on sovereignty. And here Hobbes also opposes the possibility of a sovereign international ruler who sits above sovereign State rulers. Only in the case where the league of States is a loose alliance, bound together by treaty or other agreement, is Hobbes perhaps surprisingly not opposed, and even seems to welcome the idea contrary to the way Hobbes is interpreted by international relations scholars and international lawyers.

It is perhaps especially surprising that Hobbes would regard such leagues as "legal," which could refer to the laws of nature or the civil laws. What is legal in the state of nature is merely what conduceth to peace, and Hobbes clearly sees a league of States as meeting that desideratum. If there is no super-sovereign at the international level, a State's sovereign can legally enter such international leagues, since the State's sovereignty is not undermined. Even in terms of civil law, a league of States can be seen as legal insofar as it

---

[22] Of course, the actual attacks against the United States on September 11, 2001 were at the hands of individuals who were not representing an enemy State, but a non-State actor. It is currently unclear what kind of international legal regime would protect States from non-State actors. I am grateful to Elizabeth Edenberg and Paul Morrow for discussion of this point.

[23] EW III 223, Tuck 163.

has been duly approved by each of the sovereigns who constitute the league. These individual sovereigns can legally do whatever conduceth to peace insofar as they are the makers of the law and are also cast into the role of interpreters of the law. So, it should not be surprising that Hobbes would say that a league of States can be considered legal.

It is tempting to talk about the idea of a league of States as an international civil society, on the model of the civil society of individuals coming out of the state of nature. But the lack of a power to overawe is a major difference between the league and the domestic civil society. Of course, the situation where there is no world sovereign but where many compacts or leagues are forming fits the contemporary situation quite well in the world today. Indeed, the United Nations, just as was true of the League of Nations before it, is just such a loose league of States. Given that international law is very much wrapped up with the United Nations and the various multilateral treaties that the United Nations has organized, it appears as if Hobbes could support the current regime of international law as well.

The most well known passage in *Leviathan* on international affairs seems not to be consistent with our discussion so far, and realists as well as other theorists in international relations have seized on this passage and others like it to establish their case, as we saw in the first section of this chapter. Here is what Hobbes says at the end of Chapter 13:

> But though there never had been any time, wherein particular men were in a condition of war one against another; yet in all times, kings and persons of sovereign authority, because of their independency, are in continual jealousies, and in the state and posture of gladiators; having their weapons pointing, and their eyes fixed on one another; that is, their forts, garrisons, and guns upon the frontiers of their kingdoms; and continual spies upon their neighbours, which is a posture of War. But because they uphold thereby, the industry, of their subjects; there does not follow from it, that misery, which accompanies the liberty of particular men.[24]

In the first part of this quotation, Hobbes portrays a state of nature among States,[25] where each has weapons pointing at the other in a "posture of

---

[24] EW III 115, Tuck 90.

[25] Norman Malcolm calls attention to the difference between seeing States as gladiators versus seeing Kings as gladiators. If it is Kings and other State leaders that are in parallel position to individual persons

gladiators." This image has often been used by realists in international relations who see no place for morality or law in the international state of nature—often referred to as a state of anarchy by these realist theorists. Hobbes here portrays States as perpetually distrustful of each other, with continual spying and the building of defensive installations because they are worried about probable attacks from other State leaders.

Yet in the second part of the quotation there is a door opened for the kind of argument I have been running in the chapter so far. The state of nature among States is not the same state of misery that obtained in the state of nature for individuals. In part, this means that people will not be so ready to flee from this realistic state of nature among States. But it also means that there is not such a strong need for a power to overawe all States in order for a league of States to be created. This means that the creation of loose associations of States is not ruled out, despite the distrustful posture that all States take toward each other in the state of nature for States. Indeed, this quotation should be read as providing a similar, though importantly different, account of States in the state of nature to the one that Hobbes had earlier, in Chapter 13 of *Leviathan*, provided of individual humans in the state of nature.

So, it is not necessary to read the passage from Chapter 13 about the initial distrustfulness of States as inconsistent with the passage from Chapter 22 about the prudential reasons to favor leagues of States. Indeed, the initial distrustfulness of States is what would motivate them to seek common alliances, just as is true for individual humans. The reason is the same: namely, the need to gain power through associations that makes it more likely that States will be able to defend themselves effectively once actual, as opposed to merely feared, war is started. But since Hobbes does not see the international realm as one of anarchy, a league of States is more likely to develop than a commonwealth of people. And hence, despite the famous passage about States being like gladiators, it is still at least plausible that Hobbes could support some forms of international law, such as are perhaps embodied in the International Criminal Court, which are formed by agreement among States and which are aimed at providing collective security for all the State members.

in the state of nature, then it is easier, Malcolm argues, to see that the realists can not get out of the quotation what they want. See Norman Malcolm, *Aspects of Hobbes*, Oxford: Oxford University Press, 2002, ch. 13, especially p. 443. I will not follow Malcolm's intriguing suggestion here, but will instead treat the quotation as saying that it is States that are like gladiators in international affairs.

IV. International Law in Kant's *Perpetual Peace*

In his *Dialogue*, Hobbes states emphatically that peace between one nation and another is not to be expected "because there is no Common Power in this World to punish their Injustice."[26] This argument is aimed both against constant peace as well as against the law of nations. It is both historical and logical. The historical argument is quite simple: there has never been a world sovereign, and thus there could not have been a lasting world peace based on international or any other kind of law.

At first sight, Hobbes's argument is hardly compelling, since there is no good reason why there might not be, even in the near future, the creation of a world State. Both forms of political institution, by conquest or by contract, for Hobbes, could allow for this. Hobbes has not advanced any argument against the possibility that a particularly powerful conqueror might not unite the people of the world by his conquest; nor has he shown why all the people of the world could not unite, after a particularly destructive and far-reaching war, and contract to create a world sovereign rather than a number of merely national sovereigns.

In the *Dialogue*, Hobbes is not arguing from a state of nature position, as he was in *Leviathan*, but from the position of the world as he finds it. The important difference here is that Hobbes is arguing in the *Dialogue* from the position that there are already existing nations, each with their own sovereigns. His main question is: Under what conditions would these nations unite and agree to obey a common authority? For Hobbes, one obvious answer is: due to their mutual advantage. Mutual "fear may keep them quiet for a time; but upon every visible advantage they will invade one another."[27] But the question is whether it is inevitable that these invasions occur, according to Hobbes.

The question of future states of affairs—that is, those existing after the destruction of all nations by world-wide war or the conquest of all nations by a benevolent sovereign who destroys all other sovereigns—was never much on Hobbes's mind. In this respect he examined past and present

[26] EW VI 7–8, Cropsey 57.
[27] EW VI 7–8, Cropsey 57.

events and drew his ideas of law and government from that experience. Hobbes denies that currently there are laws of nations mainly because there is no law-giver to declare them. There is clearly no established authority for these laws, nor are they promulgated anywhere. Thus the claim that there is a law of nations, for instance, stipulating that prisoners of war are to be treated according to a particular code, could only be, at best, a counsel of reason. But Hobbes does not deny the possibility of such rules, and indeed can be seen to support some of them, as I will argue in the next chapter.

At the end of the eighteenth century there were many critics of Hobbes's argument against the law of nations doctrine. Preeminent among these critics was Immanuel Kant. Late in his life Kant composed his rejoinder to Hobbes entitled *Perpetual Peace*.[28] Like Grotius, Kant argues on two levels: pragmatic and moral. His pragmatic argument is derived from essentially Hobbesian principles, thereby opening the door for a Hobbesian position different from what Hobbes actually said. Let us begin with this observation by Kant:

> A state of peace among men who live side by side, is not the natural state, which is rather to be described as a state of war; that is to say, although there is not perhaps always open hostility, yet there is a constant threatening that an outbreak might occur…the mere cessation of hostilities is no guarantee of peaceful relations…[29]

Kant, like Hobbes, looked at the past and present state of the world and saw nothing but a constant state of war between nations. Also, arguing in much the same way as we saw Hobbes argue for the basis of civil society, Kant speaks of the condition of nations without an international law:

> Nations, as states, may be judged like individuals who, living in the natural state of society—that is to say uncontrolled by external law—injure one another through their very proximity.[30]

---

[28] I will quote from Immanuel Kant, *Perpetual Peace: A Philosophical Essay*, translated by Mary Campbell Smith, London: Allen & Unwin, 1903. This translation, though somewhat dated, seems to be the best for capturing the Hobbesian language Kant sought to employ.
[29] Kant, *Perpetual Peace*, pp. 117–119.
[30] *Perpetual Peace*, p. 128.

But, from this Hobbesian conception of the relations between nations, Kant declares the possibility and moral duty of changing that relation:

> Every state, for the sake of its own security, may—and ought to—demand that its neighbor should submit itself to conditions, similar to those of the civil society where the right of every individual is guaranteed.[31]

Hobbes might have rejected this argument, but a contemporary Hobbesian could support what Kant says.

Kant admits that this vision of international harmony cannot be achieved overnight or without a great sacrifice.

> For states, in their relation to one another, there can be, according to reason, no other way of advancing from that lawless condition which unceasing war implies, than by giving up their savage lawless freedom, just as individual men have done, and yielding to the coercion of public laws.[32]

Kant even provides us with a rather good prudential argument as to why men will eventually come to choose to obey the law of nations as they did their own national laws.

> The commercial spirit cannot co-exist with war, and sooner or later it takes possession of every nation....Hence states find themselves—not, it is true, exactly from motives of morality—[seeking] to further the noble end of peace and to avert war...[33]

Thus, Kant claims that economic considerations will provide the impetus for nations to seek peace through a law of nations that would guarantee, for instance, that no nation block another's commercial progress through an embargo or restraint of trade, for instance.

Tom Sorell points out that Hobbes often speaks of the dependency of nations on one another when addressing trade.[34] Hobbes, for example, states:

---

[31] *Perpetual Peace.*
[32] *Perpetual Peace*, p. 136.
[33] *Perpetual Peace*, p. 157.
[34] Tom Sorell, *Hobbes*, London: Routledge and Kegan Paul, 1986, 2006, pp. 245–258. I thank Andrew Forcehimes for calling my attention to this point.

This matter, commonly called commodities, is partly *native*, and partly *foreign: native*, that which is to be had within the territory of the commonwealth: *foreign*, that which is imported from without. And because there is no territory under the dominion of one commonwealth, except it be of very vast extent, that produceth all things needful for the maintenance, and motion of the whole body; and few that produce not something more than necessary; the superfluous commodities to be had within, become no more superfluous, but supply these wants at home, by importation of that which may be had abroad.[35]

Hobbes saw the importance of international commerce in a similar light to the way Kant saw it. Indeed, as Noel Malcolm states, in the *Dialogue* Hobbes "recognized that trade required a system of commercial law in which subjects of different states could litigate and seek redress...And at the sovereign-to-sovereign level, Hobbes also recognized the existence of commonly agreed procedures for such matters as the payment of reparations."[36]

For these and other reasons, I follow Sorrell and Malcolm in thinking that Hobbes would not object too strongly against what Kant has set out. Hobbes would be skeptical, but he would have difficulty in disputing Kant on the level of international law and not conceding that the same arguments could then be turned against his own theory of civil law. It is my view that Hobbes's ideas actually provide grounding for international institutions in quite a similar way to that of Kant.

V. A Hobbesian Defense of International Criminal Law

The attacks on September 11, 2001 gave the United States reason to think about joining various international associations. Nevertheless, the United States continued to worry that it would so weaken itself by agreeing to the terms of such treaties as the Rome Treaty (establishing the International Criminal Court, hereinafter ICC), that it would not be able to defend its subjects against criminal sentences issued by the ICC. The United States was thus paralyzed by the hope of world peace and the fear that joining an international organization like the ICC would open itself up to harm by

---

[35] EW III 232–233, Tuck 170–171.
[36] Noel Malcolm, *Aspects of Hobbes*, Oxford: Oxford University Press, 2007, p. 452.

those who seek to exploit the weakness that comes from displaying a cooperative spirit. The United States did not worry about being a first performer, but about being a performer at all on the international stage. I will argue in this section that Hobbes can help the United States see why it is advantageous to do so nonetheless.

A Hobbesian position on international relations allows one to see what would make it rational for the United States, or other States, to join the treaty creating the ICC. After all, in Hobbes's original state of nature scenario, people do ultimately find their way out of the state of nature by establishing organizations and enforcement mechanisms that will diminish the likelihood that displays of cooperativeness will result in harm to the cooperators. Hobbes is often interpreted as holding that only a single monarch can supply the needed enforcement mechanism. But as I argued earlier, this is not Hobbes's actual position concerning the formation of leagues and other associations among States.

In the frontispiece of *Leviathan*, Hobbes portrays the sovereign as a King but only in outline, who is then filled in by the individual people who have given their consent to the social contract. Indeed, at the beginning of Chapter 18 of *Leviathan*, Hobbes says that the "sovereign power is conferred by the consent of the people assembled."[37] These people are those who will stand behind any individual King or other leader, and it is their will, not that of the King, that is crucial for peace to be secured, since the King is the stand-in for the collective will of the people.

In contemporary international law, enforcement mechanisms do not necessarily depend on there being a "world sovereign." We do not need a world monarch or other world sovereign, but only sufficient agreement among the States to provide enforcement for the rulings of international organizations such as the ICC. Joining the ICC is only problematical for the United States if there is no good enforcement mechanism in place. If the ICC has teeth, then joining it is a reasonable strategy even for, and indeed especially for, States such as the United States that fear that other States will try to take advantage of them. The best strategy to gain peace for oneself is to try to bind others not to be wrongdoers, but such binding almost always means also binding oneself. This is just what the multilateral Rome Treaty that set up the ICC has attempted to do.

[37] EW III 159, Tuck 121.

A Hobbesian position on international law could support a system of laws of nature that can be derived from the two-pronged principle: Seek peace where you can, and otherwise be ready to resort to war. What is lacking in Hobbes's account, from a contemporary perspective, is a strong defense for human rights. Indeed, Hobbes famously argues that in the state of nature, "every man has a right to every thing; even to one another's body. And therefore, so long as this natural right of every man to every thing prevails, there can be no security to any man, how strong or wise soever he be."[38] Hobbes argues that the laws of nature are mere theorems for what "conduceth to the conservation and defense of themselves."[39] For this reason, natural laws are not laws properly so-called: they are binding *"in foro interno,"* not *"in foro externo."*[40]

Nonetheless, from a Hobbesian perspective, natural laws are no less binding in terms of their reasonable restraint on violent action because of their *"in foro interno"* status. These secular natural laws bind in the conscience, but they do not bind as laws often do—that is, they do not bind because of the fear of punishment at the hands of the law-givers. Fear of the person who could punish creates a bindingness that is externally motivated. Yet the internally motivated bindingness of conscience, while weaker than things such as fear, is still a constraint for most people. And a Hobbesian can follow Hobbes in arguing that it is reasonable for humans to place constraints on what they can bargain away: "there be some rights that no man can be understood by any words, or other signs, to have abandoned or transferred."[41]

Because Hobbes did not clearly recognize a category of moral rights that could be used to ground fundamental legal norms, and because he did not think that the laws of nature were laws properly so called, he is normally seen as the first strict legal positivist rather than as a defender of natural law theory. But it seems to me that the Hobbesian, although non-standard Hobbesian, position on international relations I have been sketching sets the stage for a moral minimalism that sees certain moral or natural law principles as counseling that States bind together in leagues for their mutual advantage and protection.[42] For while the laws of nature bind only in the

[38] EW III 117, Tuck 91.
[39] EW III 147, Tuck 111.
[40] EW III 145, Tuck 110.
[41] EW III 120, Tuck 93.
[42] For an excellent defense of a similar view, see David Dyzenhaus, "Hobbes and the Legitimacy of Law," *Law and Philosophy*, vol. 20, no. 5, September 2001, pp. 461–498.

conscience, they do still bind, and can form the basis for restraint of violence, even in the international arena. A secularized and minimalist natural law theory is one that derives constraints on the use of violence from principles of human psychology and morality.

Hobbes recognized the prudential advantages of a league of States, and he also saw that such a league could be understood as "legal." More than this can also be said of a Hobbesian position on international relations. We can also say that the door is opened for non-consensual international criminal law in those cases where a sovereign is unwilling or unable to provide the protection to his subjects, which is the hallmark of sovereignty. Sovereigns effectively abdicate or relinquish their sovereignty in such cases, opening the door for some other State or international organization to cross its borders to offer just the protection that is now lacking. So, a Hobbesian position can be similar to the position Kant defended in *Perpetual Peace*. Hobbes offered tantalizing suggestions that he might support the Kantian view, as I will explore in the next chapter.

VI. Objections

In any argument for a Hobbesian defense of international law—especially international criminal law—one must face the obvious objection that international criminal law would countenance the crossing of State borders to apprehend a suspected perpetrator of an international crime, and yet this crossing of State borders appears to be a straightforward violation of sovereignty in Hobbes's view. So, the first objection I must consider is that international criminal law could not be defended on Hobbesian grounds because of the necessity that State borders must be crossed and hence State sovereignty abridged. Hobbes may support the forming of alliances, but not ones, like those involving criminal-law matters, which would countenance the crossing of State borders.

My response is that while this is an important concern, it misses the voluntarist aspect of Hobbes's philosophy. If a State reaches an agreement with another State to allow for crossing of its border for specific purposes that are mutually beneficial, then the crossing of borders is not a wrong to that State. In general, Hobbes held the view that an act is not a wrong to a person if the act is done with that person's consent. In addition, it is not necessarily an abridgement of sovereignty for the State to share power voluntarily with another State about matters that are of mutual interest, as Hobbes clearly allows in his discussion in Chapter 22 of *Leviathan* about the prudential value of States forming leagues. And on some interpretations of Hobbes, there are no rights of sovereignty between States to be worried about in any event, since States are all in the state of nature *vis-à-vis* each other.

A second related criticism is that I have not properly accounted for the idea that sovereignty for Hobbes has to do with acknowledging no one as superior in domestic affairs. Just as in Chapter 26 of *Leviathan*, Hobbes says that a sovereign can "repeal laws…when he pleaseth,"[43] so the sovereign, if he is to be truly sovereign, can negate whatever treaty into which he has previously entered, and hence cannot be bound to allow foreign officials to enter his domain in order to arrest alleged perpetrators of international crimes, even if this has been previously agreed to. For international law to function, especially international criminal law, there must be binding mechanisms to which States will adhere, such as the multi-lateral treaties that are currently the basis for most of international law.

My response is to point out that Hobbes has quite a lot to say about the reasons why people in the state of nature should not feel that they can go back on their contracts and agreements. So, while it is true that in Chapter 26 of *Leviathan*, Hobbes says: "nor is it possible for any person to be bound to himself,"[44] Hobbes also spends considerable time in Chapter 15 of *Leviathan* explaining why all are bound by the third law of nature: "*that men perform their covenants made.*"[45] And since the laws of nature are binding on everyone in the state of nature, and since sovereigns stand to other sovereigns in a state of nature, then it seems that Hobbes would be committed to thinking that sovereigns could and even should adhere to the contracts they have made with other sovereigns, though not necessarily with their own people. Indeed, Hobbes specifically says that the obligation to keep covenants is strongly supported by the laws of nature.

Third, it might be objected that international criminal law, in order to be effective, sometimes requires crossing State borders even when the State in question has not consented. After all, criminal law is a non-consensual

---

[43] EW III 252, Tuck 184.
[44] EW III 252, Tuck 184.
[45] EW III 130, Tuck 100.

form of law. Even if the State itself is engaging in criminal activity, this is not sufficient to allow other States to cross the offending State's borders and intervene. It is true that Hobbes allowed that subjects of a State may resist a sovereign who tries to kill or seriously harm them, but this does not give to others the right to intervene against a duly authorized sovereign. Hobbes is clear about this point when he says: "To resist the sword of the commonwealth, in defense of another man, guilty, or innocent, no man hath liberty."[46]

My response to this objection is to point out that if a sovereign ruler were to try to kill or oppress his subjects, that ruler would no longer be sovereign over those subjects, assuming that the sovereign is not trying to protect the rest by such action. That ruler would violate the chief duty he has, and not be entitled to demand obedience. Indeed, the sovereign would effectively be back in the state of nature *vis-à-vis* those subjects. And in the state of nature, there are no borders or stops to people coming to the aid of one another, even if those people previously lived under different sovereigns. The ruler effectively gives up his sovereignty when he demonstrates that he no longer can, or will, protect the safety of the people. Hobbes makes this quite clear in many places, especially in Chapter 30 of *Leviathan*, where maintaining the safety of the people is said to be the sovereign's chief duty.

A fourth objection is that the whole idea of international law goes against the spirit, if not the letter, of *Leviathan* in that the international domain is a domain of distrust, whereas the domain of international law must be one of trust if it is to function at all. The image of States as gladiators is not the most significant. Rather, the most significant image in *Leviathan* concerning international affairs is the image of States in perpetual distrust of one another, with their weapons pointing at each other, which is the most significant idea that Hobbes develops in *Leviathan* about the relations of States to one another.

Having weapons pointing at each other can be a sign of several things—not the least being that those who point these weapons are in a defensive posture. Being in a defensive posture is not inconsistent with still having a basis for trust. One may trust one's neighbors but still have strong locks on one's doors. Prudence cautions that one should be ready for surprises even from those one trusts. And the hope of trust does not necessarily mean that

---

[46] EW III 205, Tuck 152.

one should drop one's defensive guard. *Leviathan* has many similar apparent paradoxes—such as the very characterization of the fundamental law of nature: "*that every man, ought to endeavour peace, as far as he has hope of obtaining it; and when he cannot obtain it, that he may seek, and use, all helps, and advantages of war.*"[47] Here one is counseled to trust, but also to be ready to defend oneself, even by means of war.

A final objection is that Hobbes would not characterize international affairs as embodying "international order" as I have suggested. The members of the realist school of international relations are right to think of the Hobbesian state of nature in which States reside as one of anarchy. And in a state of anarchy, order and law have no place. The international realm is indeed a state of nature, and like all states of nature it is also a state of war, whether for individuals or for States. It is this state of war that sets the conditions that make law of any kind—especially international law—inconsistent with what Hobbes's texts say. And it is similarly the case that international order is not consistent with the Hobbesian project either.

My response is that Hobbes often says that the way out of the state of nature, at least for individual persons, is to find some mechanism by which the society can be secure in the sense that laws are administered fairly. Law and anarchy are inconsistent, but if having anarchy now means it must always be so, then civil law would never be possible. In order for there to be civil law or international law, individual humans or States must see that it is in their interest to limit or restrain themselves and come together to form a society. In my view, we are on the verge of such an agreement about forming an international society. Regardless of whether that is realistic or not, Hobbes need not be seen as opposed to an "international order" that would allow for the creation of some form of international law.

It is certainly true that Hobbes would be skeptical of the idea of a robust international law without international sovereignty. But, like Kant, he did recognize the possibility of leagues of States forming around certain issues of common concern. And just as in the case of individual people who form a civil society with a corresponding set of civil laws, States can be motivated to form a rudimentary international society with a set of limited international laws. Hobbes's skepticism is not such that he thinks individual people will never be able to leave the state of nature, and there is little reason to

---

[47] EW III 117, Tuck 92.

believe that he would also think that individual States could never be able to leave the state of war either.

In this chapter I have argued that Hobbes, or at least a Hobbesian, could defend the creation of certain international institutions, such as the International Criminal Court that was created by the Rome Treaty in the late 1990s. The theorists of international relations have chosen a bad historical example as a target for their views. Perhaps Machiavelli would be a better choice; but somehow I doubt this as well. For it is not contrary to a prudential account of international relations that States would form alliances and even leagues for the promotion of their interests. And what can be more in the interest of States than that peace would become more likely. The pursuit of peace is what drives individual people out of the state of anarchy, and it is the pursuit of peace that would also drive States out of the condition of anarchy.[48]

---

[48] I am especially grateful to Andrew Forcehimes for help with this chapter.

9
Rules of War

As I discussed in the previous chapter, Hobbes is normally thought to be one of the most notorious defenders of the view that during war there are no rules. During war the strongest should prevail, and in this sense, might makes right. If we follow this interpretation, then Hobbes would not recognize general moral rules governing the conduct of war—especially rules prohibiting cruelty in the use of violent force during war. Yet this is by no means obvious in a careful reading of Hobbes. Indeed, I will claim that Hobbes, like Grotius before him, recognizes rules of war and gives us a good start at a plausible view of universally applicable *jus in bello* rules.[1] A Hobbesian approach is somewhat preferable to a Grotian approach, since Hobbes does not assume that people are good by nature. Yet, as will become clear, a Hobbesian philosophical grounding for the rules of war sees these rules as based in the idea that unnecessary or superfluous harm should not be inflicted. Such an understanding of the basis of the rules of war does not recognize exceptions, even for those who fight on the side of a war that is clearly only defending itself and where the other side of a war is engaging in aggression.

I will argue that Hobbes laid the groundwork for some of the most important contemporary rules of war and for a distinctly moral approach to the relations among States. Hobbes is not the great supporter of realism that has denied the relevance of morality to international affairs. In this chapter I will try to mine Hobbes's texts—both *Leviathan* and the *Dialogue*—for a plausible basis for understanding the *jus in bello* rules of war, and especially a universal prohibition on cruelty.

---

[1] I do not claim, though, that Hobbes provides a basis for all of the laws of war, but only some of the most important ones.

The chapter has the following structure. First, I explain the role that the laws of nature play in Hobbes's understanding of the state of war. Second, I explain Hobbes's views of self-preservation and inflicting cruelty. Third, I reconstruct Hobbes's important insight that rationality governs all human affairs, even those concerning war. Fourth, I explicate the idea of cruelty moving from what Hobbes says to a plausible Hobbesian position. Fifth, I address recent philosophical writing on how best to understand the rules of war. Sixth, I turn to legal discussions of cruelty's place in debates about the laws of war, showing how a Hobbesian approach can ground these laws. And seventh, I respond to several objections.

I. The Laws of Nature

I begin by returning to Hobbes's discussion of the laws of nature. In Chapter 13 of *Leviathan*, where Hobbes describes the conditions of the state of nature, he says:

> Hereby it is manifest, that during the time men live without a common power to keep them all in awe, they are in that condition called war; and such a war, as is of every man, against every man…Whatsoever therefore is consequent to a time of war, where every man is enemy to every man; the same is consequent to the time, wherein men live without other security, than what their own strength, and their own invention shall furnish them withal.[2]

This state of war exists as people's natural state, before they form commonwealths, and also in the State that exists among sovereigns.[3] In this sense the state of nature and the state of war are the same for Hobbes, although the time of war in this passage is not actual fighting, but only a known disposition on the part of the parties to engage in war to protect or advance their interests.

At the beginning of Chapter 14 of *Leviathan*, Hobbes begins to set out the "laws of nature" where among other things men are commanded "*to endeavour peace.*"[4] The laws of nature are dictates of reason that tell people

[2] EW III 112–113, Tuck 88–89.
[3] EW III 115, Tuck 90.
[4] EW III 117, Tuck 92.

how to preserve their lives, where preservation is not mere sustaining of life but also contentment. Hobbes is often portrayed as linking the laws of nature to a strongly egoistic ethics.[5] Yet Hobbes says at the beginning of Chapter 14 of *Leviathan* that the laws of nature aim at peace. Of course, peace and egoism are not incompatible, but the point is that the laws of nature do not tell people how to gain advantage over others. The laws of nature are aimed at securing a situation of lasting peace for all.

In Chapter 15 of *Leviathan*, Hobbes sets out the eleventh law of nature: equity, which has played such an important role in my interpretation so far:

> *if a man be trusted to judge between man and man*, it is a precept of the law of nature, *that he deal equally between them*. For without that, the controversies of men cannot be determined but by war.[6]

Here he says that war determines how controversies are to be solved in situations where there is no person who is trusted to judge.

Hobbes then follows his discussion of equity with a discussion of the twelfth law of nature:

> And from this followeth another law, that such things as cannot be divided, be enjoyed in common, if it can be, and if the quantity of the thing permit, without stint; otherwise proportionably to the number of them that have right.[7]

Here is where proportionality first arises for Hobbes, though at this point in the text it is not elaborated. It seems, however, that proportionality is reserved for situations where controversies can be adjudicated and not to situations where there is war—seemingly leaving out many, if not all, questions of rules of war. Yet in other respects this is too easy a move, since the situation of war is one concerning the state of nature. As we will see, for Hobbes, the laws of nature apply to this state—the natural state of war— most clearly of all.

---

[5] See Gregory S. Kavka, *Hobbesian Moral and Political Theory*, Princeton, NJ: Princeton University Press, 1980.
[6] EW III 142, Tuck 108.
[7] EW III 142, Tuck 108.

The state of nature is a state coextensive with a state of war for Hobbes, unlike for Locke. But what Hobbes means by this is not that actual war exists in the state of nature, but that people will be disposed toward fighting, not constantly involved in fighting in this state. The state of nature has a set of laws—the laws of reason that regulate it. Since the state of nature is coextensive with the state of war, and since the state of nature has laws or rules, then it seems to be a fair inference that the state of war for Hobbes is not lawless but regulated by the laws of nature. In general, the laws of nature for Hobbes are just the sort of rules regulating conduct during war that the *jus in bello* has concerned throughout the history of the Just War tradition, and in international law scholarship as well, or so I will argue in what follows.

As we saw in previous chapters, there has been a debate among scholars about how to understand the laws of nature in Hobbes's work. In Hobbes's view, the laws of nature oblige only "*in foro interno*, that is to say they bind to a desire they should take place: but *in foro externo*; that is to say, to the putting them in act, not always."[8] Nonetheless, he says at the end of Chapter 15 of *Leviathan* that "the true doctrine of the laws of nature, is the true moral philosophy."[9] Hobbes says that these laws are not laws properly so called. But as dictates of reason, he clearly means for them strongly to guide conduct. International lawyers often argue today that the *jus in bello* similarly sets rules for proper conduct during war. I will take up this similarity in later sections.

In Chapter 28 of *Leviathan*, on punishments and rewards, Hobbes expands on the idea that the law of nature prohibits the punishment of the innocent. This prohibition is linked to considerations of equity: "the law that commandeth equity; that is to say, and equal distribution of justice; which in punishing the innocent is not observed."[10] Punishment is deserved only when someone has broken the law. But Hobbes seems also in this discussion to deny that the innocent have rights outside of the commonwealth. Indeed, he says that victors do not make distinctions between the innocent and non-innocent[11] when dealing with enemies, because "it is lawful by the original right of nature to make war."[12]

---

[8] EW III 145, Tuck 110.
[9] EW III 146, Tuck 111.
[10] EW III 304, Tuck 219.
[11] There is an important debate today about the various ways that a person can be innocent during war. See Jeff McMahan, *Killing in War*, Oxford: Oxford University Press, 2009.
[12] EW III 305, Tuck 219.

In Chapter 20 of *Leviathan*, Hobbes seemingly equates the state of war with the "state of mere nature."[13] In this chapter he grants to those who are in a state of war unlimited use of whatever means they need to preserve themselves. It can never be unlawful to do what is necessary to preserve one's life. This is the clear message of the beginning of Chapter 14. The prominence of pursuing peace is mixed with near license in terms of what one can do to preserve one's own peaceful condition in the state of war understood as a mere state of nature.

Here is one of the central problems in interpreting Hobbes: he seems to allow that victors can do whatever leads to the preservation of their societies; but he also holds that in a state of war, or a state of nature, there are rules nonetheless, and these are pretty clearly seen as binding moral rules. So, Hobbes is no pacifist, though he certainly argues in favor of what might be called pacifist attitudes, as I will discuss in the next chapter. But while allowing that war can be justified, he nonetheless argues also that reason dictates restraint in war, just as it does in all other human affairs. And these restraints are universal in application, as we will see. In contemporary international law, the *jus in bello* rules are also universal in scope. In my view, Hobbes presents one of the best cases for minimal and universal rules governing conduct during war, and hence his work is worthy of study for those interested in the laws of war today.

II. Hobbes on Self-Preservation and Cruelty

In reading through Hobbes's corpus, it becomes clear that there are limits to what can be done, even in war. Throughout the long historical development of the *jus in bello* branch of the Just War tradition, unnecessary suffering and superfluous injury have been condemned. And Hobbes can be seen to provide support for these rules. In Chapter 15 of *Leviathan*, he says: "it is necessary for all men that seek peace, to lay down certain rights of nature, that is to say, not to have liberty to do all they list."[14] And then, in several significant places, he discusses these limits.

A little earlier in Chapter 15 of *Leviathan*, Hobbes says that "we are forbidden to inflict punishment with any other design than for correction of

---
[13] EW III 187, Tuck 140.
[14] EW III 141, Tuck 107.

the offender, or direction of others."[15] He also says that "to inflict injury without reason" which is called "cruelty" is contrary to the seventh law of nature.[16] Here and elsewhere, Hobbes is quite clear that since the laws of nature are limitations on what it is rational to do in the state of nature, the limit on cruelty is a limit on punishment or on other attempts to cause harm to another. In Chapter 6 of *Leviathan*, he says:

> *Contempt*, or little sense of the calamity of others, is that which men call CRUELTY; proceeding from security of their own fortune. For that any man should take pleasure in other men's great harms, without other end of his own, I do not conceive it possible.[17]

Considering this and similar passages, Richard Tuck rightly says that "certain things (including pointless cruelty) were always seen by Hobbes as unlikely ever to be justifiable in terms of an agent's own preservation."[18]

In *De Cive*, Hobbes says a little more about cruelty than in *Leviathan*. Of note is this passage from *De Cive*:

> The sixth precept of the natural law is that in revenge and punishments we must have our eye not on the evil past, but the future good…But to hurt another without reason introduces a war, and is contrary to the fundamental law of nature. It is therefore a precept of the law of nature, that in revenge we look not backward, but forward. Now the breach of this law is commonly called cruelty.[19]

And a little later in the same chapter he adds the following note:

> But there are certain natural laws, whose exercise ceaseth not even in the time of war. For I cannot understand what drunkenness or cruelty, that is, revenge that respects not the future good, can advance toward peace, or the preservation of any man.[20]

In *De Cive*, Hobbes is clearer than in *Leviathan* that even in time of war, cruelty cannot be countenanced.

---

[15] EW III 140, Tuck 106.   [16] EW III 140, Tuck 106–107.   [17] EW III 47, Tuck 43–44.
[18] Tuck's Introduction to his edition of *Leviathan*, p. xxix.
[19] EW II ch. 3, para. 11.   [20] EW II ch. 3, para 26, note.

Note that in *Leviathan* Hobbes not only links cruelty to inflicting harm beyond that which advances self-preservation, but also to a disregard for the misfortunes of others. On Hobbes's account, cruelty then has two important components: 1) harm that is unnecessary for self-preservation; and 2) disregard for the needs of others. One acts cruelly when one harms another in a way that is not justified by one's own needs, and disregards the needs of others. Hobbes finds cruel behavior to be beyond the pale of how it is reasonable for people to act toward one another, even in a state of war.[21]

Thus, even though the state of nature is a state of war for Hobbes, there are limits to what individuals can do in that state. These limits are determined by first establishing what it is necessary to do in order to preserve one's own life. But not everything can be easily justified by reference to that end state. Especially if we think of harms that can be done to others, there are clear harms that could not be explained or justified by reference to self-preservation even broadly construed. Harm that is cruel, in that it is not necessary for the good of the harmer, is of this sort. In the situation of war it will turn out that these limits to what is justifiable will also apply, especially concerning such things as cruelty.

The other case mentioned in the note in *De Cive* concerns drunkenness. The person who becomes drunk does not act in a way that advances his or her self-preservation in Hobbes's account. As Lloyd has argued:

> The reason why the Law of Nature forbids drunkenness is that such intemperance impairs our exercise of the rational powers we must use to follow the Laws of Nature...Intemperance can be understood by the Laws of Nature insofar as it compromises people's ability to observe those laws. Not because it harms the agent personally; rather *only* because it may contribute to actions by individual agents that do damage to the common good, in violation of the Laws of Nature.[22]

In my view, Hobbes can be understood to analyze cruelty in a similar way.

There is a sense in which Hobbes might be thought to overstate his case when he says that in the state of nature "every man has a right to everything; even to one another's body."[23] But then we must realize that for Hobbes,

---

[21] S.A. Lloyd refers to "abstention from cruelty" as a "natural duty" for Hobbes. See her treatment of this topic in *Morality in the Philosophy of Thomas Hobbes: Cases in the Law of Nature*, New York: Cambridge University Press, 2009, p. 267.

[22] *Morality in the Philosophy of Thomas Hobbes*, p. 142.

[23] EW III 117, Tuck 91.

rights in the state of nature are mere liberties that have no correlative duties for others, and liberties are limited only by "external impediments."[24] The laws of nature are not linked to such impediments, yet they are linked to reason nonetheless. So, according to Hobbes's technical use of the terms "right" and "liberty," there is a right to everything in the state of war, yet reason counsels that we not exercise that liberty in cases where limiting our liberty is necessary for producing good for us.

It is interesting to speculate about these rules or dictates of nature, the so-called laws of nature, in respect to the limits on what one can do in the state of war. Why would there be such limits at all? Perhaps, such a thing as wanton cruelty, even during war, is actually not consistent with our own long-term self-preservation. No one wants to be the recipient of harm that is not even aimed at the good of the harmer and disregards the needs of those who are harmed. Acts of wanton cruelty will call forth retaliation or revenge that may last long after war has ended and long after there is hope for the maintenance of a lasting peace.

In Chapter 15 of *Leviathan* Hobbes indicates that people will need to rely on one another in order to achieve a lasting peace:

> in a condition of war, wherein every man to every man, for want of a common power to keep them all in awe, is an enemy, there is no man can hope by his own strength, or wit, to defend himself from destruction, without help of confederates.[25]

This quotation is part of Hobbes's well-known response to the fool, but in my view it is also part of Hobbes's less well-known defense of the limits of what it is reasonable to do in situations of war.

In a long discussion of the fourth law of nature, the law of gratitude, Hobbes gives more evidence for the view that in order to gain the sort of reconciliation that is necessary for lasting peace a person needs to act in such a way as to provide good grounds for another person's trust:

> For no man giveth, but with the intention of good to himself; because gift is voluntary; and of all voluntary acts, the object is to every man his own good; of which if men see they shall be frustrated, there will be no beginning of

---

[24] EW III 117, Tuck 91.
[25] EW III 133, Tuck 102.

benevolence, or trust; nor consequently of mutual help, nor reconciliation of one man to another; and therefore they are to remain still in the condition of *war*; which is contrary to the first and fundamental Law of Nature, which commandeth men to *seek peace*.[26]

Perhaps surprisingly, Hobbes seems to be concerned here with reconciliation in order to get out of the situation of war, and one of the key things to do is to give signs of trust. In the state of nature that exists (hypothetically) before civil society arises, such trust is not sufficient for peace. But in the (actual) situation of war between sovereigns, the idea seems to be more palatable to Hobbes.

Indeed, some of the laws of nature are addressed directly to the conditions of pursuing peace among States. For example, Hobbes declares that the fifteenth law of nature is: "*that all men that mediate peace, be allowed safe conduct.*"[27] Today, one can easily see such a remark aimed at peacekeeping forces, as well, perhaps, as those humanitarian workers who minister to those who are injured during battle—one of the main foci of the Geneva Conventions of 1948. In Hobbes's time the idea of rules during war was also certainly not uncommon. Grotius, whom Hobbes read and apparently admired, spoke at length of the laws of war, as did the scholastic writers, with whom Hobbes had less sympathy but certainly was acquainted.[28]

For Hobbes, the rules or laws in the state of nature bind morally, even as they do not bind legally, at least in a *proper* legal sense, in which they are commands of a sovereign. But that is surely also what the rules of war are today, at least for philosophers who write about them, if not also for many international lawyers. In international law the *jus in bello* has been similarly controversial as setting out laws properly so called. But as with Hobbesian laws of nature, the *jus in bello* rules are also supposed to be strong guiding norms for conduct during war. In general, Hobbes's project of describing and defending laws of nature is not dissimilar from the project in international law of describing and defending the *jus in bello*.

---

[26] EW III 138, Tuck 105.
[27] EW III 143, Tuck 108.
[28] See the first few chapters of Larry May, *War Crimes and Just War*, New York: Cambridge University Press, 2007.

III. Rationality in War

The idea that there is a limit to what soldiers can do during war is related to the idea of cruelty that we discussed in the previous section. In Hobbes's *Dialogue*, the Lawyer says:

> sensual pleasure...masters the strongest reason, and is the root of disobedience, slaughter, fraud, hypocrisy, and all manner of evil habits...The root remaining, new fruit will come forth till you be weary of punishing, and at last destroy all power that shall oppose it.[29]

The Philosopher responds: 'What hope is there of a constant peace?' And the Lawyer replies 'You are not to expect such a Peace between two Nations.'[30] Adding these quotations to those already considered in this chapter, it appears that sensual pleasures that lead to slaughter during war are contrary to reason because they interfere with what is most rational: namely, pursuit of a lasting peace. The idea that we should curb our natural desires and instead follow the path of what is rational and reasonable sets the stage for thinking that unnecessary violence should not be employed, even during war. This idea then leads easily to the idea that even in war, violent response should not be disproportionate.

In *Leviathan*, Hobbes seemed to argue for the opposite conclusion. Early in Chapter 14 he says:

> it is a precept and general rule of reason, that every man ought to endeavour peace, as far as he has hope of obtaining it; and when he cannot obtain it, that he may seek and use, all helps, and advantages of war.[31]

He goes on to say that the right of nature gives us liberty "by all means we can to defend ourselves."[32] Many have interpreted these passages to say that Hobbes believes that there are no limits to what can be done during war, but another plausible reading is that the pursuit of peace should trump such

---

[29] EW VI 7, Cropsey 57.
[30] EW VI 7, Cropsey 57.
[31] EW III 117, Tuck 91–92.
[32] EW III 117, Tuck 91–92.

considerations. And in any event, going beyond what is necessary to defend oneself has not here been countenanced.

Tom Sorell has drawn attention to the idea that for Hobbes it sometimes appears that individuals, and especially sovereigns, can engage in whatever behavior they think best. He argues:

> Even if the sovereign is not strictly answerable to his subjects or to law or to other sovereigns for what he does, he does not have the luxury of ruthlessness that is open to ordinary individuals in the state of nature....The more he acts out of narrow self-interest, and at the expense of the interests of his subjects, the more he stands to lose the power that makes such acts tempting.[33]

As we have seen in earlier chapters, sovereigns are limited by what reason dictates not to engage in behavior that would undermine sovereignty, and being cruel or ruthless is ruled out on these grounds.

Hobbes seems to connect the rational and the reasonable in *Leviathan*. For an act to be reasonable it must have some rational end, and the end must be related in the appropriate way to what is a clear good, such as self-preservation. Peace is another clear good for Hobbes. What is reasonable is that actions would aim at one or another clear good. And reason is employed to find these ends, as well as to ensure that the means we have chosen can advance those ends. So, on this understanding of rationality for Hobbes it serves both to identify means and also ends.

One obvious reason for disallowing license during war is seen in the *Dialogue*'s admonition to think about things rationally so as to secure peace, as well as in *Leviathan* Chapter 15's admonition to think about reconciliation perhaps as a way to get to war's end. In Hobbes's view there is a complex set of rational dictates concerning the behavior of those in the state of nature. The normal interpretation is that Hobbes speaks conclusively about the right of people to defend themselves. Yet, as it turns out, the first branch of the first law of nature is "*to seek peace, and follow it.*"[34] In my view, this colors all of the rest of the discussion of the laws of nature. As I indicated earlier, these laws are about how to secure peace, and self-defense is only

---

[33] Tom Sorell, "The Burdensome Freedom of Sovereigns," in *Leviathan After 350 Years*, ed. Tom Sorell and Luc Foisneau, Oxford: Oxford University Press, 2004, p. 184.
[34] EW III 117, Tuck 92.

the second, not the first, of these considerations of what it is reasonable to do in the state of nature.

Some of the laws of nature counsel in such a way that it seems hard to regard them as aimed at the (hypothetical) pre-civil state of nature. Consider, for instance, the law concerning mediation of Peace. As I explained above, this seems directed clearly at peace among sovereign States. Another kind of law, discussed only in the Review and Conclusion section of *Leviathan*, also seems hard to see in any other way than as directed at the state of war among States. Here is the passage: *"that every man is bound by nature, as much as in him lieth, to protect in war the authority, by which he is himself protected in time of Peace."*[35] This reference to war cannot really be to the (hypothetical) state of war in the pre-civil state of nature. Like the law of nature about mediation, we have here a law of nature that is addressed to war among sovereign States. And for Hobbes there are other laws of nature that are best understood as concerning both the (hypothetical) pre-civil state of nature and the (actual) state of nature among sovereign States—even those laws of nature, such as gratitude, that one would not expect to be about both states of nature.[36]

In these various laws of nature that govern behavior in the state of war among sovereign States, the rule of reason prevails. The move that I wish to make in a Hobbesian vein, but not clearly embraced by Hobbes, is that in a state of nature involving sovereign States, the laws of nature also bind individual human persons, especially those who fight in behalf of their States. Hobbes has a variety of things to say about the nature of reason, and he speaks of it in the early chapters of *Leviathan*, as follows:

> REASON, in this sense, is nothing but *reckoning*, that is adding and subtracting, of the consequences of general names agreed upon for the *marking* and *signifying* of our thoughts.[37]

When Hobbes then says that a law of nature "is a precept, or general rule, found out by reason," he can be understood most plausibly to be saying that

---

[35] EW III 703, Tuck 484.
[36] For a good attempt to categorize the different laws of nature into sets depending on whether they apply in the state of nature or civil society, see David Dyzenhaus, "Hobbes and the Legitimacy of Law," *Law and Philosophy*, vol. 20, no. 5, September 2001, pp. 461–498.
[37] EW III 30, Tuck 32

the consequences reckoned in the formulation of the laws of nature are those that best lead to a person's self-preservation and peace.

In his *Dialogue*, Hobbes also considers the type of reason that is associated with the laws of nature. At the beginning of the book, he indicates that "Equity is a certain perfect reason."[38] As we saw in earlier chapters, Hobbes distinguishes natural or universal reason from what Edward Coke had called "artificial reason"—that is, the reason that is based on long study and expert knowledge. Instead, Hobbes has his Philosopher say that "all study is rational, or nothing worth."[39] Again, what he means by reason is what is useful, or prudential, in various situations. But there is the sense that what is rational also has a universal appeal, which is in keeping with the doctrine of *Leviathan* that sees the precepts of reason as dictating what the law of nature is, and hence binding for all time. Here it is instructive to consider one last quotation from Hobbes's *Dialogue*:

> seeing every man knoweth by his own reason what actions are against the law of reason, and knoweth what punishments are by his authority for every evil action ordained; it is manifest reason, that for breaking the known laws he should suffer known punishments.[40]

To think of war as having known rules of reason is in keeping with what Hobbes sets out in *Leviathan* and the *Dialogue*.

IV. A Hobbesian View of Cruelty

On the analysis I have provided so far, Hobbesian rules of war are rational precepts concerning what practices are most likely to lead to self-preservation and peace. In this sense, these rules of war are founded in what could easily be seen as prudence. But as already indicated, Hobbes sees the laws of nature also as moral rules. Indeed, it is most plausible, I believe, to see his dictates of reason as some mixture of prudence and morality, but where there is not a complete overlap between them. In this sense, Hobbes provides a useful way to regard the dictates of reason concerning the state of war. The Hobbesian rules of war are dictates that sit in the realm of overlap of prudence and morality. Rather

---

[38] EW VI 4, Cropsey 54.
[39] EW VI 3, Cropsey 53.
[40] EW VI 122, Cropsey 141.

than seeing Hobbesian rules of war, as is traditional in Hobbes scholarship, as sanctioning license, we have seen that the Hobbesian rules of war set distinct limits on what it is wise to do in times of war among States.

One of the most significant prohibitions of the rules of war is the condemnation of cruelty—and by cruelty I mean roughly what Hobbes meant when he spoke of causing harm with disregard for the calamity of others and where harms inflicted against the other are "without other end of his own."[41] During war, cruelty is the gratuitous infliction of harm. Gratuitous infliction of harm involves infliction of harm that is not necessary for achieving a military objective. If harming another, especially in a situation of war, has the end of self-defense, then this act will not normally count as cruelty.[42]

The exception is the case where the response to a threat to self-defense is disproportionate to the threat. If harm is inflicted in excess of what is needed for self-defense, then the harm may be cruel despite having as its end self-defense. This will not be true in all cases. Cruelty is an extreme response to a given situation. There must be disregard of the needs of the person to whom the harm is directed. Acts of self-defense that are only slightly disproportionate will not count as cruel, since the need of the one inflicting the harm also has to be taken into account. But the one who is the threat to the self-preservation of another does not somehow forfeit all rights, especially in the case of innocent or non-culpable threats.

Cruelty involves the infliction of excessive or unnecessary suffering. In some cases, the line between militarily necessary and unnecessary suffering may be hard to draw, but in many cases clear guidelines can be determined. Cruelty is also gratuitous because it is undertaken in disregard for the needs and interests of others. But a defensible Hobbesian conception of cruelty will not stress other stronger notions of contempt. Indeed, Hobbes defines contempt as "neither desire, nor hate," seemingly also using the term as if it were mere disregard for the interests of others, not also hatred of the other.[43] When harm inflicted on another is clearly disproportionate to what could be seen as necessary for self-preservation understood broadly, this is

---

[41] EW III 47, Tuck 44.

[42] I thank Henry Shue for his comments on how Hobbes's notion of cruelty is closely related to necessity. Indeed, a plausible Hobbesian conception of cruelty could dispense with the element of contempt, as we understand it today, altogether.

[43] EW III 40, Tuck 39.

tantamount to showing contempt for the needs of the other, since this so clearly is contrary to the need for self-preservation of the other.

It might be that we can think of the use of cluster bombs and "exploding" bullets as acts of cruelty in this view. Cluster bombs risk inflicting unnecessary suffering, since these weapons cannot, by definition, be targeted to specific soldiers or away from civilians. Exploding bullets are, by design, likely to cause far more internal injury in those whom they hit than is necessary to take the soldier out of commission on the battlefield. Perhaps there is some deterrent value in the terror that the anticipated use of such weapons causes in enemy soldiers. But, as I have argued, the possible deterrent advantages are almost always outweighed by the costs in terms of anger and retaliation which such tactics also cause. In any event, certain weapons cause considerably more suffering than is necessary to achieve any military objective, and would be ruled out from a Hobbesian view that proscribes cruelty.

The rationale for condemning cruelty in war is partly moral and partly prudential, in keeping with Hobbes's explicit blending of these two normative categories in his laws of nature. From a moral standpoint the infliction of suffering or harm is *prima facie* wrong if it is excessive or unnecessary, since such harm fails to treat a fellow person with even a minimum of respect as a fellow person who is naturally equal to all others. From a prudential perspective, acts that antagonize one's enemies will make the pursuit of peace much harder, and it is the pursuit of peace that is the most important prudential goal. In addition, as Hobbes said, when we deal unequally with some people we give them little recourse but for continuing war.

Soldiers are trained to inflict injury—especially lethal injury—upon enemy soldiers. They are also trained to do all they can to protect their fellow soldiers and to fight doggedly for whatever military objective their superiors command them to achieve.[44] It is this training that is responsible for soldiers being tempted to engage in excessive suffering against the enemy they have been told to destroy. Yet if the objective of war is to achieve long term peace, as seems to be Hobbes's position at the beginning

---

[44] See Robin Geiss, "The Principle of Proportionality: 'Force Protection' as a Military Advantage," *Israel Law Review*, vol. 45, no. 1, 2012, pp. 78–89.

of Chapter 14 of *Leviathan*, it is paramount that limits be placed on the amount of suffering that soldiers are allowed to inflict, even if they are fighting in a just war.

Today, the standard rationale for such limitations on excessive suffering has to do with reciprocity. On this account, showing restraint toward the enemy will seemingly provide an incentive for the enemy reciprocally to show restraint toward one's fellow soldiers.[45] But Hobbes, and a Hobbesian, would be skeptical of this rationale, since in a state of war there is no basis for reciprocal trust. As Hobbes says:

> he that performeth first, has no assurance the other will perform after...And therefore he that performeth first, does but betray himself to his enemy.[46]

The hope for reciprocity, in the state of nature or of war, is not only inadvisable but, in Hobbes's view, dangerous.[47]

Instead, from a Hobbesian perspective, such restraints as those on cruelty are likely to lead to the achievement of peace, since enemy soldiers will not be antagonized by being forced to experience suffering that is not warranted by self-preservation. Indeed, such restraint will advance the goal of reconciliation which is itself crucial for achieving a lasting peace at the end of war. Soldiers presumably will experience resentment whenever an enemy inflicts suffering. But if it is clear that the suffering was unnecessary for achieving a military objective, or for defending the soldier who inflicts such suffering, and disregards the enemy's needs, the resentment will increase to such an extent that peaceful reconciliation will be made nearly impossible.

The prudential argument for restraint during war is not alone sufficient, for like the reciprocity argument there is no guarantee that reconciliation will in fact occur because of these acts of restraint. In addition, from a Hobbesian perspective there is also the moral idea that it is wrong to harm another unless it is necessary in order to avoid a loss in terms of self-defense,

---

[45] For an excellent critique of this idea, see Mark Osiel, *The End of Reciprocity*, New York: Cambridge University Press, 2010.

[46] EW III 124–125, Tuck 96.

[47] S. A Lloyd has the best defense of the central importance of reciprocity to Hobbes's system of ideas. See her book, *Morality in the Philosophy of Thomas Hobbes: Cases in the Law of Nature*, New York: Cambridge University Press, 2009.

and where proportionality is satisfied. Hobbes generally does not argue for more than minimalist restraint on this basis, but the rules of war for which I seek to provide support are also minimalist restraints. For Hobbes, and certainly for a Hobbesian, there is a close link between what is reasonable to do and what it is morally appropriate to do. The prohibition on cruelty fits this idea of being a reasonable and thus moral restraint on conduct during war. Of course, some rules of war need more than a minimal moral argument to support them. My point here is to indicate only that one very important basis for some of the rules of war can be seen to be supported from a Hobbesian perspective.

The rules of war are minimalist in the sense that they must leave a large space for possible uses of violence that are necessary for self-defense and self-preservation more generally. Battlefield situations are highly variable, especially as the "battlefield" shifts into cities where it is hard to tell who is a combatant and who is a civilian. In such situations, it may be very difficult to accomplish legitimate military goals, or even for soldiers to defend themselves, without risking civilian casualties. Still, tactics such as the intentional and unnecessary targeting of civilians are not justifiable, and will hence be reasonable to prohibit on a Hobbesian understanding of the rules of war.

Cruelty during war seems to be potentially justifiable until one realizes that built into the definition of cruelty is the idea that it serves no obvious purpose that would be related to the defense or preservation of a soldier's life. What is reasonable would include the pursuit of nearly all sufficiently important military objectives, since these objectives are related to the overall wellbeing of the soldier and the society in which the soldier lives. But there will be tactics or weapons that nonetheless should be outlawed by a prohibition on the infliction of cruel or unnecessary suffering.

V. Minimalist Rules of War

Hobbesian minimalism is the view that moral and other normative restrictions should include only what is least objectionable. The laws of nature are supposed to represent such a minimalist set of restraints. The underlying idea is that morality should not make demands that are considered to be overbearing or unnecessarily intrusive. Such more intrusive moral demands are not ruled out altogether, but when there are a large number of somewhat conflicting perspectives in a society it is thought to be prudent to try to find some moral and prudential norms that could be agreed to, rather than to have none at all due to the plurality of potentially conflicting perspectives. Hobbesian minimalism recognizes a plurality of values and value orientations, and seeks to provide the kind of view that can be adopted by many disparate perspectives which otherwise seem at odds.

Today, some have argued that the rules of war should be different for those who fight with just cause than for those who fight a war of aggression.[48] And while there may or may not be a plausible moral basis for such a view, from a Hobbesian perspective, where prudence and morality are deeply entangled, it appears that certain restraints during war are rational, regardless of on which side one fights. The Hobbesian view of the rules of war that I will seek to defend here is that all people have a right to use all means that are necessary for self-defense and self-preservation, but that all people do *not* have a right to employ tactics not necessary for self-defense and self-preservation during war, and this most especially includes a prohibition on cruelty.

The contemporary debates about the rules of war have recently focused on the question: Should there be different rules for those who are engaging in a just war as opposed to those who are fighting an aggressive war. The idea under attack is the so-called "moral equality of soldiers." This idea, popularized in contemporary debates by Michael Walzer, was also commonly held in the historical debates. The view holds that the rules of war apply equally to all combatants, regardless of which side they are on.[49] I have defended a version of this view by reference to the need to socialize soldiers to have a sense of honor in what they do so that they do not view themselves as merely hired killers. In order to foster this sense of honor, soldiers need to see themselves as members of a professional class who act for the benefit of their countries.[50]

It is common to distinguish between the law of war concerning tactics, strategies, and weapons, on the one hand, and prohibitions on who can be targeted during war, on the other hand. The first concerns the infliction

---

[48] See David Rodin, *War and Self-Defense*, Oxford: Oxford University Press, 2002; Jeff McMahan, *Killing in War*, Oxford: Oxford University Press, 2009; C.A.J. Coady, *Morality and Political Violence*, Cambridge: Cambridge University Press, 2008; and Lionel McPherson, "Innocence and Responsibility in War," *Canadian Journal of Philosophy*, vol. 34, 2004, 485–506.

[49] Michael Walzer, *Just and Unjust Wars*, New York: Basic Books, 1977.

[50] See Larry May, *War Crimes and Just War*, New York: Cambridge University Press, 2007,

of suffering on combatants, and the second concerns suffering inflicted on those who are not, or who are no longer, engaged in hostile actions. Both categories of the rules of war are ultimately supported by the proposition that war and its terrible devastation should be minimized as much as possible. In the philosophical literature, most of those who reject the moral equality of soldiers do so by claiming that only some soldiers are liable to be killed: namely, those who fight on the unjust side of a war. Philosophers have not argued explicitly that the prohibition on the infliction of unnecessary suffering should be extended only to those soldiers who fight on the just side of a war. But such matters are certainly in the air, with various philosophers questioning the prohibition on the direct targeting of civilians, and even of Red Cross medics.[51] I shall focus on the question of weapons and tactics used against soldiers, but my arguments also raise questions about the rejection of other traditional *jus in bello* doctrines.

From a Hobbesian perspective, regardless of one's final position in this debate, at least some of the rules of war should be conceptualized as reasonable and minimalist restraints that apply to all soldiers. One could deny the moral equality of soldiers thesis and still support minimalist restraints on all soldiers, where the minimum had to be met by all, but a maximalist set of restraints applied only to those who were fighting on the aggressive, as opposed to the defensive, side of a war. David Rodin has recently supported a version of the rules of war that I think would be consonant with my proposal, even though he, unlike myself, generally rejects the moral equality thesis.[52]

Socializing soldiers not to use cruel tactics that cause unnecessary suffering, and socializing them to not intentionally target innocent civilians, even though understood as minimalist restraints, will be important in instilling a sense of honor among all soldiers. And prohibiting cruelty even on the battlefield will also instill in soldiers the idea that they are only to use the immense power that they have been given either for their own self-defense or for advancing a legitimate military objective that promotes their

---

[51] See Cecile Fabre, "Guns, Food, and Liability to Attack in War," *Ethics* vol. 120 (2009): 36–63; and Helen Frowe, "Killing the Red Cross," paper presented at annual meeting of the Society for Applied Philosophy, Manchester, July 2011.

[52] David Rodin, "The Moral Equality of Soldiers: Why *In Bello* Asymmetry is Half Right," in *Just and Unjust Warriors*, ed. David Rodin and Henry Shue, Oxford: Oxford University Press, 2007.

self-preservation. A common minimum of restraint for all soldiers is in my view the key to a Hobbesian conception of the laws of nature.

In my previous writings about the rules of war, I have stressed the importance of understanding such rules as grounded in the principle of humane treatment. In the history of these debates it is normally Grotius who is thought to have best represented this idea in the seventeenth century. I have been arguing that Hobbes can also be placed in this camp. But for Hobbes this would be true only if we understand humane treatment in the minimalist way I have been exploring. A minimalist approach to the rules of war allows for such distinctions in how we understand cruelty, and sets the stage for a position on respect for the rules of war that is consistent with several different theoretical approaches.

Taking a Hobbesian minimalist approach to the rules of war helps us also in resolving some of the issues raised in contemporary theoretical debates. Even if one thinks that there might be different rules of war for those fighting on the just as opposed to the aggressive side of war, we might still reach agreement about a core of the rules of war that apply equally to all soldiers, even if there may be other rules that apply differentially. And as I said, the minimalist approach also allows for the core rules to be supported with a strong moral principle that is also acceptable from a wide variety of ethical perspectives.

I have been proceeding in a minimalist vein in order to make it more likely that the rules of war so conceived will indeed seem obvious across humanity. The Hobbesian project is just of this sort: the laws of nature are supposed to be what anyone would recognize as reasonable principles. As Hobbes says in the Introduction to *Leviathan*, he can only set out principles and then ask his reader if he "find not the same in himself." Hobbes rightly says that there is no other demonstration possible in these fields of value inquiry. This seems to me to be a highly plausible strategy for thinking about what in international legal theory is often described as the laws of humanity. In the remainder of this chapter I wish to indicate how such a minimalist understanding of the rules of war would fit with contemporary legal understandings of the laws of war.

VI. The Laws of War

Contemporary legal debates about the laws of war are often framed by reference to the so-called Lieber Code, the "Instructions for Government of Armies of the U.S. in the Field" drawn up by Francis Lieber in 1863. In the code, Lieber indicated that the guiding idea was that "military necessity does not admit of cruelty—that is, the infliction of suffering for the sake of suffering or revenge."[53] Article 16 of the Lieber Code then states: "and, in general, military necessity does not include any act of hostility which makes the return to peace unnecessarily difficult." And article 15 concludes: "Men who take up arms against one another in public war do not cease on this account to be moral beings, responsible to one another and to God." Similarly, the Hague Convention (IV) of 1907, Article 23, states: "it is especially prohibited…(e) to employ arms, projectiles, or material calculated to cause unnecessary suffering." The French term "maux superflus," here translated as "unnecessary suffering," has also been translated as "superfluous suffering."[54]

Clearly related to the points from Hobbes by which I began this chapter is the idea that the laws of war are to minimize the calamities of war—"the calamities of others" that Hobbes addressed directly in *Leviathan*. The first modern treaty on the rules of war, the St Petersburg Declaration of 1868, begins by stating "that the progress of civilizations should have the effect of alleviating as much as possible the calamities of war."[55] The example provided is telling: "the employment of arms which uselessly aggravate the suffering of disabled men." In the same document, the rules of war were said to be meant to prohibit violations of "the laws of humanity." Hobbes's discussion of the laws of nature is clearly in the same camp as laws of humanity, just as Hobbes also worried about war's calamities.

In its advisory opinion on the Legality of the Use or Threat of Nuclear Weapons, the International Court of Justice (ICJ) held that:

> 78. The cardinal principles contained in the texts constituting the fabric of humanitarian law are the following. The first is aimed at the protection of the civilian population and civilian objects and establishes the distinction between combatants and non-combatants; States must never make civilians the object of attack and must consequently never use weapons that are

---

[53] Quoted in Leslie C. Green, "International Regulation of Armed Conflicts," in *International Criminal Law: Vol. 1, Crimes*, ed. M. Cherif Bassiouni, 2nd ed., Ardsley, NY: Transactional Publishers, 1999, p. 363.
[54] See my discussion of this debate in *War Crimes and Just War*, New York: Cambridge University Press, 2007, pp. 75–79.
[55] Quoted in Green, "International Regulation of Armed Conflicts," p. 364.

incapable of distinguishing between civilian and military targets. According to the second principle, it is prohibited to cause unnecessary suffering to combatants: it is accordingly prohibited to use weapons causing them such harm or uselessly aggravating their suffering. In application of that second principle, States do not have unlimited freedom of choice of means in the weapons they use.

Here the ICJ makes it clear that the prohibition on unnecessary suffering is a cardinal principle of international law.

The ICJ then adds a statement about the relationship between the laws of war and considerations of humanity:

> 79. It is undoubtedly because a great many rules of humanitarian law applicable in armed conflict are so fundamental to the respect of the human person and "elementary considerations of humanity," as the Court put it in its Judgment of 9 April 1949 in the *Corfu Channel* case (I. C. J. Reports 1949, p. 22), that the Hague and Geneva Conventions have enjoyed a broad accession. Further, these fundamental rules are to be observed by all States whether or not they have ratified the conventions that contain them, because they constitute intransgressible principles of international customary law.

This language of being "intransgressible" is the strongest an international court can use to describe the status of these fundamental rules concerning unnecessary suffering.

The Additional Protocol I to the Geneva Conventions, Article 35 (2), states that parties to a conflict are prohibited "to employ weapons, projectiles, and material and methods of warfare of a nature to cause superfluous injury or unnecessary suffering." This seems to give even broader scope to the prohibition than had been articulated earlier in the St Petersburg Declaration and the Lieber Code. And the Convention on Prohibitions or Restrictions on the Use of Certain Conventional Weapons (CCW) states that "the right of the parties to an armed conflict to choose methods or means of warfare is not unlimited," prohibiting weapons or methods "of a nature to cause superfluous injury or unnecessary suffering."[56]

---

[56] I am very grateful to Simon O'Connor of the Norwegian Red Cross for his help in understanding these rules.

Another context where a Hobbesian minimalist understanding of the rules of war, especially concerning cruelty, arises concerns those who are confined by one party's side and hence under their control. It is especially cruel to mistreat people who are disabled prisoners of war or are otherwise dependent on one party for meeting their basic needs. It would produce unnecessary suffering to subject these prisoners to conditions that are harmful to them, and would show disregard for these needs. As under another's control, these prisoners do not pose a threat, and mistreating them can normally not be justified by reference to our own interests or any reasonable military objective. This is consistent with the way the Geneva Conventions are often understood, at least concerning its Common Article III, where cruel treatment is also singled out for prohibition.

Indeed, the Geneva Conventions articulate the idea of "outrages to human dignity," in addition to the more general idea of inhumane treatment, and the theoretical work of late has focused similarly on dignity and humane treatment. What is needed, and what a Hobbesian minimalist approach can provide, is a general grounding for the ideas of the Geneva Conventions and other important statements of the laws of war. I hope that I have supplied the beginnings of an articulation of what that grounding could be based in—namely, what is thought to be reasonable from some kind of state of nature account that is drawn in broadly Hobbesian terms.

In some respects the laws of war are an odd doctrine, since the best way to avoid unnecessary suffering is not to go to war in the first place. What is peculiar is that the laws of war, seen as laws of humanity, do not make war illegal. One could plausibly ask why the intentional large-scale taking of life that is characteristic of war is not also obviously wrong. It seems that the answer conforms to the old Augustinian Just War view that some wars need to be fought for the progress of civilizations. The war against Nazism is normally cited today as an obvious Just War. The laws of humanity, in the form of the laws of war, while not outlawing all war, do the next best thing: these rules try to make war less horrible than it would be otherwise. While I have challenged this position about the justifiability of war, I do support the laws of war nonetheless.[57]

---

[57] See Larry May, "Contingent Pacifism and the Moral Risks of Participating in War," *Public Affairs Quarterly*, vol. 25, no. 2, April 2011, pp. 95–111. Also see Larry May, "Contingent Pacifism and Selective Refusal," *Journal of Social Philosophy*, Spring 2012.

The doctrine that is central to the Geneva Conventions is based on the assumption that there will be wars, even if it is not necessarily assumed that those wars will all be necessary. And once it is assumed that there will be wars, then the doctrine underlying the Geneva Conventions, and most of the other documents on the laws of war, is to minimize suffering during war. Even though war is all about inflicting suffering, suffering should be kept to a minimum. This is clearly in keeping with the Hobbesian doctrine I set out above.

As I mentioned, the Declaration of St Petersburg in 1868 declared that the rules of war are supported by the proposition "that the progress of civilization should have the effect of alleviating as much as possible the calamities of war." To this end, it was declared:

> That the only legitimate target which States should endeavor to accomplish during war is to weaken the military forces of the enemy.
> That for this purpose it is sufficient to disable the greatest number of men.
> That this object would be exceeded by the employment of arms which uselessly aggravate the suffering of disabled men, or renders their death inevitable.
> That the employment of such arms would be contrary to the laws of humanity.[58]

The idea is supposed to be that certain rules or principles are so obvious that they can be used to proscribe behavior as a kind of law across all of humanity.

One of the most obvious universal principles of the laws of humanity is that the production of unnecessary suffering be prohibited. Again, now expressed in terms slightly different from those above, the idea is that rationality is supposed to be the basis for evaluating behavior. The challenge, then, is to find behavior that could not be construed as rational, even during war. The answer provided is that even during war it is irrational to produce suffering that is useless or to no obvious end, as well as to produce suffering that shows disregard for the needs of others. Given that rationality relates means to ends, if a given means has no reasonable end understood in terms of the legitimate aims of war, then that behavior is irrational and is to be proscribed.

---

[58] The Declaration of St Petersburg, 1868.

VII. Objections

Let us next consider a few objections to the views I have set out in order to see more of the supporting reasons for a Hobbesian account of some of the most important rules of war. First, it could be objected that calling cruel behavior irrational does not capture the full force of what is so obviously wrong with cruelty. Perhaps it might be said that it is the assault on dignity that makes cruelty so obviously wrong. Cruelty is an assault on the person and in this sense is inhumane, not merely irrational or unreasonable. My Hobbesian minimalism has not allowed for the full force of cruelty to be appreciated.

I would not disagree that this is a highly plausible way to explain the wrongness of cruelty, but there is in some respects an even more obvious basis for the wrongness. Cruelty is a subspecies of irrational and unreasonable behavior in the sense that it is pointless, or at least pointless in terms of any legitimate objective that could be articulated as counting during the course of war or armed conflict. And we should also remember that Hobbes also added that cruelty shows contempt for the needs of others, perhaps indicating that even he was grappling with the idea of dignity, even if he did not fully articulate this important moral idea, and if he misnamed the concept "contempt," which is most significant to cruelty, instead relying on the idea of what is not necessary for self-defense.

If rationality is to be any guide at all as to the normative constraints on behavior, it will surely be in cases where there is no point to the behavior. Of course, in the case of the rules of war, especially concerning cruelty, there may seem to be a point to cruel behavior. It may be thought that deterrence is made more effective the more extreme the response to harm. During war, one would seemingly gain an advantage by being known for cruelly treating those who are captured, for instance. But on any rational construal of what proper behavior during battle should be, there is no point to cruelty. Cruelty does not, at least in the long run, advance any of the goals of war related to winning and accomplishing a just peace.

A second related objection can be seen in a counter-example: the use of cruelty as a means to deter prisoners of war from attempting to escape. In the movie *Bridge Over the River Kwai* the Japanese are portrayed as employing extremely cruel treatment of Allied prisoners of war as the means to prevent them from escaping or mutinying, given that there were more prisoners of war than there were Japanese soldiers to guard them. Here, it might be said, it was not irrational for the Japanese to employ cruelty as a strategy of war, given the point of keeping prisoners of war out of battle and using the least number of soldiers possible to keep the prisoners from escaping back to the battlefield.

And yet, there are factors even here that tell against this use of cruelty being seen as rational. One of the most common objections to the use of cruelty in such situations is that it upsets the reciprocity upon which some have defended the rules of war. If the Japanese are known for mistreating prisoners of war, then Japanese prisoners of war should expect similar behavior from the Allies. As I said earlier, I do not necessarily support this reasoning, since the cruelty could be covert, or as seems to be true today, reciprocity itself may not be something that either side can expect.[59]

Another consideration is that the use of cruel tactics may be rational in the short run but not in the long run. Here I would point to various problems that emerge in *jus post bellum* thinking.[60] The most serious problem with cruelty, even if it has a short term military point, is that it makes reconciliation very difficult after war ends. As Michael Walzer has said, we must avoid

> the danger of provoking reprisals and of causing bitterness that will long outlast the fighting. The bitterness...might, of course, be the consequence of an outcome thought to be unjust...but it may also result from military conduct thought to be unnecessary, brutal, or unfair or simply "against the rules." So long as defeat follows from what are widely regarded as legitimate acts of war, it is at least possible that it will leave behind no festering resentment...[61]

The climate that leads to reprisals and bitterness, after war ends, is made much more likely if unnecessary harms are inflicted on a State's soldiers.

---

[59] See Mark Osiel, *The End of Reciprocity*, New York: Cambridge University Press, 2010. For a contrary view, see S.A. Lloyd's defense of what she calls Hobbes's "reciprocity theorem," *Morality in the Philosophy of Thomas Hobbes: Cases in the Law of Nature*, New York: Cambridge University Press, 2009, p. 273 and elsewhere.

[60] On this general topic see Larry May, *After War Ends: A Philosophical Perspective*, Cambridge: Cambridge University Press, 2012.

[61] Walzer, *Just and Unjust Wars*, New York: Basic Books, 1977, p. 132.

A third objection is that I have focused mainly on the part of the Hobbesian concept of cruelty that concerns unnecessary suffering. But there is another part that concerns showing contempt for the needs of others. One objection might be that I have failed to note that in war, respect for the needs of enemy soldiers is simply not possible when the whole point of war is to kill as many enemy soldiers as one can. If it is not cruel to kill soldiers contrary to their needs, it would similarly seem not to be cruel merely to harm enemy soldiers contrary to their needs. Indeed, it might be claimed that it is a duty of soldiers to do all they can to kill or incapacitate enemy soldiers, and that my proposal sends soldiers at best mixed messages that could undercut this important duty.

The laws of war have indeed allowed that States can go to war to protect what they perceive to be their interests, but that nonetheless there must be limits on what can occur on the battlefield. Some pacifists have found such a position incoherent. But disabling or killing during war is simply what war is about, whereas inflicting harm is not. Again, as I said above, the idea is that soldiers can be trained to kill in such a way that is not inhumane concerning the way the killing occurs. To this end, the laws of war have been articulated to do what we can to make war not so horrible. With the proper socialization, a soldier will not necessarily act in a way that is inhumane if cruelty can be avoided.

It is not necessarily cruel to kill soldiers on the battlefield, just as it is not necessarily cruel to kill a convicted murderer by lethal injection. In both cases there are ways to do the killing that show more or less regard for the needs of sentient humans who can be subjected to unusually awful forms of treatment, and where merely being killed is not necessarily one of those painful forms of treatment. While inflicting pain is not the only measure of showing contempt for the needs of others, it can be a rough approximation of whether sentient beings are being treated with disregard for their needs. Indeed, this is one of the reasons why death is often considered not as bad as torture.[62]

A fourth objection is that I have failed to see that if a soldier is a threat to the self-preservation of another soldier, there should be no limit on what can be done to him if he fights on the unjust side of a war. Soldiers who are unjust threats have forfeited their rights, and these rights include the right

---

[62] See Henry Shue, "Torture," *Philosophy & Public Affairs*, vol. 7, no. 2 (1978), pp. 124–143.

not to be treated cruelly. In defending ourselves, we do not have to be careful not to be cruel. Such care is not owed to those who threaten our lives, regardless of whether the threat is innocent or non-culpable. Self-defense trumps other considerations such as cruelty, since life is the most precious of all goods.

My response is to point out that there is indeed a conflict that will be hard to resolve here. I hold the view that there are other goods or values that are as significant as self-defense, such as humaneness. I have defended this position at length in other works.[63] Suffice it to say here that when life is not at such risk only one kind of action is reasonable, then even if life is given highest value, other moral considerations such as humaneness can be reasonably appealed to as well. The prohibition on cruelty, even during battle, is one of the considerations of humaneness that is not ruled out simply because one person has a right of self-defense and another person is acting in support of an unjust war.

The laws of war are traditionally seen to be applicable universally. I have argued that the cornerstone of some of these laws—the prohibition against cruelty and the infliction of unnecessary suffering—has a strong claim to be regarded as a universal principle. Such principles are essential for war to be waged in a humane manner and for combatants to see themselves as professional soldiers rather than merely as hired killers. Contemporary theorists who think that all the laws or rules of war should be seen as specific to which side of the war one is on need to think harder about what would constitute minimal conditions for humane wars. There may be reasons to see some of the rules of war as varying, depending on the side on which one fights, but there are also some rules of war that should be adhered to by all soldiers.

In this chapter I have looked to a seemingly unlikely source, the philosophical writings of Hobbes, to provide the beginning of an argument supporting the laws or rules of war—especially the prohibition on cruelty and other forms of unnecessary injury and suffering. From the Hobbesian understanding of the laws of nature as grounded in rationality, I attempted to provide a grounding for certain minimalist constraints during war, such as can be found in the Declaration of St Petersburg and the Geneva

---

[63] See my book, *War Crimes and Just War*, Cambridge University Press, 2007.

Conventions, as well as in many more recent statements of international law. A Hobbesian account of the rules of war is one that would stress minimalist constraints, but constraints nonetheless, despite the way that Hobbes has often been interpreted. And I have argued that such *jus in bello* minimalist prohibitions are universally applicable during wars, contrary to what some contemporary theorists seem to think.

10

The Attitude of Pacifism

In this chapter I argue against the common attempt to portray a "Hobbesian" position as involving the rationality of having pro-war attitudes. Since Hobbes's own times this has been a common way of characterizing his views, as can be seen in the work of John Eachard cited earlier.[1] In more recent times, Walter Berns has argued that Hobbes provides no rational basis for following the laws of nature.[2] Many contemporary thinkers have likewise portrayed the readiness to use violence in the "imperialist" mentality as essentially Hobbesian.[3] As has been true throughout this book, I am also concerned to rebut the general trend in Hobbes scholarship to portray him as an illiberal absolutist.

It is well known that Hobbes contended that the human condition can be described as "the war of every one against every one." It is thus contended that Hobbes is the great defender of the use of violence, especially in situations where there is no law, such as exists in the relations between nations. I will argue that there is an important difference between Hobbes's view of the attitude we should take toward peace versus the attitude that we should take toward war. It is my contention that Hobbes has been unfairly characterized as the promoter of pro-attitudes toward war and violence, when in fact the more fundamental attitude he defends is that of a pro-attitude toward peace.

While Hobbes never uses the term "pacifism," I think that he is committed to a common tenet of this doctrine. Pacifism concerns the development

---

[1] See, for example, John Eachard, *Mr. Hobbs's State of Nature Considered* (1672), ed. Peter Ure, Liverpool: Liverpool University Press, 1958.

[2] See his essay in Strauss and Cropsey's *History of Political Philosophy*, Chicago, IL: Rand McNally & Company, 1963, p. 355.

[3] For example, see Hans Morgenthau, *Politics Among Nations*, New York: Alfred A. Knopf, 1965, p. 56.

of attitudes of cooperation and restraint toward the use of violence. Having attitudes of peace is the view that violence should be used only as a last resort to defend oneself from serious harm or in protecting others from serious harm. It is true that Hobbes differs from some pacifists in thinking that people always retain the natural right to use all means necessary to preserve their lives, and even that it "is forbidden to do that which is destructive of his life." Nonetheless, Hobbes clearly defends another tenet of some forms of pacifism, such as contingent pacifism,[4] which sets, as one of its tenets, the limits of one's peace-seeking at the point where one risks serious harm to self. Indeed, Hobbes does not even defend the use of violence to prevent serious harm to others, but carefully restricts the domain of legitimate violence to the protection of self. In what follows I will examine first what Hobbes says about attitudes in general, before turning to the attitudes toward peace-seeking which he believes people in and out of the state of nature should adopt.

I. Attitudes and Moral Psychology

Hobbes's moral psychology does not employ the term "attitude," but the various things that are said about passions, opinions, and appetites (as well as what is said about dispositions) can be interpreted as providing a view of our attitudes, especially the attitude toward war and peace. Appetite (or desire) concerns endeavor toward a particular object.[5] Some appetites are inborn and some are learned,[6] but in both cases all people call those things "good" that they have an appetite for, just as they call those things "bad" that they have an aversion toward.[7] So appetite (or its opposite aversion) encompasses a large part of what today are called attitudes. But, appetites are merely simple passions until they are mixed with opinion or belief.[8]

Hobbes says that opinions are presuppositions concerning whether a thing will be or will not be, has been or has not been.[9] Opinion leads up

---

[4] See my paper "Contingent Pacifism and the Moral Risks of Participating in War," *Public Affairs Quarterly*, vol. 25, no. 2, April 2011, pp. 95–111. Also see "Contingent Pacifism and Selective Refusal," *Journal of Social Philosophy*, vol. 43, no. 1, Spring 2012, pp. 1–18.
[5] EW III 39, Tuck 38.
[6] EW III 40, Tuck 39.
[7] EW III 41, Tuck 39.
[8] For a very good collection of Hobbes's writings on these topics see *Body, Man, and Citizen*, ed. R. S. Peters, New York: Collier Books, 1962.
[9] EW III 52, Tuck 47.

to judgment, just as appetite leads up to willing. And when appetite and opinion are mixed together there is, such as in the case of hope, a disposition of the mind toward a certain thing conjoined with the opinion that that thing will be attained. In general the opinion that a thing is attainable is conjoined with the will that it be attained. When such mixtures of opinion and appetite are not merely momentary but become a disposition or virtue of character, then we have something like what contemporary social psychologists call an attitude.

Moral virtues are merely another name for what Hobbes calls the laws of nature.[10] These are dispositions that are partly based on passion and partly based on reason.[11] All moral virtues or laws of nature incline people toward peace and harmony. The passion of aversion operates to make us fear death, and our appetites lead us to desire commodious living. Reason leads us to form the opinion that this is what can be had if we reach agreement with our fellow humans, and out of this springs the mixed psychological state (combining appetite and opinion) of hope, which ultimately causes us to seek peace. The disposition to seek peace thus has the three components (cognitive, evaluative, and conative) normally associated with attitudes. I will speak throughout the rest of this chapter of the attitude of pacifism as equivalent to the disposition (as understood from the above analysis) to seek peace.

What is of most interest to me is to set out Hobbes's analysis, as well as his defense, of the attitude of pacifism. The second law of nature seems to be clearly addressed to the dispositions or attitudes that Hobbes thinks are rational in the state of nature. This law holds

> that a man be willing, when others are so too, as far-forth, as for peace, and defence of himself he shall think it necessary, to lay down his right to all things; and be contented with so much liberty against other men, as he would allow other men against himself.[12]

Here we have a clear statement of the desirability of people having positive attitudes toward peace, whenever one does not thereby jeopardize one's own self-defense. This attitude is said to be rational, since it is necessary to offset the natural tendency that all people have to distrust one another. That

[10] EW III 146, Tuck 111.
[11] EW III 116, Tuck 90.
[12] EW III 118, Tuck 92.

Hobbes views this attitude as one of favoring cooperation is also seen at the end of the paragraph which contains the passage just cited: namely, that all people follow "that law of the Gospel; *whatsoever you require that others should do to you, that do ye to them.*"[13]

So we have two components to the attitude of pacifism that Hobbes encourages all people to adopt. First, all of us should be willing to give up our claim to all things, whenever peace can be secured thereby without jeopardizing self-defense. And second, all of us should be willing to do for others whatever we would ask that these others do for us. The first is a negative attitude toward always exercising one's liberty so as to gain advantage over another, and the second is a positive attitude toward cooperation with these others. It is true, of course, that when a person's self-defense is jeopardized by such non-combative and cooperative attitudes, all bets are off, and people should be ready to return to war and distrust. But the fundamental part of the first law of nature is that one continue to develop peace-seeking attitudes, and this is said to be necessary for the attainment of society with all its benefits. Thus, contrary to the way that Hobbes is normally interpreted, the attitude of pacifism plays an important role in his social contract argument in the central chapters of *Leviathan*.

II. Trust, First Performance, and Peace

One of the chief reasons that Hobbes is not recognized as a proponent of pacifism is that he argues against the initiation of peace by any single person who has no guarantee that others will act likewise. And it seems reasonable to think that if Hobbes rejects the desirability of first performance to the social contract, he seems to show himself to be opposed to the attitudes of cooperation and trust that I have admitted to be essential to the attitude of pacifism. In this section I will indicate why Hobbes's position on first performance is not inconsistent with support for the attitude of pacifism.

In Chapter 14 of *Leviathan* Hobbes sets out his argument against first performance as follows:

> For he that performeth first, has no assurance the other will perform after; because the bonds of words are too weak to bridle men's ambition, avarice,

---
[13] EW III 118, Tuck 92.

anger, and other passions, without the fear of some coercive power; which in the condition of mere nature, where all men are equal, and judges of the justness of their own fears, cannot properly be supposed. And therefore he which performeth first, does but betray himself to his enemy; contrary to the right, he can never abandon, of defending his life, and means of living.[14]

Here it is clear that criticism is brought against first performance of contracts only in the state of nature. Furthermore, the criticism is made because first performance jeopardizes self-defense. And it should also be noted that it is assumed that there is no alternative basis for trusting other persons than merely what they have said, and that this pales by comparison with the natural tendencies people have toward avarice, ambition, and anger. But the kind of pacifist attitudes I am attributing to Hobbes makes exception for just this case where self-defense is jeopardized.

The cooperative part of the attitude of pacifism is only challenged by the problem of first performance if a person never has a reason to think that self-defense can be secured at the same time that one is cooperating. And we know that this is certainly not Hobbes's position, since he says that

> in a civil estate, where there is a power set up to constrain those who would otherwise violate their faith, that fear is no more reasonable; and for that cause, he which by the covenant is to perform first, is obliged to do so.[15]

More importantly, even in the state of nature where no such power exists, it is still important to have the attitude of pacifism, for without it people will not be inclined to enter into such covenants in the first place. Thus, even though it is unreasonable to cooperate unilaterally in the state of nature, it is still important to have the attitude of pacifism in this state, and such an attitude is consistent with Hobbes's critique of first performance.

Hobbes makes this point explicit when he says that it is natural for people to seek those conditions that will lead them out of the state of war.

> Whosoever therefore holds, that it had been best to have continued in that state in which all things were lawful for all men, he contradicts himself. For every man by

---

[14] EW III 124–125, Tuck 96.
[15] EW III 125, Tuck 96.

natural necessity desires that which is good for him; nor is there any that esteems a war of all against all, which necessarily adheres to such a state, to be good for him.[16]

Hobbes also holds that right reasoning about what is good for us (namely peace) is just as natural as are those passions that lead us to go to war against each other in the state of nature.

> Therefore true reason is a certain law; which, since it is no less a part of human nature, than any other faculty or affection of the mind, is also termed natural. Therefore the *law of nature*, that I may define it, is the dictate of right reason, conversant about those things which are either to be done or omitted for the constant preservation of life and members, as much as in us lies.[17]

In a footnote to this passage from *De Cive*, Hobbes says that:

> the whole breach of the laws of nature consists in the false reasoning, or rather folly of those men, who see not those duties they are necessarily to perform towards others in order to their own conservation.[18]

These passages show that Hobbes saw the need for people in the state of nature to seek their own long-term preservation by developing the dispositions to seek peace whenever such peace could possibly be had without risk to self-defense. Unilateral cooperation is condemned in the state of nature, but failure to seek cooperation is equally condemned by Hobbes.

Hobbes does not hold that people are by nature sociable, and this may also be thought to make it unlikely that he supports the development of positive attitudes toward peace. As I have reconstructed Hobbes's position, the natural predispositions toward avarice, ambition, and anger initially find themselves dictating the way that we will conduct our lives. People eventually discover, however, that these natural passions are inconsistent with the natural desire to attain long-term stability in one's life.[19] What is natural is a person's reasonable expectation that she will want to turn her attention to things other than warring against her fellow humans. So, while we do not

---

[16] De Cive, EW II 12, ch. I, para. 13.
[17] De Cive, EW II 16, ch. II, para. 1.
[18] De Cive, EW II 16 note, ch. II, note to para. 1.
[19] This is grounded perhaps only in a *modus vivendi*, but such a grounding is thoroughly in line with a Hobbesian minimalism.

have natural social dispositions, we are naturally led to see the reasonableness of developing them, though at the same time holding firmly to our worries about our continued self-defense.

Here is the great Hobbesian predicament: people are not naturally inclined to trust others, because they fear the loss of self-defense that often comes through trust; but it is necessary to develop such trusting dispositions in order to attain any lasting hope of self-preservation. My interpretation is that Hobbes advocates the development of positive attitudes toward peace as a bridge toward long-term preservation, but that such attitudes should not be allowed to overwhelm completely our natural tendencies to be very cautious wherever the trust of others is concerned. In the next section I will reconstruct Hobbes's reasons for thinking that pacifist attitudes should be developed, even in light of what he says about the foolishness of developing other social tendencies.

III. The Reasonableness of Developing Pacifist Attitudes

In the state of nature it is certainly unreasonable to have an unrestricted positive attitude toward doing violence to others, or at least to be known as someone who has such an attitude. Rather, it is reasonable to develop an attitude that restricts the time when violence is looked upon favorably, generally seeing violence as a last resort. In discussing the fourth law of nature in *De Cive*, Hobbes says "that it is a precept of nature, that every man accommodate himself to others."[20] Such statements are some of the best evidence for thinking that Hobbes is not opposed to the development of pacifist attitudes, but in every discussion of this sort there is appended a discussion of the proper limits of these attitudes.

De Cive's fifth law of nature provides the best articulation of the limits placed on the attitudes of pacifism. Here is an important passage:

> The pardon of what is past, or the remission of an offense, is nothing else than the granting of peace to him that asketh it, after he hath warred against us, and now is become penitent. But peace granted to him that repents not, that is, *to him that retains a hostile mind*, or that gives not caution for the future, that is, seeks

[20] De Cive, EW II 36, ch. III para. 9.

not peace, but opportunity; is not properly peace, but fear, and therefore is not commanded by nature. Now to him that will not pardon the penitent and that gives future caution, peace itself it seems is not pleasing: which is contrary to the natural law.[21]

Here it is said that a person should not remain ready to do violence to another person even if that person has recently done violence to us. Rather, such a violent attitude would only make sense if the aggressor does not repent and ask to be forgiven for the aggression.

But if someone aggresses and does not apologize, such a person gives indication that he or she is not a reasonable person, and such a person should not be afforded the trust that is normally given to those who are reasonable. Those who are unrepentant are not to be trusted, because they have not only acted violently in the past but display pro-war attitudes concerning their future acts. Unrepentant aggressors must be treated with extreme caution, and in their case we should remain ready to act violently to thwart their aggressions and to pay them back in kind. Since they are unreasonable, they are unlikely to respond in predictable ways to any other posture on our part.

The discussion in *Leviathan* of the argument of the fool can be cited as further confirming evidence for my claim that Hobbes condemns those who maintain unrestricted positive attitudes toward violence and against cooperation. The third law of nature, "*that men perform their covenants made*," defines the limits of justice,[22] defined as "*the constant will of giving to every man his own*."[23] In discussing this law of nature, Hobbes considers a possible counter-objection.

> The fool hath said in his heart, there is no such thing as justice; and sometimes also with his tongue; seriously alleging, that every man's conservation, and contentment, being committed to his own care, there could be no reason, why every man might not do what conduced thereunto: and therefore also to make, or not make; keep, or not keep covenants, was not against reason, when it conduced to one's own benefit.[24]

---

[21] De Cive, EW II 37, ch. III, para. 10, my italics.
[22] EW III, 130, Tuck 100.
[23] EW III 131, Tuck 101.
[24] EW III 132, Tuck 101.

Hobbes's response to the fool is quite complex, but what concerns me is what Hobbes says about the fool's position taken in the state of nature.

> in a condition of war, wherein every man to every man, for want of a common power to keep them all in awe, is an enemy, there is no man who can hope by his own strength, or wit, to defend himself from destruction, without the help of confederates; where every one expects the same defense by the confederation, that any one else does: and therefore he which declares he thinks it reason to deceive those that help him, can in reason expect no other means of safety, than what can be had from his own single power.[25]

Here Hobbes quite clearly tries to show the unreasonableness of continuing to act in an uncooperative manner in the face of the cooperativeness of others. Even in the state of nature, such behavior is unreasonable, because it is ultimately self-destructive. Drawing on Hobbes's strategy here, I want to show next what it is that is unreasonable about not adopting those attitudes of pacifism that I set out at the beginning of this chapter.

The person who continues to hold anti-pacifist attitudes displays to others both a lack of interest in confederation, and also, for that reason, he or she displays to others that it would be a bad bet to trust him or her. There is thus no good reason to treat this person in any other way than as an enemy—that is, someone toward whom others should not restrain their violent impulses. Yet, if we are regarded by others in this way, then our long-term self-preservation will not be advanced. Such a result will not be something that any reasonable person would choose. Indeed, we can now see why it is that all the laws of nature are said to lead to the same thing: developing the habits and attitudes that incline toward peace. This is made explicit in *The Elements of Law* (*De Corpore Politico*), when Hobbes says that concerning "the law of nature, the sum whereof consisteth in making peace."[26] And then, in *De Cive*, he says

> because dominions were constituted for peace's sake, and peace was sought after for safety's sake he, who being placed in authority, shall use his power otherwise than to the safety of the people, will act against the reasons of peace, that is to say, against the laws of nature."[27]

---

[25] EW III 133–134, Tuck 102.
[26] EW IV 87, ch. II, para. 2.
[27] EW II 166–167, ch. XIII, para. 2.

All the laws of nature lead to the same result, peace, and all these laws are reasonable on the same grounds: namely, they advance long-term self-preservation for each person who follows these laws. The natural passions, especially avarice, ambition, and anger, lead only to short-term gain for individual persons. Natural reason acts as a constraint on these passions, rectifying the excesses into which the unbridled passions would lead us. In this sense, then, the laws of nature are all reasonable, and insofar as the laws of nature lead people to adopt pacifist attitudes, these attitudes are also reasonable.

IV. The Choice between Peace and War

It has been contended for over 300 years that Hobbes is the great opponent of trust and cooperation. But how can this traditional reading of Hobbes be defended, given what I have argued in this chapter? Perhaps the most interesting strategy would be to contend that the laws of nature are not binding on anyone unless there is complete assurance that everyone will follow the dictates of these laws. And since in the state of nature there is no assurance of this sort, then it is never a good idea to trust another person or to be the first to indicate that you are willing to cooperate rather than fight with these others.

As Gregory Kavka has pointed out, the chief problem for any cooperative venture in the state of nature is in securing compliance.[28] Mutual cooperation is indeed a better bet than is mutual non-cooperation. But since mutuality cannot be guaranteed in the state of nature, individual non-cooperation is a better strategy than is individual cooperation. Kavka's reconstruction of Hobbes's argument against the fool, which I discussed previously, highlights the important point that Hobbes is there only arguing for the rationality of second-party cooperation, not first-party cooperation (what I called "first performance"). Without some assurance of compliance, first-party cooperation is not rational, which means that we would never even get to the problem of second-party cooperation in the state of nature.

Indeed, Kavka's point is correct if we are considering the question of how people should come to act in the state of nature, but throughout this chapter

---

[28] Gregory S. Kavka, *Hobbesian Moral and Political Theory*, Princeton, NJ : Princeton University Press, 1986, p. 127.

I have been considering the question of what attitudes people should take toward their future actions. It is not clear that this second question must be answered in the same way as the first question. It may be rational for some person to be the first to give evidence that he or she has *pro-attitudes* toward cooperation, even though it is not rational for this same person to be the first to *act* in a cooperative manner. In the remainder of this section I will defend such a claim both by reference to Hobbes's texts and, in the next section, by a Hobbesian argument which is at least not inconsistent with Hobbes's texts.

In *Leviathan* Hobbes defines the state of war which generally characterizes the state of nature in the following way:

> For WAR, consisteth not in battle only, or the act of fighting; but in a tract of time, wherein the will to contend by battle is sufficiently known...so the nature of war, consisteth not in actual fighting; but in the known disposition thereto, during all the time there is no assurance to the contrary. All the other time is PEACE.[29]

Here the state of war is characterized in terms of dispositions or inclinations to fight. But these are more than just inclinations, since to be able to fight effectively, people must be able to discriminate between different contexts. The addition of this cognitive content makes it reasonable to say that Hobbes's state of war is defined as that state where everyone has pro-war attitudes. These attitudes arise due to our natural passions of anger and avarice, which are motivations for short-term gain.

War continues to hold sway as long as there are no assurances that people have different attitudes. For Hobbes, the state of war remains as long as it is known that most or all people have pro-war attitudes. The antidote to this state of war must involve some assurance that people generally do not have these attitudes. It seems reasonable to interpret Hobbes as holding that the first thing that must be done is to make it generally known that people have peace-seeking attitudes. The first law of nature can then be understood as enjoining people to take on these peace-seeking attitudes, and of letting others know that they have these attitudes rather than the pro-war attitudes of what could be called a first-striker.

---

[29] EW III 113, Tuck 88–89.

V. The Problem of the First Peace-Seeker

From a Hobbesian perspective, while there may be a temporary disadvantage in being publicly known as less inclined toward violence than others in one's society, this disadvantage can be greatly (although not completely) offset by also making it publicly known that one retains a pro-attitude toward violence used in one's self-defense. Thus, while the first person to display peace-seeking attitudes opens himself or herself up to possible exploitation by those who do not have such attitudes, such a person with pacifist attitudes does not risk his or her life, and hence cannot properly be said to be acting irrationally, especially given the potential for long-term gain that will result once one person has publicly indicated that he or she does not have pro-war attitudes.

It might be claimed that someone having pacifist attitudes still does not act rationally in the state of nature, since such a person places herself at a disadvantage relative to others. Any voluntary move to disadvantage oneself is seemingly at odds with the general principle regulating the state of nature: act only on that maxim that will advance your own interests. I have given reasons for thinking that even Hobbes did not hold to such a bold principle. But even if we accept this as the regulative principle of the state of nature, there is reason to think that this principle will not rule out the development of pacifist attitudes. Indeed, the larger point of this chapter is that Hobbes and contemporary Hobbesians are committed to view the development of moral attitudes as a reasonable strategy, perhaps despite what seemed to be the case earlier in this chapter, even in the rarified air of the state of nature.

Kavka claimed that the laws of nature—those precepts of reason that are coextensive with morality within the state of nature—should all be understood as having an important qualification which would tell against my claims so far. He says: "An agent is required to act as the main clauses of these laws of nature require (that is, is obliged *in foro externo*) when and only when others are doing the same."[30] In the spirit of his Hobbesian enterprise, Kavka also endorses this claim that he attributes to Hobbes. But, in my view, Kavka merely exacerbates the problem of first performance,

---

[30] Kavka, *Hobbesian Moral and Political Theory*, p. 346.

and is thus not in keeping with the spirit of Hobbes's project. For now, not only moral behavior but also moral dispositions and attitudes are not rational to be developed unless someone else developed them first. Yet this would literally never happen, since on this view it is always irrational for any person first to contemplate doing so unless it is clear that others will do the same.

This problem—which we might call the problem of the first peace-seeker (to distinguish it from the problem of the first performer)—only becomes important if we think that it is a disadvantage, on balance, not to be continuously aggressive, or to be ready to be aggressive, toward others in the state of nature. It is true that Hobbes claims that conquest and pre-emptive attack are justified by a broad right of self-preservation,[31] but it seems to me that he could not recommend such a strategy to all who populate the state of nature. Conquest and pre-emptive strikes, unlike purely defensive uses of violence, do not clearly advance long-term self-preservation and are thus not clearly rational strategies to pursue. This is true even in situations where others are engaging in these non-defensive uses of violence. The first peace-seeker is a rational person in that he or she stands ready to try to break the cycle of escalating aggression (aggression/defense/counter-aggression) as a first move toward the establishment of peace—something that every rational person desires. Unlike the "first performer" who must literally lay down his or her arms, the "first peace-seeker," on balance, does not risk major short-term loss.

Thus we can begin to see why Hobbes claims that the first and most fundamental law of nature (elsewhere called precept of reason) is "to seek peace." As he is quick to add, it is not reasonable to lay down one's right to all things if others do not do likewise, "for that were to expose himself to prey, which no man is bound to, rather than to dispose himself to peace."[32] One possible reading of this passage is that Hobbes is contrasting the act of first performance that exposes a person to prey, with the disposition or attitude toward peace, which does not necessarily involve such a risk. In any event, it seems to me that such a position is not inconsistent with what Hobbes has held, at least on the interpretation I offered above, in *Leviathan*, *De Cive*, and *The Elements of Law*.

---

[31] Kavka, *Hobbesian Moral and Political Theory*, p. 316.
[32] EW III 118, Tuck, 92.

The advantage to be gained by first indicating that one has peace-seeking attitudes is considerable. By one's example, one helps others to develop similar attitudes, and this opens the door to the kind of limited trust upon which the social contract seems to be based. It is not my contention that such attitudes are sufficient for getting out of the state of nature. As Hobbes says, we will still need a power strong enough to overawe in order for first performance to be a rational strategy. But why would one even think of being a first performer if one continued to have pro-war attitudes. True, fear of the continued state of war might bring us quite a ways, but it is not enough to get the idea of cooperation first implanted. Such an idea seems sorely lacking when everyone has pro-war attitudes.

It could be contended that the mere desire for long-term self-preservation is sufficient to motivate people to begin to think of mutual contracts enforced by a sovereign. Such a strategy, however, neglects the very powerful short-term motivators of anger, avarice, and revenge. It is true that fear of the sovereign will offset these motivations in civil society, but why would people think of subjecting themselves to a sovereign in the first place if their pro-war attitudes remained and were focused only on the short-term? As long as a person's attention remains focused on the short-term, fear is unlikely to provide sufficient motivation. Something very strong is needed to overcome these pro-war attitudes long enough for people even to consider establishing a society. And while there may be other possibilities I have not considered, a fundamental change in disposition or attitude, which Hobbes himself discusses as the first law of nature leading to peace, can provide the missing motivation. Such attitude changes must normally be included along with the fear of the continuing state of war, but such changes are not themselves sufficient for achieving peace. In general though, people not only have to see the desirability of getting out of the state of nature, but have to be inclined to stop being war-like, which means that they must develop peace-seeking attitudes.

I will conclude this chapter with some brief remarks on why public displays of the attitudes of pacifism are not enough, in Hobbes's view, to secure peace. In Chapter 17 of *Leviathan*, Hobbes clearly indicates that the laws of nature are not sufficient to secure peace, since people will continue to be driven by their natural passions of "partiality, pride, revenge, and the like. And covenants, without the sword, are but words, and of no strength to secure a man at all."[33] While Hobbes does provide, I believe, good reason to adopt pacifist attitudes, adopting these attitudes still puts us in no better shape than those who promise, without consideration (as is true of assumpsit), to keep to a bargain. The reason for this, in both cases, is the same: the signs by which a person indicates pro-peace attitudes or good-faith promising are not, by themselves, of the sort that it is reasonable to trust. In addition, a power to overawe is also necessary on a Hobbesian account.

Think of the types of sign which can be used publicly to display one's pro-peace attitudes. A person could make a speech to this effect, but this would be "mere words" which could be as easily withdrawn as they could be made, as Hobbes tells us. There could be some act, such as laying down one's weapons, but such an act, insofar as it opens up a person to attack in a way that merely expressing an attitude does not, is an unreasonable thing to do in the state of nature. There are no signs that can be used that do not fall prey either to the charge that they are mere words and hence do not go far enough, or that they are acts of first performance and hence go too far. From all of this it follows that Hobbes's defense of the importance of peace-seeking attitudes does not replace his defense of the strong arm of the sovereign.

Finally, it is also important to realize that Hobbes's defense of pacifist attitudes is not a defense of pacifism itself. The pacifist is normally thought to be someone who takes the actions which Hobbes thinks it unreasonable to take, at least in the state of nature, whereas the person with pacifist attitudes merely stands ready to act in a pacifist manner, but only when certain conditions have been met. Yet, standing ready to act in a pacifist manner is already quite an advance over those avaricious souls who are normally thought to populate Hobbes's state of nature. Overcoming war-like dispositions is the first step toward the attainment of peace, for it makes people more likely to search for those conditions under which peaceful conduct can become rational. If people do not follow the first law of nature, and if they thereby retain their pro-war attitudes, they will not think of cooperation and trust as valuable things to be pursued, and they will not search for the context in which cooperation and trust can be reasonably undertaken.

Hobbes is not the great defender of the unlimited use of violence he is often portrayed to be, and he is also not a defender of the value of pro-war

[33] EW III 154, Tuck 117.

attitudes, but he does remain skeptically worried about the possible hidden intents of even the most apparently peace-loving people. Nonetheless, as I have tried to show, Hobbes thinks that developing pacifist attitudes is one of the most rational things to do in the state of nature. He thereby provides a fascinating prudential and moral defense of peace-seeking attitudes—a defense that is especially poignant today.

Concluding Thoughts

Hobbes has been studied by those interested in politics and morality for three and a half centuries; yet he has often been dismissed or neglected by those interested in law, or misunderstood by those interested in international relations. I have found Hobbes's views on law to be fascinating for more than thirty-five years, since my graduate studies; and my interest in Hobbes on international relations extends back further, to my undergraduate years. Throughout my career I have thought about law and politics through a lens supplied by Hobbes, and now I feel I have paid my dues by defending him against his harshest detractors. But even those who have criticized Hobbes have normally paid respect for his intellect. Let me end, in the remaining few pages of this book, by attempting to explain what I think is Hobbes's enduring appeal.

First, Hobbes is a systematic thinker of the sort that is nearly unheard of among today's philosophers. This explains, in part, why he is such fun to teach. My students generally begin by being very skeptical of my enthusiasm for Hobbes, who after all is regarded by many to be the worst of the Early Modern thinkers for deriving reactionary views supposedly from universal premises. Very quickly, however, students have become entangled in Hobbes's web, as he attempts to provide a coherent view that provides intriguing answers to most of the debated political questions, and to do so often from metaphysical or epistemological premises that students of philosophy expect and yet rarely find. It is the systematic character of his writing that is the most intoxicating. On some level, all the parts fit together, and one gets a metaphysics, an epistemology, an ethics, a politics, a jurisprudence, and to a certain extent, a theology. So in order to approach Hobbes on his own terms one has to commit oneself not just to some political beliefs but to a world view.

Second, like a very good novelist or poet, Hobbes rewards the reader each new time one encounters his writing, no matter how many times that is (and in my case it is an annual event to reread *Leviathan*). The views are intricate and the arguments incredibly subtle. But what is true of very few other philosophers, Hobbes's views evolve before your eyes, changing if only in minor ways but later cumulatively in major ways, the further one gets into his texts. Stylistically, Hobbes is a truly great writer—perhaps one of the very best to have written in the English language. And yet, to give him his due one must also remember that he was the first to write philosophy in the English vernacular.

Third, rarely has there been a philosopher whose thought experiments were so naturally suited to philosophizing, especially about politics, morality, and law. Like Plato's cave or the ring of Gyges, Hobbes's state of nature and social contract captivate. Today, it is rare indeed to find such imagination in philosophical writing. Arendt, Nozick, and Rawls could spark the imagination as well, but it remains to be seen whether or not they will still be doing so three and a half centuries later, as Hobbes is still doing. Those who are open to be captivated will be held breathless. There are arguments presented to support nearly everything, so that if one is analytically inclined one will definitely not be disappointed.

Fourth, while I had spent several years thinking of myself as a student of philosophy, it was not until I encountered Hobbes in a serious way, and found myself fighting with him over and over in my doctoral dissertation, that I began to think of myself as a philosopher. My impression is that this is often true of graduate students who have a serious encounter with Hobbes's writings. He presents his ideas in such a way that one is forced to fight with him, if for no other reason than to convince oneself that his seemingly audacious ideas could hold any truth, or to try to find a more plausible interpretation through his voluminous writings.

Finally, Hobbes is thoroughly engaged with the world around him, especially the political and legal events of his time. When I was in graduate school it was controversial to try to bring one's philosophizing into contact with contemporary events. But I, and many other younger philosophers, rebelled, and I found in Hobbes a fellow traveler who was also an inspiring model of how to do very good philosophy but still connect with that world. Today, Hobbes would fit in well with the very best of political philosophers, who are definitely no longer reluctant to bring theory to practice. In this sense, Quentin Skinner is right to stress Hobbes's rhetoric, though I have preferred to avoid it in this book, more out of ignorance of what rhetoric is all about than out of a disdain for those who can mix rhetoric with reasoned argumentation.

In this book I have tried to provide my own somewhat idiosyncratic reading of Hobbes's texts. I was inspired, as I have often said throughout the book, by how badly Hobbes has been misread or misunderstood, especially by those who have written with an ideological agenda, but not always. I regard the work of Hedley Bull, Hans Morgenthau, and Charles Beitz as some of the best work in international relations theory. But I also found it amazing that they and I could read Hobbes's texts and find such a different story. This is not meant as a criticism of them or of Hobbes. In my view, the very best philosophy is so complex and nuanced that several different stories can be constructed from its parts.

In the course of this book I have developed two main lines of interpretation of Hobbes that are not often advanced. First, I have argued that Hobbes is not a strict legal positivist, as he is so often characterized. But I have also argued that he is also not a natural lawyer—at least not of the sort that the scholastics were. Instead, he holds a position very similar to that of Lon Fuller, who famously said that natural law was best understood as a procedural doctrine rather than a substantive one. Hobbes's views about the limits of lawmakers are nearly all procedural, even as they are also connected to his unique view of secular laws of nature.

In the introduction I surveyed the main ways in which, on my interpretation, Hobbes argued for a limited Leviathan. One of the crucial issues concerns what to think of the concept of equity in Hobbes's writings. For Hobbes, equity is primarily a law of nature—at least in *Leviathan* and *De Cive*—and in this respect, equity is a limit on sovereign law-making that is enforced largely by self-imposed limits by sovereigns on their own actions. But in Hobbes's later work, especially the *Dialogue*, equity as a natural law concept is linked somewhat with the courts of equity in seventeenth-century England. It is, of course, still true that the sovereign controls these courts, but Hobbes sees equity courts as the place where unfairness or arbitrariness, as a matter of iniquity, can be countered, even though not as a matter of injustice.

We can see the different strains in Hobbes's position if we again confront the quotation from *De Cive* that is the epigram at the beginning of my book:

> Most men grant, that a government ought not to be divided; but they would have it moderated and bounded by some limits. Truly it is very reasonable it should be so...for my part, I wish that not only kings, but all other persons, endued with supreme authority, would so temper themselves...within the limits of natural and divine law.[1]

Hobbes begins this quotation by affirming that it is reasonable that a government be moderated or bounded by some limits. On first sight, this looks to be the kind of remark by Hobbes that would cause serious trouble for interpreters who see his sovereign as an absolute ruler who is not limited.

Yet the second part of the quotation from the epigram seems greatly to lessen the impact of the limitations on sovereignty, since we are told that these limitations are those that are self-imposed. As I said in the introductory chapter, if the point is that sovereigns are counseled to temper themselves, then this does not look much like a serious limitation on sovereignty. But then the third part of the quotation can be seen to address this worry insofar as Hobbes links limitations on sovereignty with the strictures of natural and divine law, which in his view are universally binding. And so we are back to the question of how binding are the principles of natural law, especially the principle of equity.

I have argued that Hobbes can be seen as taking equity more seriously than other laws of nature because of the things he says about equity in *Leviathan* and especially in the *Dialogue*. First, equity is the main law of nature that binds the sovereign. At least in part this is because the sovereign is one who is to judge cases, or at least to appoint those who will judge cases, and equity is the principle that governs such matters when the application of the law to certain facts leads to results that were not those contemplated by those who drafted the law.

Equity has been understood, at least since Aristotle, to play this role in adjudication, and the development of equity in Anglo-American jurisprudence has mirrored this. Indeed, the initial head of the Court of Equity, the Lord Chancellor, was initially a cleric who was thought to be best able to apply the divine and natural law to cases that had already been subjected to adjudication on strictly positivist grounds. In the century before Hobbes wrote, the head of the Court of Equity was still the King's Chancellor,

---

[1] EW II 96 note, ch.VII, note to para. 4.

but the role was filled with non-clerics, who, like Thomas Moore, were appointed for their status as moral exemplars in English society as well as for their legal knowledge.

This first main issue that my book has investigated—namely, whether and to what extent the principles of equity really bind the Hobbesian sovereign—can be understood by noting that Thomas Moore, though appointed by King Henry VIII, and dependent on this sovereign for his power as Chancellor and head of a Court of Equity, was able to exercise independent judgment and counter the wishes of the King concerning his desire to have his marriage annulled. Ultimately, the King succeeded in having Moore replaced by someone who would do the King's bidding, and of course, Moore was powerless to prevent his own beheading. But Thomas Moore is remembered for the exercise of his independent judgment, even in the face of the King's wrath.

It is tempting to think that Hobbes has Henry VIII in mind when he urges sovereign princes to limit themselves and follow the principle of equity lest they weaken themselves and undermine their sovereignty, as seems to have happened to Henry VIII. In a certain sense, Henry should have imposed limits on himself consistent with natural and divine law. When he did not, the consequences were that he ran afoul of his own Chancellor—the conscience of the King and the one entrusted to uphold equity. As the King had appointed the Chancellor, the King could fire him and appoint someone else. But in my view, Hobbes would say that the King had acted unreasonably and imprudently, in addition to violating moral law. The Hobbesian sovereign thus risked political turmoil and dissent that would weaken his sovereign power and make it harder for him to act in the interest of the people's safety. But it is not clear how much more one can say from a Hobbesian standpoint. If this means that Henry VIII was an absolute sovereign, then at the very least one should reassess what exactly the term "absolute" means here. I argued for a stronger conclusion: namely, that the sovereign is truly limited by such considerations, but not necessarily in the way that contemporary scholars often think of limitations on sovereignty today.

My second main line of interpretation is to show that Hobbes's view of international affairs is neither that of a realist nor a cosmopolitan. Hobbes is not a realist who advocates an amoral or immoral international policy. He opens the door for the kind of limited social contract of States or of sovereigns that is quite a bit like what we find today. The best way to see this is to use the analogy between States and individual persons who find their way out of the state of nature by forming a commonwealth. Individual States could do the same, especially since Hobbes says that the risks of cooperation in forming a society among States at the international level are not as great as at the level of forming a society among individual persons.

And Hobbes is definitely not a cosmopolitan, since he is not a proponent of a world State, though he does not completely rule this option out altogether. Hobbes clearly counsels against sovereigns giving up sovereignty, indeed Hobbes talks of the duty that sovereigns have not to weaken their power. Hobbes makes it clear that sovereigns act wrongly when they deny themselves some "necessary power" for maintaining the peace of the commonwealth,[2] and he is also clear that it would not be "legal" for a sovereign to agree to a power that could overawe it.[3]

Like his contemporary Grotius, Hobbes is best seen as a defender of what is today called "the society of States" view[4]—a middle position between realism and cosmopolitanism in international relations theory. I argued that Hobbes did, and a Hobbesian easily could, support loose associations of States, or leagues as Hobbes put it,[5] such as exist today. Of course, realists could accept such a world. But in my view, Hobbes would support such a world order on moral as well as prudential grounds, in ways that are quite contrary to the way that many realists understand international relations, especially by those who think that ultimately those relations are grounded only in self-interest and that we are still left with a rough anarchy among states.

The linchpin of the Hobbesian account of international affairs that I develop is that serious consequences can follow when sovereigns violate equity, in the sense that they fail to protect their subjects or citizens. As I have indicated many times, the chief duty of the sovereign on Hobbes's account is to provide for the safety of the people. When the safety of the people cannot be maintained, then Hobbes is clear that the obligation of the citizenry also is at an end.

[2] EW III 309, Tuck 222.
[3] EW III 223, Tuck 163–164.
[4] See Simon Caney, *Justice Beyond Borders: A Global Political Theory*, Oxford: Oxford University Press, 2005, pp 10–13.
[5] EW III 223, Tuck 163.

> The obligation of subjects to the sovereign, is said to last as long as, and no longer, than the power lasteth, by which he is able to protect them. For the right men have by nature to protect themselves, when none else can protect them, can by no covenant be relinquished...The end of obedience is protection...And though sovereignty, in the intention of them that make it, be immortal; yet is it in its own nature, not only subject to violent death, by foreign war; but also through the ignorance and passions of men.[6]

In such cases where the sovereign cannot or does not protect the subjects or citizens, there is a sense that rulers abdicate sovereignty.

When sovereignty is abdicated there is an opening for international organizations even to take on the role of prosecuting rulers (now effectively deposed) that attack or fail to protect the citizenry. As Hobbes says, when

> there is no farther protection of subjects in their loyalty, then is the commonwealth dissolved, and every man at liberty to protect himself by such sources as his discretion shall suggest unto him...For he that want protection, may seek it anywhere.[7]

If subjects or citizens can seek protection anywhere once their own sovereign fails to provide such protection, it is certainly possible for people to seek safety and peace through some international institution.

A Hobbesian position, of the sort I have defended, is not antithetical to international institutions nor even to international leagues set up to achieve common goals or purposes. Indeed, I have argued elsewhere that there is an interesting Hobbesian argument in favor of international criminal law for such acts that constitute crimes against humanity.[8] I also think that Hobbes's ideas about cruelty can be mined to support the types of prohibitions found today in the sources of International Humanitarian Law. Such arguments could also be extended further to international organizations such as the World Trade Organization, especially given what Hobbes says about the importance of distribution and trade for the "sustentation of a

---

[6] EW III
[7] EW III 321–322, Tuck 230.
[8] See Larry May, *Crimes Against Humanity: A Normative Account*, New York: Cambridge University Press, 2005, Chapter 1.

commonwealth."[9] Thus, it seems odd indeed that Hobbes has been characterized as the *bête noire* of international law.

Reading Hobbes in a sympathetic way, as I have tried to do, leads to significant challenges to the orthodox ways that Hobbes has been characterized in law and international affairs, as well as in many other areas of scholarship. This is not to say, of course, that all these orthodox interpretations of Hobbes have been shown to be incorrect. That has not been my purpose. Instead, I have simply tried to determine what can be said for an alternative reading of Hobbes that is also supported by a reading of his texts.

I am sure that most of my readers will wish to disagree with me about the broad interpretive arguments that are contained in this book. But that does not bother me. What I hope to have done is to challenge my readers to look once more at Hobbes's texts. We can all benefit from yet another reading of *Leviathan*, and for most, I imagine, a first look at the *Dialogue*. I am grateful to have found Hobbes early in my studies and to have learned so much over my career from his engrossing texts. I wish the same to anyone else who embarks on the same journey.

[9] EW III 237, Tuck 174.

Bibliography

Andrew, Edward G., "Hobbes on Conscience Within the Law and Without," *Canadian Journal of Political Science*, vol. 32, no. 2, June 1999, pp. 203–225.

Arend, Anthony Clark, and Beck, Robert J., *International Law and the Use of Force*, New York: Routledge, 1993.

Aquinas, Saint Thomas, *Treatise on Law: Summa Theologica, Questions 90–97*, Washington, DC: Regnery Gateway, 1970.

Baier, Annette, "Secular Faith," *Canadian Journal of Philosophy*, vol. 10, no. 1, 1980.

Baildon, W.P. (ed.), *The Publications of the Selden Society* (V896), Select Cases in Chancery 1364–1471 10, London, 1896.

Bassiouni, M. Cherif, "The Perennial Conflict Between International Criminal Justice and Realpolitik," *Georgia State Law Review*, vol. 22, no. 3, Spring 2006, pp. 541–560.

Beitz, Charles, *Political Theory and International Relations*, Princeton, NJ: Princeton University Press, 1979, 1999.

Berman, Harold J., *Law and Revolution, Vol. II*, Cambridge, MA: Harvard University Press, 2003.

Bodin, Jean, *The Six Bookes of a Commonwealle*, ed. K. D. McRae, Cambridge, MA: Harvard University Press, 1962.

Bowie, John, *Hobbes and His Critics: A Study in Seventeenth-Century Constitutionalism*, London: Jonathan Cape, 1951.

Bramhall, John, "The Catching of Leviathan, Or the Great Whale," in G. A. J. Rogers (ed.), *Leviathan: Contemporary Responses to the Political Theory of Thomas Hobbes*, Bristol: Thoemmes Press, 1995.

Bull, Hedley, *The Anarchical Society*, New York: Columbia University Press, 1977.

Caney, Simon, *Justice Beyond Borders: A Global Political Theory*, Oxford: Oxford University Press, 2005.

Clark, Andrew (ed.), *"Brief Lives" Chiefly of Contemporaries, set down by John Aubrey between the years of 1669 and 1696*, Oxford: Clarendon Press, 1898.

Coady, C. A. J., "Objecting Morally," *The Journal of Ethics*, vol. 1, no. 4, 1997, pp. 375–397.

Coady, C. A. J., *Morality and Political Violence*, Cambridge: Cambridge University Press, 2008.

Coke, Edward, *Institutes of the Laws of England*, London: J. & W. T. Clarke, 1823.

Coke, Edward, "Prohibitions del Roy" (1607), in *Selected Writings and Speeches of Sir Edward Coke*, ed. Stephen Sheppard, Indianapolis, IN: Liberty Fund, 2003, vol. I, pp. 478–481.

Cromarie, Alan, and Skinner, Quentin (eds.), *Thomas Hobbes: Writings on Common Law and Hereditary Right*, Oxford: Oxford University Press, 2005.

Curran, Eleanor, *Reclaiming the Rights of the Hobbesian Subject*, New York: Palgrave/Macmillan, 2007.

Darwall, Stephen, *The British Moralists and the Internal "Ought": 1640–1740*, Cambridge: Cambridge University Press, 1995.

Deigh, John, "Reason and Ethics in Hobbes's *Leviathan*," *Journal of the History of Philosophy*, vol. 34, no. 1, January 1996, pp. 33–60.

Dold, G.W. F., *Stipulations for a Third Party*, London: Stevens and Sons, 1948.

Dyzenhaus, David, "Hobbes and the Legitimacy of Law," *Law and Philosophy*, vol. 20, no. 5, September 2001, pp. 461–498.

Eachard, John, *Mr. Hobbes's State of Nature Considered (1672)*, ed. Peter Ure, Liverpool: Liverpool University Press, 1958.

Fabre, Cecile, "Guns, Food, and Liability to Attack in War," *Ethics*, vol. 120, October 2009, pp. 36–63.

Finkelstein, Claire, "A Puzzle about Hobbes on Self-Defense," *Pacific Philosophical Quarterly*, vol. 82, nos. 3–4, 2000, pp. 332–361.

Finkelstein, Claire (ed.), *Hobbes on Law*, Surrey: Ashgate Press, 2005.

Fox-Decent, Evan, "Hobbes's Relational Theory: Beneath Power and Consent," in David Dyzenhaus and Thomas Poole (eds.), *Hobbes and the Law*, Cambridge: Cambridge University Press, 2012.

Frowe, Helen, "Killing the Red Cross," Paper presented at annual meeting of the Society for Applied Philosophy, Manchester, July 2011.

Fuller, Lon, "Positivism and Fidelity to Law," *Harvard Law Review*, vol. 71, no. 4, February 1958, pp. 630–672.

Fuller, Lon, *The Morality of Law*, New Haven, CT: Yale University Press, 1964.

Gauthier, David P., *The Logic of Leviathan*, Oxford: Oxford University Press, 1969.

Gauthier, David P., "Three Against Justice: The Foole, The Sensible Knave, and the Lydian Shepherd," *Midwest Studies in Philosophy*, vol. 7, 1982.

Geiss, Robin, "The Principle of Proportionality: 'Force Protection' as a Military Advantage," *Israel Law Review*, vol. 45, no. 1, 2012, pp. 78–89.

Gert, Bernard, *Hobbes: Prince of Peace*, Cambridge: Polity Press, 2010.

Gert, Bernard (ed.), *Man and Citizen*, Garden City, NY: Anchor Books, 1972.

Goldsmith, M. M., *Hobbes's Science of Politics*, New York: Columbia University Press, 1966.

Green, Leslie C., "International Regulation of Armed Conflicts," in M. Cherif Bassiouni (ed.), *International Criminal Law: Vol. 1, Crimes*, 2nd. ed., Ardsley, New York: Transactional Publishers, 1999.

Grotius, Hugo, *De Jury Belli Ac Pacis (On the Law of War and Peace) (1625)*, trans. Francis W. Kelsey, Oxford: Clarendon Press, 1925.

Grotius, Hugo, *De Jure Belli Ac Pacis (On the Rights of War and Peace) (1625)*, ed. Richard Tuck, Indianapolis, IN: Liberty Fund, 2005.

Hart, H. L. A., *The Concept of Law*, Oxford: Clarendon Press, 1960.

Hobbes, Thomas, "De Cive," in Sir William Molesworth (ed.), *The English Works of Thomas Hobbes, Vol.* II, London: John Bohn, 1839.

Hobbes, Thomas, "Leviathan," in Sir William Molesworth (ed.), *The English Works of Thomas Hobbes Vol.* III, London: John Bohn, 1839.

Hobbes, Thomas, "De Corpore Politico, or the Elements of Law," in Sir William Molesworth (ed.), *The English Works of Thomas Hobbes, Vol. IV*, London: John Bohn, 1839.

Hobbes, Thomas, "Human Nature or the Fundamental Elements of Policy," in Sir William Molesworth (ed.), *The English Works of Thomas Hobbes, Vol. IV*, London: John Bohn, 1839.

Hobbes, Thomas, "A Dialogue Between a Philosopher and a Student of the Common Laws of England," in Sir William Molesworth (ed.), *The English Works of Thomas Hobbes, Vol. VI*, London: John Bohn, 1839.

Hobbes, Thomas, "Behemoth: The History of the Causes of the Civil Wars of England," in Sir William Molesworth (ed.), *The English Works of Thomas Hobbes, vol. VI*, London: John Bohn, 1839.

Hobbes, Thomas, *A Dialogue Between a Philosopher and a Student of the Common Laws of England*, ed. Joseph Cropsey, Chicago: University of Chicago Press, 1971.

Hobbes, Thomas, "De Homine," in B. Gert (ed.), *Man and Citizen*, Garden City, New York: Anchor Books, 1972.

Hobbes, Thomas, *Leviathan*, ed. Richard Tuck, Cambridge: Cambridge University Press, 1996.

Hobbes, Thomas, "Questions Relative to Hereditary Right," in Alan Cromarie and Quentin Skinner (eds.), *Thomas Hobbes: Writings on Common Law and Hereditary Right*, Oxford: Clarendon Press, 2005.

Hoekstra, Kinch, "Hobbes on Law, Nature, and Reason," *Journal of the History of Philosophy*, vol. 41, no. 1, 2003, pp. 111–120.

Hoekstra, Kinch, "The *de facto* Turn in Hobbes's Political Philosophy," in Tom Sorell and Luc Foisneau (eds.), *Leviathan After 350 Years*, Oxford: Clarendon Press, 2004.

Holdsworth, William S., *The History of English Law*, 5 vols., London and Boston: Methuen, 1924.

Holmes, Oliver Wendell, *The Common Law*, ed. Mark DeWolfe Howe, Boston, MA: Little Brown, 1963.

Hood, Francis C., *The Divine Politics of Thomas Hobbes*, Oxford: Oxford University Press, 1964.

Hooker, Richard, *The Laws of Ecclesiastical Polity*, ed. R.A. Houk, New York: Columbia University Press, 1931.

Kant, Immanuel, *Perpetual Peace: A Philosophical Essay*, trans. Mary Campbell Smith, London: Allen & Unwin, 1903.
Kavka, Gregory S., *Hobbesian Moral and Political Theory*, Princeton, New Jersey: Princeton University Press, 1986.
Klimchuk, Dennis, "Hobbes on Equity," in David Dyzenhaus and Thomas Poole (eds.), *Hobbes and the Law*, Cambridge: Cambridge University Press, 2012.
Ladenson, Robert, "In Defense of a Hobbesian Conception of Law," *Philosophy and Public Affairs*, vol. 9, no. 2, Winter 1980, pp. 134–159.
Lloyd, S.A., *Morality in the Philosophy of Thomas Hobbes: Cases in the Law of Nature*, New York: Cambridge University Press, 2009.
Locke, John, *Essay Concerning Human Understanding (1689)*, ed. Peter H. Nidditch, Oxford: Oxford University Press, 1975.
Locke, John, *Second Treatise of Government (1690)*, ed. C.B. Macpherson, Indianapolis, Indiana: Hackett Publishing Co., 1980.
McMahan, Jeff, *Killing in War*, Oxford: Oxford University Press, 2009.
McPherson, Lionel, "Innocence and Responsibility in War," *Canadian Journal of Philosophy*, vol. 34, 2004, 485–506.
Maitland, F.W., and Pollock, Sir Frederick, *The History of English Law Before the Time of Edward I*, 2nd ed., vol. 2, Cambridge: Cambridge University Press, 1909.
Malcolm, Noel, *Aspects of Hobbes*, Oxford: Oxford University Press, 2002.
May, Larry, *The Morality of Groups*, Notre Dame, IN: University of Notre Dame Press, 1987.
May, Larry, "Hobbes on Fidelity to Law," *Hobbes Studies*, vol. 5, no. 1, 1992, pp. 77–89.
May, Larry, *Crimes Against Humanity: A Normative Account*, New York: Cambridge University Press, 2005.
May, Larry, *War Crimes and Just War*, New York: Cambridge University Press, 2007.
May, Larry, "Contingent Pacifism and the Moral Risks of Participating in War," *Public Affairs Quarterly*, vol. 25, no. 2, April 2011, pp. 95–111.
May, Larry, "Contingent Pacifism and Selective Refusal," *Journal of Social Philosophy*, vol. 42, no. 1, Spring 2012, pp. 1–18.
May, Larry, *After War Ends: A Philosophical Perspective*, Cambridge: Cambridge University Press, 2012.
Molesworth, Sir William (ed.), *The English Works of Thomas Hobbes*, London: John Bohn, 1839.
Morgenthau, Hans, *Politics Among Nations*, New York: McGraw Hill, 1948.
Murphy, Mark, "Desire and Ethics in Hobbes's *Leviathan*: A Response to Professor Deigh," *Journal of the History of Philosophy*, vol. 38, no. 2, 2000, pp. 259–268.
Oakeshott, Michael, *Hobbes on Civil Association*, Berkeley: University of California Press, 1975.

Osiel, Mark, *The End of Reciprocity*, New York: Cambridge University Press, 2010.
Peters, R.S. (ed.), *Body, Man, and Citizen*, New York: Collier Books, 1962.
Pettit, Philip, *Made with Words: Hobbes on Language, Mind, and Politics*, Princeton, NJ: Princeton University Press, 2008.
Plamenatz, John, *Man and Society*, 2 vols., New York: McGraw Hill, 1963.
Pollock, Frederick, "Reflections by the Lord Chief Justice Hale on Mr. Hobbes His Dialogue on the Laws," *The Law Quarterly Review*, 1921, pp. 274–303.
Poole, Thomas, "Hobbes on Law and Prerogative," in David Dyzenhaus and Thomas Poole (eds.), *Hobbes and the Law*, Cambridge: Cambridge University Press, 2012.
Prall, Stuart E., "The Development of Equity in Tudor England," *The American Journal of Legal History*, vol. 8, no. 1, 1964, pp. 1–19.
Rawls, John, *A Theory of Justice*, Cambridge, MA: Harvard University Press, 1971.
Rodin, David, *Self-Defense and War*, Oxford: Oxford University Press, 2002.
Rodin, David, "The Moral Equality of Soldiers: Why *In Bello* Asymmetry is Half Right," in David Rodin and Henry Shue (eds.), *Just and Unjust Warriors*, Oxford: Oxford University Press, 2007.
Rousseau, Jean-Jacques, *The Social Contract and Discourses*, trans. G. D. H. Cole, New York: Everyman Library, 1913.
Sartre, Jean-Paul, *Critique of Dialectical Reason (1960)*, trans. Alan Sheridan-Smith, London: Verso/NLB Press, 1976.
Shue, Henry, "Torture," *Philosophy & Public Affairs*, vol. 7, no. 2, 1978, pp. 124–143.
Skinner, Quentin, *Reason and Rhetoric in the Philosophy of Hobbes*, Cambridge: Cambridge University Press, 1996.
Skinner, Quentin, *Visions of Politics III: Hobbes and Civil Science*, Cambridge: Cambridge University Press, 2002.
Skinner, Quentin, *Hobbes and Republican Liberty*, Cambridge: Cambridge University Press, 2008.
Sorell, Tom, *Hobbes*, London: Routledge and Kegan Paul, 1986, 2006.
Sorell, Tom, "The Burdensome Freedom of Sovereigns," in Tom Sorell and Luc Foisneau (eds.), *Leviathan After 350 Years*, Oxford: Oxford University Press, 2004.
Sreedhar, Susanne, *Hobbes on Resistance: Defying the Leviathan*, Cambridge: Cambridge University Press, 2010.
Strauss, Leo and Cropsey, Joseph (eds.), *History of Political Philosophy*, Chicago: Rand McNally & Company, 1963.
Taylor, A. E., "The Ethical Doctrine of Hobbes," *Philosophy*, vol. 13, no. 52, October 1938, pp. 406–424.
Taylor, A. E., "The Ethical Doctrine," in K. C. Brown (ed.), *Hobbes Studies*, Oxford: Basil Blackwell, 1965, pp. 35–55.

Thompson, George and Williston, Samuel, *Williston on Contracts*, 2nd ed., New York: Barker, Voorhis and Co., 1936.

Tuck, Richard, *Philosophy and Government 1572–1651*, Cambridge: Cambridge University Press, 1993.

von Gierke, Otto, *The Development of Political Theory*, trans. Bernard Freyd, New York: W.W. Norton, 1939.

van Mill, David, *Liberty, Rationality, and Agency in Hobbes's Leviathan*, Albany, NY: State University of New York, 2001.

Walzer, Michael, *Just and Unjust Wars*, New York: Basic Books, 1977.

Warrender, Howard, *The Political Philosophy of Hobbes: His Theory of Obligation*, Oxford: Clarendon Press, 1957.

Watkins, W. N., *Hobbes's System of Ideas: A Study in the Political Significance of Philosophical Theories*, London: Hutchinson & Co., 1965.

Yale, D. E. C., "Hobbes and Hale on Law, Legislation, and the Sovereign," *Cambridge Law Journal*, vol. 31, no. 1, April 1972, pp. 121–156.

Index

absolute
  power 22–3, 97
  rights 36–7
  sovereignty 21, 65, 83, 99, 141, 151–2, 243–4
actor 64, 140, 168
  artificial, see *artificial*
  v. author 160–2, 164
aggression 195, 212–14
Alexander the Great 94, 176
Allied forces 219–20
altruism 37, 45, 142
anarchy 12, 17, 126, 175, 183, 193–4, 245
anima legis 97
Aquinas, Thomas 16, 20, 30, 47, 90, 108–11
Arendt, Hannah 241
aristocracy 140, 165, 171
Aristotle 69, 88, 149, 243
artificial
  actor 156
  collective agent 54, 156, 164
  person 71, 90–1, 156, 160–1, 164, 166
  reason 90–2, 139–56
assembly 3, 9, 52, 54–5, 63–4, 71, 125, 140, 165–6, 168–71, 181
assumpsit 15, 21, 23–5, 49–50
Athens 95
Aubrey, John 88
Austin, John 108
authority
  and consent 34, 48, 65, 105
  and distributive justice 93
  and God 110–12
  and joint action 17, 156, 158, 160, 163–5, 171
  and law-making 10, 71, 76, 82, 92, 94, 96–8, 104, 106, 120, 127, 146, 148
  and the sovereign 2, 13, 25, 49, 66–8, 81, 84, 94, 99, 108, 119, 151, 154, 162, 172, 182, 232, 243
  and stage play analogy 161, 164
  and transfer rights 55, 161
  and war 206
  common 184
  criterion 103, 115, 119
  legal 16, 78, 95, 114, 122, 124–5, 147, 185, 207
  moral 36
  of Church and State 47
Authorization 2, 21, 34–5, 52, 55, 64–5, 106, 110, 116, 143, 155–72
  of law/of punishment 131

Bacon, Francis 78–9, 98, 116–17
Baildon, W. P. 29, 77
Bassiouni, Cherif 177

Bastille 17, 156, 168, 170
Behemoth 112
Beitz, Charles 175–6, 242
belief 135, 225
  and knowledge 91, 110
Bentham, Jeremy 108
Berns, Walter 224
Bodin, Jean 16, 21–3, 39
Bracton, H. 100, 104, 143
Bridge Over the River Kwai 219
Bull, Hedley 17, 177, 242

canon law 97, 111–13
Chancery Court 75, 77–9
Charles I 98–9
checks and balances 152
the Church 46–7, 97, 112
Cicero 87
civilians, see *soldiers*
civil law
  and concept of law 85, 103–4
  and international law 173, 181, 187, 193
  and laws of nature 5, 120, 122, 181
  and morality 34–5, 38–9, 43, 73, 83, 123
  creation of 71, 77
  "Of Civil Laws," see *Leviathan*
civil society 29, 38, 43–5, 46, 53, 58, 70–1, 73, 83, 94, 133, 157, 237
  international 42, 174, 179, 180, 182, 185–6, 193, 203
coercion 40, 70, 101, 119, 177, 186, 228
Coke, Edward
  and common law 87–9, 100, 113–16, 144
  and divided sovereignty 16–17, 79, 92, 96–8, 141, 143, 145–9, 151, 153–4
  and natural/artificial reason 90–1, 139, 142, 144, 207
collective action, see *joint action*
collective agency 156–7, 170, 172
collectivity 156, 159, 164–5, 167–8, 172
commonwealth
  and contracts 5, 63, 64, 68, 198
  and custom 91
  and international law 12, 181, 183, 187, 192, 245, 247
  and the sovereign 6, 8, 11, 132, 140
  by acquisition 96, 105
  disobedience in 127–30
  obligation to 35, 71, 111, 121–2, 131, 134
community 158, 172, 177, 180
compliance 233
conscience 5–6, 14–15, 20, 32–3, 35–6, 47, 79, 83, 124–5, 134, 189–90
  public/private 34–6, 124

conscientious objection 153
  selective 124–5, 132, 134, 137
conscription 128–9, 131, 133
consent
  and collectivities 163–5, 168
  and Grotius 157–9
  and international law 188, 190–1
  and Lever v. Heys, see Lever v. Heys
  and moral obligation 20
  and the origin of law 97
  and the sovereign 23, 48, 64–6, 97–8, 100, 166, 188
  implicit/explicit 22–3, 60, 105–6, 149, 151, 157, 166, 168
  to be governed 52–4
Constitution 39, 48–9, 62, 65–6, 95, 156
  American 152–4
constitutional
  contract 16, 49, 56–8, 60, 62–5, 68
  law 95
  limitation 14, 39, 62, 65, 68
  scheme 56, 66
contempt 200, 208–9, 219, 221
contentment 43, 197, 231
contradiction 15, 33, 37, 41, 46, 53, 114, 119, 228
  and absurdity 15, 33
contract
  law 21, 23
  original 52–5, 64, 102, 105
  social 2, 16, 20, 25, 27, 34, 40, 43–4, 46, 48–9, 51–66, 91, 109, 125, 179, 227, 237, 241, 244
  The Social Contract and Discourses, see Rousseau, Jean-Jacques
  theory 16, 20, 25, 48, 66
  third party beneficiary 24–5, 37, 49–52, 62, 64
Convention on Prohibitions or Restrictions on the Use of Certain Conventional Weapons (CCW) 216
coordination 168–71
  problem 152
Corfu Channel Case 216
cosmopolitanism 244–5
counsel 7–8, 180, 185, 206
Court of Star Chamber 79
covenant
  and contracts 57–63, 161, 179, 228, 237
  and justice 29, 70–1, 231
  and obedience 34, 43–4, 71, 122–3, 127, 133, 246
  and original contract 52, 102, 105
  based rulerships 22
  between states 11–12, 181, 191
crimes against humanity 246
Cromarie, Alan 86
Cromwell, Oliver 98, 147
Cropsey, Joseph 86, 89

cruelty 3, 7, 12–13, 29, 195–6, 199–202, 204–5, 207–15, 217, 220–2
custom 23, 28, 72, 85, 91, 97, 114, 144, 147–9, 151, 216

death penalty 16, 32, 87, 122, 125, 127–30
De Cive 3, 5, 13–15, 39, 68, 74, 89, 94, 108, 126, 164, 181, 200–1, 229–30, 232, 236
De Corpore Politico 14–15, 34, 124, 132–3, 232, 236
de facto theory 106
De Homine 75, 89, 133
De Jure Belli ac Pacis 157
democracy 48, 140, 165
desires 26, 46, 73, 106, 133, 140, 176, 208, 225, 237, 244
  and laws of nature 14, 33, 132, 198
  for commodious living 28, 226
  for peace 31–2, 135, 236
  natural 133, 142, 204, 229
deterrence 209, 219
A Dialogue Between a Philosopher and a Student of the Common Laws of England 1, 16, 247
  and Coke and Hale 86, 96, 116, 139, 141, 149
  and consent 105
  and *de facto* theory 106
  and equity 6, 9–10, 41, 67, 74, 77, 79, 82, 102, 242–3
  and international law 184, 187
  and laws of nature 76, 118
  and reason 207
  and the concept of law 38, 85, 89–90, 95, 99, 103–4, 107–8, 111–13, 117, 119
  and the sources of law 93–4
  and the sovereign 2–3, 17, 41, 68, 75, 120–1, 146, 151–2
  and war 195, 204–5
  "*De Legibus*" 89
  "Of the Laws of Reason" 87
  role of participants in 88, 100
dignity 217, 219
disability 215, 217–18, 221
disobedience 90, 107, 113, 118, 127–30, 133–8, 204
divine law 13–15, 76, 95, 109–10, 243–5
Divine Right of Kings 95, 141, 143, 153
Dold, G.W.F. 49–50
drunkenness 13, 200–1
due process 10–11
  procedural/substantive 9, 79
Dutton v. Poole 49
duty
  and contracts 24, 51, 62–3, 59
  and international law 186, 221
  in the state of nature 202, 229
  of the sovereign 2–6, 8, 11, 39–41, 51–2, 56, 65–6, 68, 73–4, 78, 81, 83, 120, 124–7, 134, 192, 245

Dyzenhaus, David 9, 121

Eachard, John 45, 224
egoism 133, 136, 141–2, 197
Egypt Uprising 167, 171
England 38, 45, 67, 69, 83, 94, 96, 98–9, 112, 145, 147, 149, 150–2
  laws of 1–2, 21, 23, 87–8, 94, 96–7, 99–100, 111–12, 114, 120, 143–7, 149, 242
English Civil War 98, 112
equality 5, 74, 151, 176–7, 198
  and rights 46, 178
  natural 44, 141, 179, 209, 228
  of treatment 6, 41, 73, 82, 209
  of prudence/strength/hope 25–6, 28
equity
  and justice 1, 16, 20, 25, 35, 67–84, 90, 119
  and law of nature 5–6, 67, 73, 76–8, 83, 109, 117, 119–20, 197, 242–3
  and law of reason 78, 81, 89, 97, 118, 120, 297
  and laws 41, 67, 69, 75, 79–81, 90, 114, 118–19, 121, 148, 198
  and the sovereign 1, 4, 6, 16, 35, 40, 67, 74, 81, 83, 109, 118, 242–3, 245
  Court of 6, 10, 70, 75, 77–80, 102, 118, 242–4
  principles of 41, 75, 82–3, 121, 243–4
execution, see *death penalty*
experience 26, 90–1, 116, 141–4, 185, 210
experts 141–4, 152
ex post facto 7, 107

fairness 41, 67, 69, 75, 78, 81–3, 118, 158, 242
fear 29, 123, 128, 187–8, 230–1
  of coercion 228
  of death 28, 87, 130, 179, 226
  of others 26–7, 184
  of punishment 37, 46, 125, 189
  of self-contradiction 15
  of the sovereign 132, 237
  of war 183, 237
Fenner, Edward 50
fidelity to law 14, 16, 122–38
first performer 57–9, 61–3, 174, 178–81, 188, 210, 227–8, 233, 235–7
first striker 234
Founding Fathers 153–4
freedom 71, 81, 145, 186, 216
free gift 59–60, 62–3, 68
free rider 125
Fool 43, 202, 231–3
Fuller, Lon 1, 9, 16, 42, 82, 121–2, 137–9, 154, 173, 242

Gauthier, David 131
Geneva Conventions 12, 17, 203, 216–18, 222
  Additional Protocol I 216
  Common Article III 217
Gert, Bernard 139–42, 153

gladiators 25, 174, 182–3, 192
God 3, 20, 22, 30, 45, 47, 96, 109–14, 117–19, 142–3, 215
good
  and morality 13, 37–8, 42, 141, 225, 229
  and peace 124, 137, 205
  common 137, 142, 166, 201
  laws 4–5, 40, 47, 74–5, 80
  of the people 5, 75, 81, 127, 137
  subjective theory of 28–9, 72–3
gratitude 5, 202, 206
Grotius, Hugo 156–60, 165–6, 172, 185, 195, 203, 214, 245

habit 72, 93, 204, 232
  of obedience 124, 132–3, 135
Hague Convention 215–16
happiness 40, 68, 126
Henry IV 114
Henry VIII 112, 244
heresy 87
Hitler, Adolf 177
Holdsworth, William 86
Hood, Francis C. 118
Hooker, Richard 16, 21–3, 53
humaneness 214, 217, 219, 221–2
human rights 189

identity
  common 169
  group 172
  shared 167
imperialism 94, 224
in foro externo, see *law of nature*
in foro interno, see *law of nature*
Institutes of the Laws of England 145
individualism 22, 54, 157, 159
intent
  authorial 156, 162–3, 167, 171–2
  and contract 54, 61
  and joint action 168
  and violation of law 127, 129–30, 135–6, 246
  in war 211, 213, 217
  of the law 80–1, 120
International Court of Justice (ICJ) 215–16
International Criminal Court (ICC) 173, 177, 183, 187–8, 194
international law
  criminal 12, 17–18, 173–4, 177, 180, 187, 190–1, 246
  humanitarian 216, 246
international relations 1, 11–13, 173–7, 181–2, 188–90, 193–5, 240, 242, 245

Japan 219–20
joint action 156–72
jus in bello 195, 198–9, 203, 213, 223
jus post bellum 220

just cause 181, 212
justice
 and goodness 5, 40, 74–5, 82
 and equity 1, 16, 20, 41, 67–83, 90, 119, 198, 242
 and laws of nature 5, 122, 231
 and the law 25, 27, 29, 90–1, 93, 107–8, 119, 131
 and the sovereign 4, 35, 40, 91, 94, 101–3
 courts of 77, 102, 118, 144
 international 184
 international court of, see *International Court of Justice (ICJ)*
 natural 6, 83, 123
justification
 and origin of law 95
 hypothetical 66
 moral 49, 66, 175
 of contracts 44, 48
 of cruelty 13, 200–1, 211, 217
 of disobedience 90, 122, 127–31, 134–6
 of international law 18
 of war 199, 217, 236
Justinian 94
just war 198–9, 210, 212, 217, 222
 Augustinian 217

Kant, Immanuel 42, 174, 184–7, 190, 193
Kavka, Gregory 233, 235
King in Parliament 147, 150, 152, 154
King's Bench 17, 24, 50, 77, 79, 86
knowledge 22, 29, 106, 115, 158, 207
 of authority 110–11
 of law 85, 88–92, 146, 244
 of morality 29–30, 44

law of nature
 and civil law 120, 122
 and contracts 11, 36, 44, 70, 191, 231
 and equity 5–6, 10, 68, 73, 75–6, 82, 118–19, 162, 197, 242–3
 and law of reason 30, 32, 44, 46, 68, 89, 117–18, 121, 132, 179, 196, 200, 202, 214, 222, 226, 229, 235
 and morality 4, 10, 28, 47, 123, 207, 226
 and right of nature 30–1
 and peace 18, 35, 45, 118, 120, 124, 126–7, 178, 193, 196–7, 200, 203, 205, 227, 230, 232, 234, 236–8
 and punishment 9
 and status as law 32, 35, 72, 117, 121, 181, 189
 and war 198, 200–1, 203, 206, 209, 211, 214–15, 224, 238
 in foro interno/externo 5, 14, 32–3, 189, 198, 235
league of states 12, 181–3, 188–91, 193–4, 245–6

League of Nations 182
legal positivism 1, 6, 16, 35, 42, 67, 83, 108, 121, 189, 242–3
legitimacy
 and contracts 24, 44, 58, 60
 and war 211, 213, 218–20, 225
 of decision making procedure 48
 of disobedience 128, 136–7
 of institutions 155
 of laws 74, 106–7, 113, 120–2, 127, 130, 132
 of punishment 157
 of self-defense 134
 of the sovereign 1, 4, 40, 48, 65, 81, 97, 105, 121, 129, 163, 173
Lever v. Heys 24, 50
Leviathan
 and collective agency 156, 171
 and contracts 16, 34, 49–51, 56–7, 65, 179
 and ethics 28–9
 and equity/morality 40–1, 47, 67, 72–5, 82, 102, 122, 197, 242–3
 and international relations/war 12–13, 174, 176, 178, 181, 183, 191–2, 195, 198–202, 204–7, 210, 214–15, 227, 234, 236
 and justice 101, 108, 231
 and law 14, 25, 27, 95, 104, 107, 110, 112, 115, 126–8, 130–1, 162
 and laws of nature 31–3, 35, 70, 117–18, 120, 122, 193, 196–8, 237
 and sovereignty 2–3, 5–9, 11, 15, 17, 23, 75, 78, 91, 99, 139–40, 146–7, 149, 151–2, 188
 v. *Dialogue* 1, 16, 68, 76, 85, 87–90, 94, 102–3, 105, 118–19, 184, 247
liberalism 137, 224
liberty 31, 36, 44, 46, 68, 75, 81, 84, 123–5, 136, 145, 180, 182, 192, 199, 202, 226–7
 defending 83, 204, 246
 to disobey 129–30, 135
 harmless 126–7, 154
license 55, 199, 205, 208
Lieber Code 17, 214–16
Lieber, Francis 215
Lloyd, S.A. 201
Locke, John 42, 44–5, 56, 66, 121, 166, 198
Long Parliament 139, 147, 149

Machiavelli, Niccolo 8, 194
Magna Carta 88–9, 94, 96, 145–6, 148, 151
Magna Charta see *Magna Carta*
Malcolm, Noel 187
maux superflus 215
minimalism 138–9, 154–5, 189, 190, 199, 211–14, 217, 222–3, 229
 Hobbesian, 211–12, 219
mob 168–72
monarchy 3, 22, 98, 140–1, 147, 151, 152, 154, 165–6, 169, 171

Moore, Thomas 244
Morgenthau, Hans 17, 176, 242
motivation 25–6, 35, 37–8, 46, 180, 183, 186, 189, 193, 234, 237
Mubarak, Hosni 171
multitude 17, 56, 63–4, 140, 156, 160, 163–72
Napoleon I 177
Nazism 137, 217
New England Town Meeting 167, 171
nominalism 59, 99, 137
norms 47, 189, 203, 212
Nozick, Robert 241

obligation
    and promises/contracts 20–2, 24, 34, 37, 43, 59–61, 133, 191
    international 177
    legal 9, 47, 107, 109–12, 119–23, 125, 127, 130–1, 135
    moral 23, 30, 32–3, 37, 46, 123, 175
    of the sovereign 4, 8, 52, 245
    political 48–9, 66
    to obey 12, 22, 35, 129, 132–3, 135–6, 138, 246
opinion 30, 115, 225–6
organization 59
    international 187–8, 190, 246
    of groups 159
ownership 58–9, 61, 64, 93–4, 101, 161–4, 170, 172

pacifism 13, 18, 199, 221, 224–5, 226–39
    contingent 225
Paris 168, 172
Parliament 3, 52, 94, 98, 106–7, 140, 145–7, 149–50, 152
passions 27–8, 43, 64, 225–6, 228–9, 233–4, 237, 246
peace
    and fidelity to law 35, 124–5, 129–30, 133–8
    and laws of nature 5, 18, 28, 31–2, 37, 45, 64, 71, 93, 120, 126, 164, 181, 193, 196–7, 199, 231, 233, 237
    and prudence 44
    and the sovereign 3, 41, 68, 108, 127, 140, 141, 143, 152, 182
    and war 13, 36, 186, 200, 202, 204–7, 209–10, 215, 219, 233
    first seeker of 180, 227, 235–6
    international 174, 178–9, 184–5, 187–9, 194, 203, 231, 245–6
    seeking attitudes 123, 132, 224–7, 229, 230, 232, 234–5, 237–9
Perpetual Peace, A Philosophical Essay 42, 184–5, 190
Physician's Case 50
Plato 88, 122, 135–6, 149, 241

pleasure 30, 44, 200, 204
plurality 52, 212
Pollock, F. 86
Pope 112–13
Pophan, John 50
positive law 9, 22, 73, 95, 100, 102–3, 109–11, 118, 120–1
precedent 75, 77, 114, 144, 148, 152
precept 6, 30–2, 74, 109, 197, 200, 204, 206–7, 230, 235–6
prisoners of war 185, 217, 219–20
Prohibitions del Roy 142
promise
    and contracts 15, 23–4, 32, 50, 58–63, 71, 179, 238
    and morality 33–4, 72, 133, 136
    in law v. in fact 51
    mutual 37
promulgation 103, 106–7, 111, 114–15, 120
proportionality 197, 204, 208, 2011
Provender v. Wood 50–1
prudence
    and first performance 61
    and international relations 175, 181, 183, 190–2, 194, 245
    and law and morality 15, 20–47, 83, 244
    and limiting sovereign 7–8, 66, 150, 154
    and selective conscientious objection 124
    and war 186, 207, 209, 210–12, 239
psychology 25–6, 38, 190
    moral 225
public interest
    v. private interest 140–1
punishment 35, 60, 93, 102, 118, 128, 131, 157, 200, 204, 207
    fear of 37, 46, 125, 135, 189
    of the innocent 3, 9–11, 79, 198
    of the sovereign 46, 109, 114

Queen Elizabeth 112

rationality 35, 75, 119–20, 201, 236
    and law 87–8, 93, 100, 105, 123, 222
    and reason 204–5
    in state of nature 45, 126, 175, 179, 181, 188, 200, 210, 226, 233–5, 239
    in war 196, 204–7, 212, 218–20, 224, 234, 237–8
    of attitudes 226, 236
    of people 26, 32, 43, 46, 141–2, 243, 236
Rawls, John 49, 241
reciprocity 5, 37, 58, 150, 210, 220
reconciliation 202–3, 205, 210, 220
Red Cross 13, 213
regicide 139
repentance 230–1

representation 17, 63–4, 73, 110, 123, 132, 138, 140, 156–72
responsibility 17, 68, 98, 156–60, 168, 215
restraint 123, 126, 189–90, 199, 210–14, 225
revenge 13, 200, 202, 215, 237
right of nature 12, 31, 35, 124, 198–9, 204, 246
Rodin, David 213
Rome 94, 112, 176
  Treaty of 177, 187–8, 194
Rousseau 96
  The Social Contract and Discourses 96

safety
  individual 26, 127, 130, 132, 137, 178, 246
  of the innocent 45
  of the King 143
  of the people 3–4, 6, 40–1, 46–7, 65, 68, 74, 78, 82–4, 115, 119–20, 126, 151, 178, 192, 232, 244–5
St Petersburg Declaration 17, 215–16, 218, 222
Sartre, Jean-Paul 170
self-defense 36, 111, 128–9, 131, 137, 179, 202, 205, 208, 210, 212–13, 219, 222, 226–30, 235
self-destruction 31, 71, 129, 142, 225, 232
self-interest 25–6, 28, 35, 42–4, 46–7, 135, 142, 150, 180, 193, 196, 205, 235, 245
  common 167–70, 191, 246
self-preservation
  and fidelity to law 35, 44, 81–2, 125, 132, 134, 137
  and justice 71, 93
  and natural law 164
  in the state of nature 31, 36, 38, 42, 45, 199, 229–30, 232–3, 236–7
  in war 196, 199, 200–2, 205, 207–12, 214, 221, 225
September 11, 2001 180, 187
Skinner, Quentin 86, 153, 241
"society of States" view 245
soldiers 127–8, 131, 133, 136, 204, 209–11, 220–22
  moral equality of 212–14
  v. civilians 209, 211, 213, 215–16
solidarity 167–70
Solon 94–5
Sorell, Tom 186, 205
sovereignty 8, 11, 16–17, 21–2, 39, 41, 64–6, 68, 77–8, 119, 121, 125, 130–1, 136, 138, 152, 155, 172–3, 205
  abdicating 12, 120, 190, 192, 245–6
  and artificial reason 139, 143–6, 153–4
  divided 14, 23, 98–9, 141, 143, 145, 147, 149–54, 181
  limits of 1–3, 5–6, 10–14, 17, 23, 42, 48, 66, 76, 147, 153, 180–1, 243–4
  of states 177, 181, 190–1, 193

stage play, see *authority*
Starkey *v.* Mill 24
state of nature
  and state of war 26–8, 36, 45, 73, 83, 196, 198–9, 201–2, 210, 225, 229, 234, 237
  as hypothetical 25, 94, 99, 105, 241
  contracts in 25, 29, 37, 48, 52–4, 56–7, 64, 174, 191, 228
  international 173, 176–7, 180, 182–4, 188–9, 191–2
  law in 29, 35, 70, 124, 181
  morality in 31–2, 69, 76, 203, 235
  rationality in 44, 175, 179, 197, 200, 205–6, 217, 226, 230, 232, 235, 238–9
Statute law 76–7, 79–80, 88–9, 92–3, 99–101, 105, 107, 113, 115–18, 120
Succession 97, 99, 108
summa ratio 92, 97

Tahrir Square 171–2
Taylor, A. E. 69, 89, 118
torture 221
trade 186–7, 246
trust 3, 50, 127, 244
  and contracts 57–8, 61, 64, 179, 237
  between individuals 27, 57–8, 73, 124, 174, 178–80, 193, 202, 210, 226–8, 230–3, 237
  between states 179, 181, 183, 192
  in state of nature 27, 64, 73, 174, 180, 183, 203, 210, 228, 233
  to judge 73, 197
Tuck, Richard 200

ultra vires action 164, 171
United Nations 182
United States 141, 180, 187–8
universalism 1, 91, 195, 199, 207, 222–3, 240, 243

virtue 5, 29, 35, 47, 109, 133, 226

Walzer, Michael 212, 220
Warrender, Howard 118
Whitehall, John 95–6
Will 7, 31–4, 46, 52–3, 60–1, 71–2, 101, 103, 108, 125, 145, 149, 158, 169, 226, 231, 234
  artificial 91
  of God 95, 110–2
  common 52–3, 64, 125, 158, 169, 171, 188
William the Conqueror 94, 96–7, 99, 105
words
  and actor/author 160–3
  and promising 15, 34, 37, 54, 57, 59, 61, 227
  mere 59–60, 129–30, 237–8
World Trade Organization 246